# Aspects of Twentieth-Century Music

**RICHARD DELONE**  *Indiana University*
**VERNON KLIEWER**  *Indiana University*
**HORACE REISBERG**
**MARY WENNERSTROM**  *Indiana University*
**ALLEN WINOLD**  *Indiana University*

Coordinating Editor
**GARY E. WITTLICH**  *Indiana University*

*PRENTICE-HALL, INC., Englewood Cliffs, New Jersey*

*Library of Congress Cataloging in Publication Data*

Main entry under title:

Aspects of 20th-century music.

Bibliography: p.
CONTENTS: Wennerstrom, M. Form in 20th-century
music.—DeLone, R. Timbre and texture in 20th-century
music.—Winold, A. Rhythm in 20th-century music. [etc.]
1. Music—History and criticism—20th century.
I. Delone, Richard Peter.  II. Wittlich, Gary,
1934- ed.  II. Title.
ML197.A8        780'.904        i74-12401
ISBN 0-13-049346-5

Printed in the United States of America

10  9  8  7  6  5  4  3  2


PRENTICE-HALL INTERNATIONAL, INC., *London*
PRENTICE-HALL OF AUSTRALIA, PTY. LTD., *Sydney*
PRENTICE-HALL OF CANADA, LTD., *Toronto*
PRENTICE-HALL OF INDIA PRIVATE LIMITED, *New Delhi*
PRENTICE-HALL OF JAPAN, INC., *Tokyo*
PRENTICE-HALL OF SOUTHEAST ASIA (PTE.) LTD., *Singapore*

*To the memory of a colleague,*

*Phillip T. Beach*

# Contents

# Preface

We stand in the midst of one of the most revolutionary of all periods in the history of art music. At no time in the past have so many conceptually opposing musical developments existed side by side: tonal vs. atonal music; highly organized (serial) vs. freely organized (chance) vs. probabalistic (stochastic) music; music for traditional instruments vs. music for electronic instruments; and even music with sounding elements vs. music without sound! Such a plurality of compositional approaches naturally puts the listener in a difficult position—he is often confronted with music for which he has very little of the experience necessary for bringing intelligible order to the perceived sound. It is for this reason that performers are often unwilling to perform this music, or if performed, that listeners are unwilling (or unable) to hear it. How, after all, are we to understand a new (or even relatively new) language without experience?

In order to help resolve some of the questions raised by music of the twentieth century, we have conceived this book, the primary purpose of which is to study this century's music from the point of view of its structure. We have made no attempt to deal with individual or collective styles or to survey systematically the literature of this period, nor have we dealt with the various mechanical devices and the techniques of manipulating sounds in the composition of electroacoustic music. Rather, we have addressed ourselves specifically to the question of how form, timbre and texture, rhythm, line, chord, and ordering procedures are dealt with by twentieth-century composers in a wide variety of musical works from early to very recent examples.

The organization of the book is essentially from general to specific. The initial chapter on form, for example, deals with overall forming principles, with changing formal concepts moving from the more to the less traditional, and for the most part with complete works or movements thereof. The following chapter deals with timbral and textural details as they apply to a wide variety of compositions. As the topics of the following chapters become more specific, particularly as they are concerned with single as opposed to multiple dimensions of musical structure, their contents are more detailed. In all cases, the general approach is from essentially traditional to more novel and/or more complex manifestations of a topic.

A common concern of each chapter is the desire of its author to communicate an analytical way of looking at music. As music is the product of human thought, so must music be studied thoughtfully. This is particularly true for music of this century since often the newer ideas of structuring musical materials have few, if any, precedents in music of the past. In some instances, notably in the concluding chapter, we have introduced terms that may be unfamiliar to the reader. In all cases we have applied these terms in an attempt to make our presentation more lucid and consistent and to provide linguistic aids for the student. At the end of each chapter, we have provided a list of works for further study and a list of references, some annotated, to which the student may refer for additional consideration of each topic.

The use of this book will vary with the particular situation in which it may be used. We believe that, ideally, the book should serve as a text for a course of at least one semester's duration on the undergraduate level or on the graduate level of study though it may also find use as a supplement to music literature courses. The ordering of contents is left to the discretion of the individual or the teacher. Each chapter is complete in itself and does not depend necessarily on any other chapter for the general understanding of its contents. We suggest either taking the chapters in order, beginning with generalizations and moving to more specific details of musical structure, or beginning with a particular work (say one from the first chapter) and using each of the other chapters as a source of information for dealing with the details of that work. In any event, we strongly urge that the point of departure for any discussion be the sounding music itself. Further, we suggest that all work be accompanied by additional analysis and writing assignments made by the teacher.

The task of acknowledging all those who have made this book a reality is a difficult one. Since each of the authors is a teacher and a composer or performer (or both), we must necessarily cite the contributions of our teachers and our students. We acknowledge also the patience and encouragement of the members of our families during the course of writing this book. To those who have provided clerical assistance, especially Sandra Redmon, Velda Hall, Marilen Wegner, and Carole Wright, we also extend our thanks. And finally, we acknowledge the stimulation and encouragement given the authors by each other. Probably no multiply-authored text has been put together with more cooperation and less disagreement.

GARY WITTLICH *for the Authors*

# chapter one

# Form in
# Twentieth-Century Music

MARY WENNERSTROM

## CONCEPTS OF FORM

The form of a musical composition is one of the most important and frequently-discussed factors in the creation of an art work. Form implies the organization of materials into a meaningful whole—a whole that can be apprehended aurally as an aesthetic complex. Although this complex is the result of many small events, the resultant shape is more than the sum of disparate parts. The shape of a musical art work is a fascinating construction that exists in time and is a complete organism representing only itself.

Composers have had many different views of "form," and the differences between analyses of form and the actual musical substance have provided a rather bewildering array of terms and labels. Traditionally analysts have discussed "themes," sections (phrases, periods, etc.), and familiar plans of ternary or sonata-allegro arrangements of material. Useful as these terms are, a distinction must be made between *forms* (abstract formal designs) and *form* (the principles and procedures of combining materials). Forms, as abstract patterns, are more easily discussed and have become the subject for numerous books and essays. Form, as a study of underlying processes, is not easily categorized, for indeed each musical composition possesses a somewhat special shape and arrangement of materials.

This dichotomy between form and forms is particularly apparent in

**1**

twentieth-century music, where there are often no familiar "plans" of themes, no clearly-articulated divisions, and sometimes no evident developmental procedures. This lack of a familiar abstract design has led some writers to conclude, with a critical note, that contemporary music *has* no form, and has led other more enthusiastic musicians to state that form is only part of the "old music," a relative of major-minor tonality, which is dispensable in the "new music." Both of these views are incomplete and in a sense erroneous. Any art work that exists in time has *some* shape to it, even though a familiar pattern may not be immediately obvious. While certain *forms* (formal designs) may be dependent upon a tonal scheme, form, as a process of relationships, is a universal procedure of integration that is required for meaningful apprehension by a listener.

The understanding of twentieth-century music requires first an understanding of the materials which are being employed. The listener must start with the idea that *any* event in *any* parameter (pitch, duration, timbre, dynamics) can have a formative function in the music and can contribute to the resultant shape of the piece. This unlimited source of material at the composer's disposal demands close attention from a performer or listener, since it is easy to confuse the scale and importance of events going on in the work. In a thirty-second Webern work, every pitch event is important, and two measures lasting only a few seconds may represent the "exposition" of material. In a twenty-minute Penderecki work, individual pitch events may not be as important as the total dynamic or textural result, and sections may be three or four minutes in length. This sort of diversity in the scope of materials and in the scale of composition is new in the twentieth century, and is something which must be taken into consideration before studying a contemporary work.

Another new aspect of form in the twentieth century is the different approaches to the process of structure. Western music has in general, up until the twentieth century, depended on an architectonic combination of parts; a musical work has been regarded as a series of units which are put together to form a whole. This architectural approach to musical design incorporates several valid ideas; a piece of music needs sectionalization in order for the listener to comprehend the pattern being presented, since no one can retain large units of sound without smaller shaping divisions. Some of the greatest works of Western music—Beethoven quartets, Bach fugues, Brahms symphonies—are exciting in their architectural design, and represent the highest sort of architectonic building. Each section has a purpose and fits with every other section to form a large complex constructed out of the principles of restatement, variation, and contrast. While this idea of design is still valid for many twentieth-century works, form as a *process* rather than as an architectural shape is also present in many composers' thinking. Edgar Varèse, for example, regards form as a *resultant*—the consequence of the interaction of opposing forces—rather than as a pattern of parts. "There is an idea, the basis of an internal structure, expanded and split into different shapes or groups of sound constantly changing in shape, direction, and speed, attracted and repulsed by various forces. The form of the work is a consequence of this interaction. Possible musical forms are as limitless as the exterior forms of crystals."[1] This formal approach allows a germinal idea to be split into its different components of melody, rhythm, timbre, etc., each element developed and changed according to an individual pattern. Structure then is a result of an ever-changing presentation of consistent material.

Other contemporary composers think of "form" in music as an unpredictable element which can incorporate variable time lengths and can include the performer(s) and sometimes the audience in the structuring process. Christian Wolff says, "Form is a theatrical event of a certain length, and the length itself may be unpredictable."[2] Such a philosophy is obvious in aleatory or mathematically-controlled plans that depend more on a method or a process than on a carefully-constructed, architectonic plan. In John Cage's work there is often a merging of the sounds of the world with the sounds of a composition so that no structured time dimension is audible or desired. Earle Brown writes that he consciously introduces an ambiguous parameter into composition, which he describes as "the human will and capacities for responsible action (both technical and esthetic) as a parameter acting and reacting upon the physical parameters which the composer has described in the score."[3] Thus the composition is the result of no *one* rationale but is a product of the interaction of several wills (the composer's, the performer's).

All of these concepts of form lead to a broader approach to analysis and study of twentieth-century music. It is usually not profitable to look for a traditional "label" to describe every composition, and the first emphasis should be on a comprehension of the shaping processes, often combined with a study of the composer's approach to structure. These processes can be discovered by studying the materials of the work, the relationships between sets of materials and within them, and the ways in which the materials are combined. Any sound event can have a formative function and the kinds of materials emphasized in each piece are of first importance in delineating a recognizable sound complex. Several of the other chapters of this book study the variety of possibilities in twentieth-century music within single parameters.

The relationships and combinations of materials are more complex. Although these relationships often depend on a study of individual pieces, certain procedures, such as quick contrasts, interpolation of new material, and layering of ideas, have become part of the twentieth-century musical

[1]Edgar Varèse, "The Liberation of Sound," *Perspectives of New Music*, V (Fall, Winter, 1966), 16.

[2]Christian Wolff, "On Form," *die Reihe*, VII (1960), 26.

[3]Earle Brown, "Form in New Music," *Source*, I (January, 1967), 49.

language. In addition, the consistent principles of restatement, contrast, and variation are valid for this as well as for any other century. While contrast elements are usually not too difficult to discern, restatements and variants of previous material may be less obvious and may depend on rhythmic transformation, pitch displacement, or on only dynamic or timbral return. All parameters may operate concurrently or may have different plans of restatement and contrast. All of these possibilities provide challenging and exciting opportunities for understanding the musical structure and demand that the knowledgeable listener or performer have a broad spectrum of approaches at his disposal.

Structure in the music of the twentieth century is a result of a combination of old "forms," new vocabulary, and innovative shaping processes. Traditional shapes, such as ternary, rondo, and sonata-allegro, are still operative in much music. Variational methods are evident not only in "theme and variation" works but in pervasive techniques of motive transformation, permutations of sets, and contrapuntal reworkings of material. Innovative processes such as layering and interpolation produce block forms or the multifaceted "crystallization" of which Varèse speaks. In addition, the open forms which result from aleatory operations and "works-in-progress" constitute a new dimension in composition in the twentieth century.

Although any discussion of form cannot adequately describe all of these possibilities in a short space of time, representative works can present processes of analysis and possible ways of thinking about form. Several compositions have been chosen which demonstrate first a use of more traditional designs, although the materials involved are often quite different from those of previous centuries. Secondly, works which depend on more peculiarly twentieth-century operations are examined for structural components. In each piece the parameters interact in different ways and yet manifest some constancy in their use of contrast and unity by return. Twentieth-century music has many new materials and a number of innovative formative processes, but it also adheres to many of the strong structural principles of Western music, often with a new freedom of approach. To understand this music, the musician must literally be ready for any sound or event and must be able to attempt a synthesis of elements. The works discussed here demonstrate a few interesting examples from the vast and exciting array of twentieth-century works.[4]

---

[4]Works chosen for analysis here are not found in any anthology except for the Stravinsky *L'Histoire du Soldat* excerpt. These works, however, are very similar to compositions in various anthologies (Burkhart, Wennerstrom, etc.), and the procedures suggested can be applied to the music in these books or to any twentieth-century work. Twentieth-century composers whose formal operations are very close to earlier models of form and whose materials in most instances make the formal schemes quite obvious have not been discussed here.

## SECTIONAL FORMS

The procedure of using various arrangements of rather clear-cut sections of music to create form has long been an established principle in composition. The most familiar example is the traditional "ternary" form—A B A—which combines elements of contrast and restatement into a balanced whole. Rondo forms are an extension of this combinational procedure, with longer patterns of alternating contrast and return.

All of these ideas are still present in twentieth-century music. Many examples exist of standard ternary patterns, with various modifications, and the idea of a constant return that is the basis of rondo form is still a viable one. However, in addition to the obvious examples of complete restatements, where pitch, texture, rhythm, and instrumentation usually work together, composers have also worked with forms which emphasize the return of elements of only timbre or dynamics rather than pitch, or forms in which the various parameters have separate patterns of return.

One of these pieces is *Movements* for Piano and Orchestra by Igor Stravinsky. Composed in 1959, it is an example of Stravinsky's more recent serial output. The work is in five movements, connected by interludes, each of which exploits a different instrumental timbre. Movement IV, reproduced in Ex. 1-1, falls into three sections that are distinguished primarily by

**EXAMPLE 1-1.** Stravinsky: *Movements* (1958–59), IV, complete (mm. 96–135). Copyright 1960 by Hawkes & Son (London) Ltd. Reprinted by permission of Boosey & Hawkes, Inc.

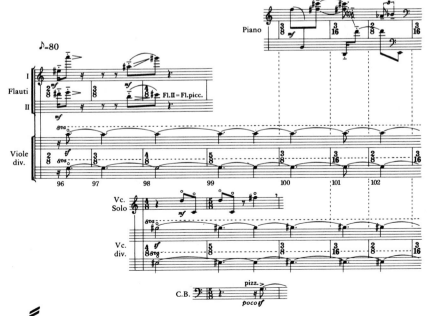

**EXAMPLE 1-1** continued.

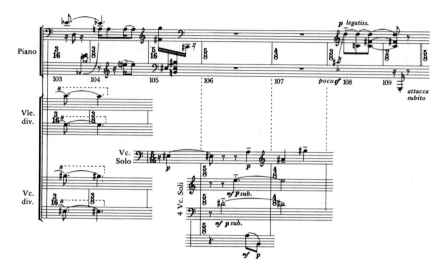

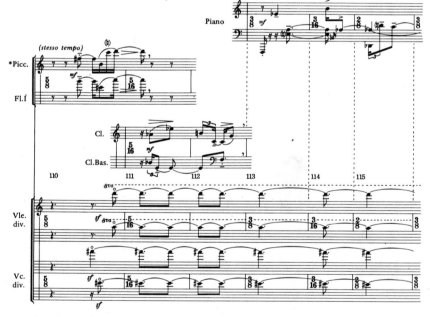

*sounds octave higher.

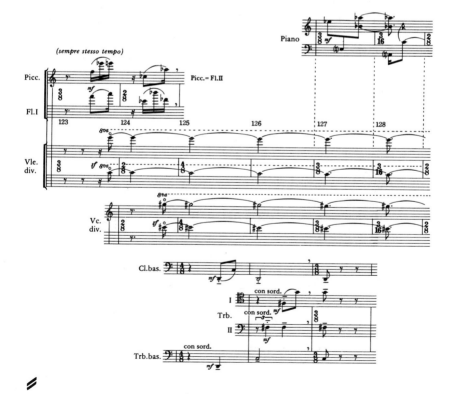

**EXAMPLE 1-1** continued.

instrumentation and dynamics. Each section makes use of layers of timbre, superimposed on top of one another. The orchestra is divided into flutes and high strings (playing harmonics), low strings, and piano, with occasional entrances of low wind instruments substituting for the low strings. These instrumental layers are diagrammed in Fig. 1-1.

IV.  A.  96–109
  Flutes_____

  String harmonics_____

| | Solo Cello | Piano | Solo Cello | Piano |
|---|---|---|---|---|
| sf-mf | mf | mf | p | p |

  A′.  110–122
  Flutes_____

  String harmonics_____

| | Clarinets | Piano | Solo Celli | Piano |
|---|---|---|---|---|
| sf-mf | mf | mf | mf-p | p |

  A″.  123–135
  Flutes_____

  String harmonics_____

| | Bass clarinet Trombones | Piano | Solo Celli and Basses | Piano |
|---|---|---|---|---|
| sf-mf | mf | mf | mf | mf |

**FIGURE 1-1.** Stravinsky: *Movements* (1958–59), IV; Sectionalization by Instrumentation and Dynamics.

The movement divides into three sections, each following basically the same plan of instrumentation and dynamics. The most audibly distinctive events occur at the beginnings of the sections, where the flutes are in a high register and the strings attack the high harmonics *sf*. Notice that while these harmonics all form perfect intervals, producing a consistency of sonority, each beginning otherwise employs almost completely different pitches and rhythms. Stravinsky creates a strophic sectional form (in this case A A' A'') by an emphasis on certain instrumental colors.

The sections follow essentially similar patterns. A solo instrument or small group of instruments is followed by a rhythmically active statement in the piano. The cadences all include solo celli and piano, with a lowering of the dynamic level. In addition, these cadence sections all begin with minor sevenths and end on a long sonority, punctuated by one note, that centers around D, C, and F♯.

This part of Stravinsky's *Movements* demonstrates a clear three-section form and illustrates how this shape is created most prominently by the return of a specific instrumental and dynamic plan. The compositional procedure also reveals a concept of "layering" that is basic to much of Stravinsky's music. Stravinsky characteristically superimposes or juxtaposes layers or units of sound, and works with different patterns of continuation and development in each layer. In this part the flutes and strings function as a background, against which the solo instruments start, are interrupted by the piano, and then continue to a cadence. The piano, on the other hand, is interrupted by the strings before reaching *its* cadence. Stravinsky has made use of various concepts of layers in all of his music, but in the more recent music even the layout of the score demonstrates these divisions (see Ex. 1-1), as each instrumental group has its own position on the score, and appears only when it is playing.

This emphasis on dynamics and timbre in the creation of form can easily be transferred to electronic music, where specific pitch and rhythmic events are often hard to perceive. In spite of the rather unfamiliar medium (or perhaps because of it), some composers of electronic music have relied on very clear-cut shapes in their music. One example is the ballet suite *Evolutions* by the Dutch composer Henk Badings. The suite is made up of six short movements, each rather traditional in form although the sound sources are completely electronic. The fourth movement, "Intermezzo," has a very clear A B A' design. The A sections are generally soft and are based on pure, lyric sounds (sine waves). The B section is louder, and has a higher density level (both horizontally and vertically), besides having more percussive timbral characteristics. Both A sections have an underlying pedal, above which almost tertian arpeggios ascend; the A' section has a melody added to the other components, although the pitch elements in this section are different from those in the first section. A diagram of this movement is given in Fig. 1-2.[5]

In this "Intermezzo," form is delineated not so much by specific pitch or rhythmic events as by recognizable sound characteristics, particularly timbre and texture. Sectional designs such as this are certainly a continuation of traditional shapes and are sometimes easier to hear than the ternary forms of the late nineteenth century.

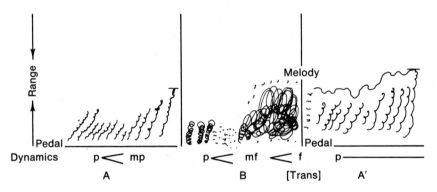

**FIGURE 1-2.** Badings: *Evolutions* (1958), "Intermezzo"; Sectionalization by Texture and Dynamics.

A last example of sectional design is again from Stravinsky's work, in this case from an early composition, *L'Histoire du Soldat* (1918), written for a chamber group of seven instruments. This suite consists of a number of related short pieces, connected by a narrative. The last piece in the suite, the "Triumphal March of the Devil," illustrates Stravinsky's subtle use of motives in a pattern that resembles a rondo design. Here, however, instead of depending on clear-cut, separated sections, Stravinsky merges one idea into another and transforms each idea as it returns. Ex. 1-2 is the first fifteen bars of the march, in which the basic material of the movement is presented; Fig. 1-3 illustrates how these ideas are combined in the work.

[5]This diagram is taken from the recording on Limelight LS-86055 (Mercury), realized in the Philips' laboratory at Eindhoven.

**EXAMPLE 1-2.** Stravinsky: *L'Histoire du Soldat* (1918), "Triumphal March of the Devil," mm. 1–15. Used by permission of J. & W. Chester Ltd., London.

**EXAMPLE 1-2** continued.

| Measures | 1-3 | 4-5 | 6-7 | 8-15 | 16-18 | 19-27 | 28-29 | 30-39 | 40-41 | | 98-112 |
|---|---|---|---|---|---|---|---|---|---|---|---|
| Melodic-Rhythmic Motives | A | B | C | B′ | A | B″ | A′ | B″ | C′ | | B″ |
| Instrumentation | Tutti | VI, C.B., Trb, | Cor, VI. | VI, C.B., Trb, Perc. | Tutti | VI, Perc. | Tutti | VI, Perc. | Cor, VI, Perc, CI, Fg. | | Perc. |
| Dynamics | ff | | | | | | | | | | |

| Measures | 42-44 | 45-46 | 47-48 | 49-56 | 57-76 | 77-84 | 85-95 | 96-97 |
|---|---|---|---|---|---|---|---|---|
| Melodic-Rhythmic Motives | A | B | C | B′ | B″ | C′ | B″ | A′ |
| Instrumentation | Tutti | VI, C.B., Trb. | Cor, VI. | VI, C.B., Trb, Perc. | VI, Perc. Cor, VI, Perc, CI, Fg. (Trb, C.B.) | | VI, Perc. | Cor, CI, Fg. Cor, Perc. |
| Dynamics | ff —————————————————————— pp | | | | | | | |

**FIGURE 1-3.** Stravinsky: *L'Histoire du Soldat* (1918), "Triumphal March of the Devil"; Sectionalization by Melodic-Rhythmic Motives, Instrumentation, and Dynamics.

13

The A idea in this movement (mm. 1–3) is a repeated-note figure that occurs previously in the suite (see the "Royal March," opening and mm. 97–101). The figure is initially stated *ff* by all the instruments, and the opening three measures return almost exactly at m. 16 and exactly at m. 42. At m. 28 there is a loud tutti return, shortened; at m. 96 only the opening phrase returns, *pp* (Ex. 1-3). In the course of the march Stravinsky shortens the opening unit and reduces its instrumentation and volume, while increasingly emphasizing the other material.

**EXAMPLE 1-3.** Stravinsky: *L'Histoire du Soldat* (1918), "Triumphal March of the Devil," mm. 28–29; 96–97. Used by permission of J. & W. Chester Ltd., London.

The B and C material (mm. 4–5 and 6–7 respectively) is most readily recognized by its instrumentation. The short violin double stops predominate in both units of material, with the C sections adding a short melodic fragment in the cornet. Stravinsky develops this contrasting material by combining the violin with various instruments, more frequently with only the battery of percussion, until at the end the percussion (the "devil's drums") wins out and silences the rest of the ensemble. The cornet melody (C) recurs at odd intervals and near the end is reiterated in varied versions by all the instruments (Ex. 1-4). The B and C units sometimes function together in a B C B′ arrangement (mm. 4–15, 45–56, 57–95) and sometimes as separate bits of material.

On a large scale, the March is divided into two sections by the exact return of mm. 1–15 in mm. 42–56. After this restatement, Stravinsky reorders the material of mm. 19–41 in mm. 57–97, omitting the return of A material found in mm. 16–18. The original ordering of B″ A′ B″ C′ becomes B″ C′ B″ A′, with the B and C sections extended and the A section shortened. The work ends with a coda of percussion alone.

Stravinsky's ingenious combination of sound units is based on recognizable melodic-rhythmic, textural, timbral, and dynamic characteristics. Fig. 1-3 indicates that these sound units sometimes function as complete entities and sometimes are broken apart. Only pitch and rhythm, and not instrumentation or dynamics, may return as in m. 96, or several different motives may emphasize the same timbral characteristics, such as the violin and percussion. In addition, although there is a clear pulse throughout, it is hard to predict

**EXAMPLE 1-4.** Stravinsky: *L'Histoire du Soldat* (1918), "Triumphal March of the Devil," mm. 75–84. Used by permission of J. & W. Chester Ltd., London.

how the pulse will be grouped or how long each section will be. This constant lengthening and shortening of material is a characteristic of Stravinsky's which makes his music always interesting. In this movement the indicated dynamics are consistently loud throughout (although the effective dynamic level varies with the instrumentation), until the volume diminishes to an echo at the last statement of A. Instrumentation and texture are interdependent, while the melodic-rhythmic material has its own independent pattern. Thus although "rondo" describes the general shape of the movement, a simple letter scheme cannot demonstrate the subtleties at work here. The processes involved are not only the intermittent return factor, but also the variation and extension of the contrasting material and the rather independent plans of the different parameters.

## DEVELOPMENTAL FORMS

The process of development is one that has been essential to music from its beginning. Chant, for instance, is frequently constructed from modifications of the same small groups of notes, and these procedures of permutation have carried through many centuries into much music of the twentieth century. Some composers, such as Bartók and Stravinsky, base many of their works on a network of interrelated motives that take on new appearances within and between movements by transformations of rhythm, dynamics, and instrumentation. It is difficult to separate developmental procedures from variational ones, since both terms indicate some transformation of initial material with a retention of certain essential original features. Indeed, it is perhaps impossible to distinguish between these intertwined techniques as *processes*; as form-creating devices, however, it is possible to distinguish developmental sections (units in which small bits of material are treated to many *different* presentations and combinations) from variational sections (units which are dependent on basically *one* type of presentation of material, if not on the retention of an entire phrase structure or shape).

Traditionally the "form" in which development plays the largest role is the sonata-movement design, with a basic plan of exposition of material, development of it, and recapitulation. These parts should not be related to the simple sectional ternary form, for they have a much different purpose; indeed in the more complex manifestations of this plan, developmental ideas permeate not only the "development" section but also the other parts of the form. In Haydn's works, for instance, the melodic material of the exposition is often related, one theme being a variant of the other, with contrast created by changes in the other parameters. Beethoven, especially in his later works, depends on short motives for the generating impetus of the composition and often develops material extensively before the real "development" section. The sonata-movement form has been very useful to many composers because of its organic quality, since the basis of the form is the presentation of certain material, its growth through a number of changes, and its restatement in something close to its original form. Each composer who has dealt with the form has given it a slightly different interpretation and balance, and this developmental pattern has been the basis for many of the major works of the eighteenth and nineteenth centuries.

Twentieth-century composers too have been attracted to the sonata-movement pattern and have employed the underlying ideas of statement-development-restatement for their own creative purposes. Some writers believe that this form depends on the duality of tonal centers inherent in music based on functional tonality, and of course the contrast of tonal centers in the exposition and the reconciliation to tonic in the recapitulation are important features of the structure. However, if we accept the underlying processes of the form, which have a general applicability, it is obvious that this formal design is still prevalent in twentieth-century music, even without the element of contrast found in previous tonal systems. It is not difficult to make a connection between the sonata designs of late Beethoven (particularly his quartets) and works such as the string quartets of Béla Bartók.

Bartók has written many large-scale works, with movements frequently in a sonata design or in some form of his own rondo-sonata pattern. One set of works, the six completed string quartets, stands out as a monument of twentieth-century chamber music. The quartet medium occupied Bartók's thinking throughout his career: the first quartet was written in 1908, the sixth quartet was written in 1939, and Bartók was planning a new quartet when he died in 1945. The six quartets are outstanding examples of writing for the medium, and also demonstrate techniques that Bartók employs in his full-scale works for other combinations.

The Fifth Quartet was written in a month in 1934 to fulfill a commission for the Elizabeth Sprague Coolidge Foundation. Although perhaps not as well known as the Fourth and Sixth Quartets, the Fifth has much the same architectural plan as the Fourth and many of the more aurally accessible features of the Sixth. The Fifth Quartet has five movements (Allegro, Adagio Molto, Scherzo, Andante, and Finale), and the whole assumes the plan of an arch: Movements I and V are related, as are Movements II and IV, with the Scherzo-Trio-Scherzo (Movement III) forming the center of the arch. Bartók uses this large design in many of his works, and it is continued in such procedures as motivic interconnections and mirroring.

The first movement of the quartet is itself an arch form, presenting most of the material of the entire quartet, and demonstrates on a smaller scale the organic growth and structure of the five movements. In addition to its arch shape, the first movement is a complex of interrelated materials that has the general shape of a sonata design, with a specific "developmental section" combined with almost continuous growth and change in the basic material. The recapitulation returns the elements of the exposition in reverse order, creating the arch; in addition, the material recurs completely inverted, both texturally and melodically.

No simple labeling of exposition-development-recapitulation-coda can describe the complex of relationships in this movement, but the general scheme is a point from which to begin a discussion. Figure 1-4 is a diagram of the movement, including the large sections and their smaller components, with measure numbers, and a listing of pitch focus, dynamics, tempo, and timing in seconds for each section.

The exposition (mm. 1–58) is itself a composite of many factors. Ex. 1-5 illustrates the main material of the movement. Although this material is quite diverse rhythmically, texturally, and dynamically, there are definite interrelationships in the underlying intervallic and contoural structure. Particularly interesting is the growth of material in mm. 1–13 and the connection of this material with that of the contrasting section in mm. 44–45. Ex. 1-6 illustrates these connections by superimposing the motives. An opening repeated B♭ is embellished with an important whole-step upper neighbor (motive 1). The repetitions are then spun out into a melodic line which ascends from B♭ to E, using a minor third and a chromatic line (motive 2), followed by a series of perfect fourths (motive 3). In mm. 8–9 a

**EXPOSITION (1–58) / DEVELOPMENT (59–132)**

| Sections | EXPOSITION (1–58) | | | | | | DEVELOPMENT (59–132) | | | | | |
|---|---|---|---|---|---|---|---|---|---|---|---|---|
| | **I.** | | | | | **II.** | | | | | | |
| Measures | 1–13 | 14–23 | 23–24 | 25–36 | 37–44 | 44–58 | 59–69 | 69–86 | 86–103 | 103–109 | 109–126 | 126–132 |
| Motives | A | B | A | C | A | | A frag. | A frag. and II | C and A frag. | A frag. | A frag. | Return of A, inverted |
| Pitch Focus | [Bb–E] | F#–C# | C# | C– (Eb–A) | C–F# | [Bb–F] | [E] | (G–Bb) | G | half-steps | E | [F–E] |
| Dynamics / Tempo: ♩ = 132 | f / 132 | p / 120 | ff / 120 | f / 132 | ff / 132 | p / 112 | f / 138, 160 | f / 160 | ff / 132 | f / 138 | ff / 120, 150 | ff / 132 |
| Bartók's Timings (in seconds) | 24.5 | | 22 | 35 | | 49 | 41.5 | | 74 | | | 13 |

**RECAPITULATION (132–176) / CODA (177–218)**

| Sections | RECAPITULATION (132–176) | | | CODA (177–218) | | |
|---|---|---|---|---|---|---|
| | **II.** | | **I.** | | | |
| Measures | 132–146 | 147–159 | 159–176 | 177–201 | 202–209 | 210–218 |
| Motives | Inverted | C, inverted | A, inverted | A and II frag. | dev. of motive | A |
| Pitch Focus | F#–C | Gb–C (Eb–A) | Bb–E | A–Eb | | [Bb–E–Bb] |
| Dynamics / Tempo: ♩ = | p / 112 | f / 132 | ff / 132 | p, cresc. to f / 168, 184 | f / 168 | ff / 138 |
| Bartók's Timings (in seconds) | 47 | 24 | 31 | 33.5 | | 30 |

FIGURE 1-4. Bartók: String Quartet No. 5 (1934), First Movement; Form.

**EXAMPLE 1-5.** Bartók : String Quartet No. 5 (1934), I, mm. 1–28 ; 44–47. Copyright 1936 by Universal Edition ; Renewed 1963. Copyright and Renewal assigned to Boosey & Hawkes, Inc., for the U.S.A. Reprinted by permission. Permission granted by Universal Edition A.G., Vienna, for all countries of the world except USA.

**EXAMPLE 1-5** continued.

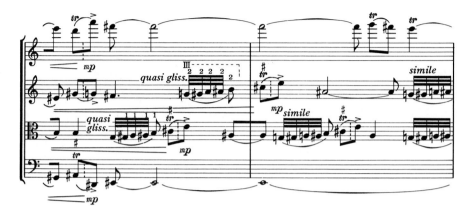

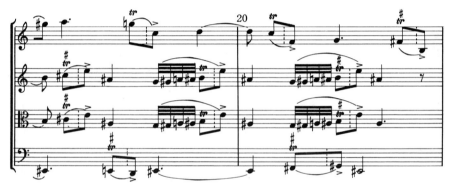

**EXAMPLE 1-5** continued.

pattern begins that uses these same intervals, in a different order but with a similar contour, in a new rhythmic setting (motives 4 and 5). Each part of this growing line has been numbered, because Bartók deals with these ideas as separate entities in the course of the piece. The last line in Ex. 1-6 is the contrasting "theme" beginning in mm. 44–45. Although this section provides the greatest contrast in the exposition because it is quieter, slower, and texturally less dense than the material surrounding it, the melodic material and certain rhythmic elements have been retained from the opening thirteen measures. The ascending major second (D-E), minor third (D-F) and chromatic line are all present, and the descending perfect fifth of motive 5 (A♭ — G♭ — E♭ — D♭) has been retained in an embellished and extended

$$A♭ \underset{M2}{\longleftrightarrow} G♭ \underset{m3}{\longleftrightarrow} E♭ \underset{M2}{\longleftrightarrow} D♭$$

form. A similarity of contour and register also unites the two sections.

**EXAMPLE 1-6.** Bartók: String Quartet No. 5, I; Melodic correspondences in the exposition. Copyright 1936 by Universal Edition; Renewed 1963. Copyright and Renewal assigned to Boosey & Hawkes, Inc., for the U.S.A. Reprinted by permission. Permission granted by Universal Edition A.G., Vienna, for all countries of the world except USA.

The first group of material in the exposition is a long one (see Fig. 1-4), presenting the A material and two contrasting ideas (mm. 14–23 and 25–36) in a rondo-like succession. Measures 25–36 return intact, inverted, in the recapitulation, but the music in mm. 14–23 never returns in this movement. However, this section has larger ramifications. Melodic motives from m. 15 (e.g. 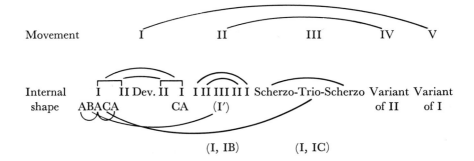 ) occur prominently in the second movement (see Movement II, m. 27 ff.). Ideas from both of these contrasting sections (mm. 14–23 and 25–36) can be found in various parts of the second and third movements, which are in themselves arch shapes. The first movement thus generates material for the whole quartet, and the concept of development and change is not limited to a "development section." Figure 1-5 illustrates some of the interrelationships of the five movements.

Movement  I  II  III  IV  V

Internal  I  II Dev. II  I  I II III II I  Scherzo-Trio-Scherzo  Variant  Variant
shape  ABACA  CA  (I′)  of II  of I

(I, IB)  (I, IC)

**FIGURE 1-5.** Bartók: String Quartet No. 5; Interrelationships among the five movements.

In the first movement, however, there is also a clear-cut section of development where Bartók employs ingenious recombinations of the material of the exposition. Bartók first breaks apart the opening material and works with it in various combinations of textures, sometimes reusing fragments in an ostinato. At m. 86, for example, the rhythmic ostinato from m. 25 is used as an accompaniment to motives 4 and 5, presented *ff* in octaves in the violins. After "stacking up" motive 4 in ascending half steps and inverting this procedure (Ex. 1-7, mm. 103–109), Bartók begins some interesting motivic alterations. Measure 109 is motive 5, inverted; in m. 111 this motive becomes decorated to serve as an accompanimental figure to motive 1 (Ex. 1-7, mm. 112–118). Measures 119–125 combine motive 1, inverted, with motive 5 in its original form and treat this line to canon and inversion. This reordering and reworking of motivic material is the essence of the developmental procedure, and Bartók provides exciting and masterful examples of many different techniques in this development section.

**EXAMPLE 1-7.** Bartók: String Quartet No. 5, I, mm. 103–122. Copyright 1936 by Universal Edition; Renewed 1963. Copyright and Renewal assigned to Boosey & Hawkes, Inc., for the U.S.A. Reprinted by permission. Permission granted by Universal Edition A.G., Vienna, for all countries of the world except USA.

**EXAMPLE 1-7** continued.

Più mosso ♩ =150
120

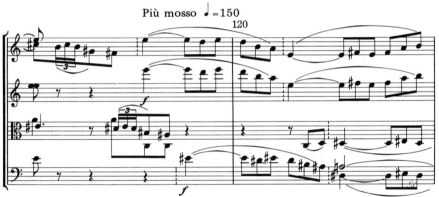

Measure 126 is the interior climax of the movement, at a point closer to the end than to the beginning of the movement. This section returns the first idea (motives 1, 2, and 3) in inversion, in preparation for the return of all the ideas inverted, and also serves as the tonal opposition to the B♭ tonic of the movement. Although major-minor tonality is not operative here, definite pitch centers occur (see Fig. 1-4). B♭ is the underlying tonal center, and E is most often pitted against the tonic as a "dominant"—the symmetrical opposite of B♭. This tritonic polarity is obvious in the first melodic material, which outlines B♭-E, in the first vertical interval of the piece (m. 5), and in other tritones of the exposition (particularly F♯-C). The exposition ends on an F major $\frac{6}{4}$ chord, which moves immediately to the repeated E at the beginning of the development and then into unstable pitch areas. Measure 126 returns to the F-E combination which began the development in the form of the vertical interval of a minor second.

Measures 132–146 are a return of mm. 44–58, inverted melodically and texturally (the order of entries of the material is reversed). Measures 147–159 are the return, inverted, of mm. 25–36; again, textural inversion takes place with a pedal on g♭¹ instead of C in the cello line. The inverted return of the opening material begins in m. 159 on B♭, punctuated by a diminished triad. Measure 172 introduces the variant of motive 5 found in the development (m. 111), again on E—a motive which leads to an "allegro molto" coda. The coda is based on a motive derived from the pitches of motive 4 and the rhythm of the "second theme" (Ex. 1-8). This motive is developed in a frenzied pace of imitation, inversion, fragmentation, extension, and combination with motive 1.

**EXAMPLE 1-8.** Bartók: String Quartet No. 5, I; Coda motive (m. 177). Copyright 1936 by Universal Edition; Renewed 1963, Copyright and Renewal assigned to Boosey & Hawkes, Inc., for the U.S.A. Reprinted by permission. Permission granted by Universal Edition A.G., Vienna, for all countries of the world except USA.

The closing of the movement (Ex. 1-9) presents an interesting synthesis of the materials of the movement, and an unmistakable return to the B♭-E central tritone, with a final emphasis on B♭. Measures 209–210 and the closing measure both present the coda motive in its original and inverted form, going from E to B♭ in contrary motion. Measures 211–215 are a recapitulation of the opening five measures, incorporating the repeated B♭ and all the pitches of motive 2, reordered to emphasize the major second of motive 1, ascending and descending (D♭-E♭-D♭

E♮-D♮-E♮).

**EXAMPLE 1-9.** Bartók: String Quartet No. 5, I, mm. 209–218. Copyright 1936 by Universal Edition; Renewed 1963. Copyright and Renewal assigned to Boosey & Hawkes, Inc., for the U.S.A. Reprinted by permission. Permission granted by Universal Edition A.G., Vienna, for all countries of the world except USA.

The complex of relationships in this quartet produces a fascinating cohesive structure that can be approached as one approaches late Beethoven works or any other form that involves motivic interrelationships and developments. The peculiarly Bartókian features—the arch form and the inversion of restated materials—can be found in many of Bartók's other works (e.g., Music for Strings, Percussion, and Celesta, Fourth String Quartet, and the Violin Concerto). In fact, the concept of developing materials, not only in separate sections but almost as soon as they are presented, is typical of almost all of Bartók's music. This kind of form has a built-in unity and cohesion, and depends for contrast on dynamic, timbral, and temporal variety. Bartók's works, like this quartet, have a peculiar sense of symmetry without having exactly balanced sections or a predictable ordering of parts.[6] The force of the rhythmic and melodic activity drives the music into unique shapes, but Bartók's sense of form creates patterns out of these impulses just at the point where they threaten to overflow their boundaries. The deeply-rooted melodic and harmonic connections establish a clear, if definitely contemporary, pitch order, and the large-scale temporal shaping produces a marvelous aurally-apprehensible organism.

Halsey Stevens says, in writing about the Fifth Quartet:

> The problems of musical form, unlike those of the graphic and plastic arts which are fixed in time, are principally those of relating the sound-materials to those which have been heard and those which are to come. The attributes of unity, variety, balance, all are perceptible only by an act of will. The understanding of the shape of music is not attained by relaxing and allowing the sounds to flow through one like electricity through a wire. Such a procedure may provide a pleasant tingle now and then by momentary combinations of sound, but the meaning of the music, as expressed in the interrelationship of its parts, is irrevocably lost.
>
> Thus it is necessary, for a valid appreciation of a musical work, to become aware of what is happening in it at every moment. Fortunately, most compositions are not so complex that their basic structure is excessively difficult to perceive. From movement to movement, the Bartók quartets offer no really serious listening prob-

---

[6]The first movement of this fifth quartet depends for its proportions on the golden mean (or golden section), a ratio of $\frac{a}{b} = \frac{a+b}{a}$, where $\underline{a}$ is the longer part of a unit, $\underline{b}$ the shorter part, and $\underline{a} + \underline{b}$ the total unit. This ratio applies almost exactly to the time lengths of parts of this movement (see Bartók's timing in seconds in Fig. 1-4): between the exposition plus development and the recapitulation plus coda (longer section-shorter section); between the material in the exposition under I and II (longer-shorter); between the major divisions of the development (shorter-longer); between the material of the recapitulation under II and I (shorter-longer); and between the recapitulation and the coda (longer-shorter). Proportional relationships based on this particular well-known ratio are extremely prevalent in Bartók's works and are in many cases the underlying basis of form and balance. This proportion has been explained and extended into pitch and other parameters in an article by Erno Lendvai, "Duality and Synthesis in the Music of Béla Bartók," in *Module, Proportion, Symmetry, Rhythm,* pp. 174–193, and in his book, *Béla Bartók: An Analysis of His Music* (London: Kahn and Averill, 1971).

lem, but the interrelationships of the movements, so vital to the conception, is likely to be overlooked because of their temporal separation. Yet, once perceived, these relationships make the structure meaningful as a whole, which is infinitely greater than the sum of its individual parts.[7]

This quotation is appropriate for all music, particularly all twentieth-century music, where the understanding of the whole comes from active listening participation. It is especially appropriate to large-scale works, such as this Bartók quartet, in which more dimensions of the music are revealed upon each examination.

## VARIATIONAL FORMS

The variational processes of transformation have a great deal in common with many developmental procedures. The idea of variation-development finds its way into twentieth-century music at all levels of composition, since many pieces are constructed completely out of ever-varied presentations of the same basic idea. These ideas can be as specific as the maintenance of one series of pitches, or can center on a more general concept, such as melodic contour. The retention of one element through a series of changes creates form that is hard to categorize, since the process of transformation is usually more important than sectionalization or than any sort of "return."

A wide spectrum of contemporary works makes use of variational procedures. Some writers have indeed viewed every serial piece as a "variation," and in one sense this idea is true. Something is retained throughout (a pitch ordering) while many other elements are changed. However, since serialism itself can generate so many different kinds of vertical and horizontal pitch groupings, and since the other elements of composition are almost limitless, it is perhaps too inclusive a statement to say that every serial work is in "variation" form. There are, however, several different manifestations of variational ideas in the twentieth century, and some interesting approaches to the old problem of unity and variety.

Traditionally "variation form" has been most often considered as the "theme and variations" or as one of the passacaglia-chaconne processes. Twentieth-century composers have maintained an interest in these ideas. Thematic structures of a certain length and phrase structure are sometimes preserved exactly throughout a set of variations (Schoenberg, Variations for Orchestra); in other works, the general phrase patterning is constant without an exact retention of any element (Bartók, Concerto for Violin, II). Melodic lines too are important factors in the variational procedure: repeated melodic bass patterns are found in passacaglias by such diverse composers as Britten,

---

[7]Halsey Stevens, *The Life and Music of Béla Bartók*, rev. ed. (London: Oxford University Press, 1964), pp. 191–192.

Hindemith, and Schoenberg, and the principle can be extended to the ostinati of Stravinsky's music. A series of notes of varying lengths is often employed with or without specific contour manifestations (see the variation movements of Stravinsky's Sonata for Two Pianos and Concerto for Two Pianos.) Harmonic pattern retention, on the other hand, is not common in the twentieth century except in certain areas of jazz (the twelve-bar blues, for example, can be viewed as an extension of the chaconne procedure).

In addition to these more straightforward variation techniques, composers have also dealt with "variation" as a complex of interrelated small units. There is often no "theme" as such, only basic generating material. The only difference between this sort of procedure and a continuous developmental piece is the sectionalization; the variation works are divided into specific sections ("variations") which are internally unified by a similar method of presentation (texture, rhythm, etc.). At times the composer will maintain a rather consistent phrase pattern throughout at least some of these sections (Copland, Piano Variations; Dallapiccola, Variations for Orchestra), but in other instances there are no discernible phrase patterns. This procedure depends not on the statement and varied restatements of a complete idea but on the grouping of several sections, none of which is really the "theme" but all of which have a similarity of material and are constructed from different arrangements of small musical ideas.

One of the most complex arrangements of this sort is demonstrated by Webern's Variations for Orchestra, Op. 30. This work, written in 1940, is a "theme" and six variations, which Webern speaks of as being arranged in a kind of combination ternary and sonata design. The "theme" of the work, mm. 1–20 (Ex. 1-10), is itself a complex of relationships and illustrates several twentieth-century practices related to serialism and to motivic development. This work is based on a symmetrical twelve-tone series which is a composite of smaller units. As can be seen in Ex. 1-11, the last six notes of the row are the retrograde inversion of the first six notes, so that there are only twenty-four forms of the series rather than the customary forty-eight (the retrograde forms are the same as the inverted ones, and the retrograde inversions the same as the prime forms). The row is constructed completely of minor seconds (interval class one) and minor thirds (interval class three), with the first four notes serving as a basic pattern. This symmetrical four-note pattern occurs at other places in the row, too (notes 4–7, 6–9, and 9–12), and serves as a real generating force for the entire piece. This *a* set (A, B♭, D♭, C), one of Webern's favorite patterns, and the *b* set (B, D, E♭, G♭) generate the whole composition.[8]

---

[8] See Chapter Six, Section 2.3, for a more complete explanation of sets and for a method of symbolizing them. The *a* and *b* sets in Webern's Variations, Op. 30, are (0134) and (0347); both include the minor and major third combination.

**EXAMPLE 1-10.** Webern: Variations for Orchestra, Op. 30, mm. 1–20 ("Theme"). © 1956, Universal Edition. Used by permission of the publisher. Theodore Presser Company sole representative United States, Canada and Mexico.

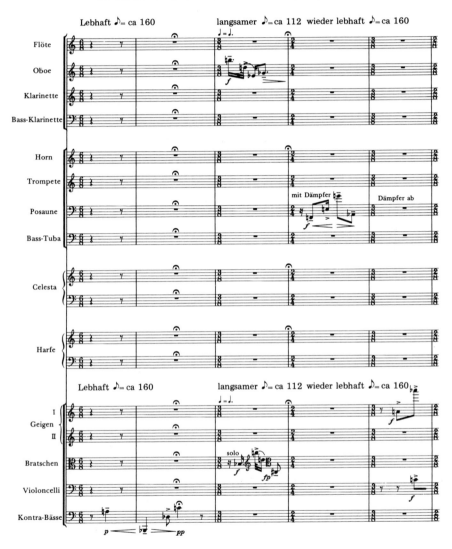

**EXAMPLE 1-10** continued.

**EXAMPLE 1-10** continued.

**EXAMPLE 1-11.** Webern: Variations for Orchestra, Op. 30 (1940); Series and motivic relationships.

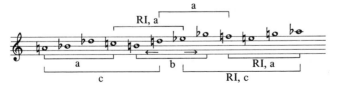

Webern's employment of serial procedure is dependent on these micro-structures that he has created within the row. Measures 1–20 of the Variations (Ex. 1-10) illustrate his complete reliance on the four-note sets from the row—all either of the *a* or *b* type. The four notes are generally presented as lines in one instrument, although the theme is punctuated by two vertical sonorities, one in m. 12 (a *b* collection) and one in m. 15 (an *a* set). The chord in m. 20 (an *a* set) leads directly to Variation I, where it forms an accompanimental background to a melodic line. Although all of these four-note groups combine to form permutations of complete twelve-tone rows, the emphasis is not so much on a twelve-tone series as on the sets of four notes, varied by instrumentation, rhythm, octave displacement, and dynamics.

In addition to the closely-woven pitch structure of this work, there is a tight rhythmic arrangement of parts. The opening bass motive presents one rhythmic pattern ( ♩ ♩ ♪♪ ) and the oboe line in m. 2 a second pattern ( ♫.♩♫. ), in which the first group ( ♫.♩ ) is retrograded and augmented to produce the second ( ♫. ). The second pattern is presented again in m. 2 in the viola, in a rhythmic canon at the 16th. These two rhythmic patterns are the only ones in the theme, and are presented in permutations similar to the changes in the pitch parameter. Figure 1-6 illustrates the rhythm of each four-note pitch pattern in mm. 1–20, also giving the dynamics, pitch set (*a* or *b*), and instrumentation. These rhythms employ retrograde, augmentation, and diminution, along with exact restatement, in much the same way that the pitch sets undergo retrograde, inversion, and restatement. As Webern himself states, "Everything in the piece is derived from the two phrases stated in the first two bars by double bass and oboe!"[9]

Although the first twenty measures of this work have definite interrelationships and seem to group into phrases, exact sectionalization is hard to determine. Webern refers to this section as a "period," evidently thinking of two rather balanced parts, but numerous overlapping features create grouping here (e.g., tempo, dynamics, fermatas, contour, and the punctuation points of the chords). The strongest separation sets apart mm. 10–12, which are the loudest and most dense of the passage. Perhaps more important than an exact breakdown into sections is the weaving together of the pitch and rhythmic motives into a complex that makes sense through Webern's unerring sense of timing.

Measures 19–20 serve as a connection to the first variation, introducing ideas of the next section. Example 1-12 is the beginning of the first variation (mm. 21–55), which, since no new material is present, depends for contrast

[9]Webern in a letter to Willi Reich, March 3, 1941. Quoted in Walter Kolneder, *Anton Webern*, tr. Humphrey Searle (Berkeley: University of California Press, 1968), p. 155.

| Dynamics | Pitch Set | Rhythmic Pattern I | Instrument, measure |
|----------|-----------|--------------------|---------------------|
| *p* | a | | Bass, 1 |
| *f* | a | | Trombone, 3 |
| *f* | a | Canon | Violin, 4—5 |
| *f* | b | | Cello, 4—5 |
| *p* ▷ a | | Canon | Violin, 7—9 |
| *p* ▷ a | | | Harp, Bass, 8—9 |
| *f* | a | Canon | Cello, 10—11 |
| *f* | a | | Tuba, Trombone, 10—11 |
| | | | Chord (b), m.12 ( *sf* ) |
| *p* ▷ a | | Canon | Tuba, 13—14 |
| *p* ▷ a | | | Harp, Viola, 13—14 |
| *f* ◁ a | | | Violin, 15—16 |
| | | | Chord (a), m.15 ( *sf* ) |
| *pp* | a | | Violin, 19—20 |
| | | | Chord, (a), m.20 leads to Variation I (*pp*) |

| Dynamics | Pitch Set | Rhythmic Pattern II | Instrument, measure |
|----------|-----------|---------------------|---------------------|
| *f* | b | Canon | Oboe, 2 |
| *f* | a | | Viola, 2 |
| *sf* ▷ *p* | b | | Bass Clarinet, 6 |
| *f* ◁ b | | | Winds, 11—12 |
| *p* ▷ b | | Canon | Bass Clarinet, 17—18 |
| *p* ▷ b | | | Oboe, 17—18 |

**FIGURE 1-6.** Webern: Variations for Orchestra, Op. 30. Theme (mm. 1–20); Dynamics, Pitch, Rhythm, Instrumentation.

on a different mode of presentation. This whole section is unified by its texture, a melodic line stated over repeated four-note chords. This new textural presentation contrasts with the linear nature of the theme. However, the basic ideas have still been retained. Measures 21–23, in the violin line, are simply a rhythmic augmentation and retrograde of the bass line of m. 1, with the pitches exactly maintained. Measures 24–26, violins, are an exact augmentation of m. 2, with the pitches of the viola line retained. The trombone line of m. 3 occurs in measures 27–30, clarinet part, and the cello line

**EXAMPLE 1-12.** Webern: Variations for Orchestra, Op. 30, mm. 18–34 (end of Theme and beginning of Variation I). © 1956, Universal Edition. Used by permission of the publisher. Theodore Presser Company sole representative United States, Canada and Mexico.

**EXAMPLE 1-12** continued.

of mm. 4–5 appears in the trumpet in mm. 31–34. Although Webern does not keep a measure-by-measure correspondence throughout this variation, and the two sections are of differing lengths, there is a clear retention of elements from the theme with a contrasting method of presentation.

As Webern shortens and lengthens the variations later in the work and develops the material more extensively, the relationship to the theme becomes less aurally apparent. Variation II (mm. 56–73) emphasizes only vertical elements in the form of four-note chords, creating a shorter "bridge" variation. Variation III (mm. 74–109), by contrast, is completely linear, with an almost monophonic texture. The four-note rhythmic and pitch sets have been broken down into three- and even two-note patterns, effecting a much more fragmentary use of materials and less density than in any of the previous sections.

Variation IV (mm. 110–134) returns to four-note groups, and employs a much thicker texture, created by the overlapping of a number of contrapuntal parts. This variation uses no chords; however chordal elements return in Variation V as punctuations to the linear elements. Variation V (mm. 135–145) is almost completely at a *p* or *pp* dynamic level, and, like Variation II, is a short transitional variation to what Webern calls a coda. This sixth variation (mm. 146–180) summarizes many of the ideas of the preceding sections but depends particularly on long three- and four-note simultaneities, some formed from a new superposition of two *a* pitch sets.

The theme of these Webern variations incorporates motivic variational procedures which are typical of many of Webern's works, both serial and non-serial. The sectional variational principle extends these interrelationships to a higher structural level. Many twentieth-century works employ similar processes, either in works labeled as "Variations" or in more subtle manifestations. This sort of unobtrusive variational method is especially prevalent in the early works of Webern and Schoenberg, where the resultant form is a product of an almost psychological, inner continuity of time.

Example 1-13 is the fourth of a set of short piano works, Op. 19, written by Schoenberg in 1911. This piece is one of the most concentrated expressions of Schoenberg's thought, and is similar to much of Webern's early work. In such compositions, every event is important and nothing can be overlooked or taken for granted. Although both Webern and Schoenberg are strongly rooted in a nineteenth-century Germanic romantic tradition, the more conventional aspects of their music are often overlooked because of the freedom of transformation and the different approach to pitch order.

Op. 19, No. 4, is clearly divided into three sections (phrases) by the silence which follows the lines in mm. 5 and 9. These divisions create rather traditional "four-bar phrases," the first and second prepared by an anacrusis and the first extended at the cadence. Each of these phrases, although it is not apparent at first glance, uses the same material, and the short piece is in essence three "variations" of one idea.

**EXAMPLE 1-13.** Schoenberg: *Sechs kleine Klavierstücke,* Op. 19 (1911), IV. Copyright 1913 by Wien Universal Edition. Renewed 1940 by Arnold Schoenberg. Used by permission of Belmont Music Publishers, Los Angeles, California 90049.

The most obvious connection between the three phrases is the contour of
the melodic line. In each case a melodic pattern is presented monophonically,
interrupted by two chords at certain strategic spots, and in each case the line
is a descending one, made up of three descending parts. Figure 1-7 illustrates
these contoural patterns graphically. Measures 1–5 descend first, after an
ascending third, from $a^2$ to $a^1$; then, after another ascending third, from $e^2$
down to $e^1$; and finally, in a continuation of this line, from $d^2$ down to $f\#^1$, a
smaller descent. The ascending third, filled in ($f\#^1 - g\#^1 - a\#^1$), creates a
cadential pattern of expectation. These three descending shapes are carried
out again in mm. 5–9. An ascending third ($b^1 - d^2$) initiates a small descent
(m. 6 is a varied restatement of the notes and contour of the end of the first
phrase, mm. 3–4). Measure 7 is a descent of an octave ($a^1 - a$), using an
exact transposition of the first part of m. 3. Measures 8–9 contain the final
descent of a seventh, to the lowest melodic point in the piece. The cadence
here ($b, c^1, d^1, e$) may be compared with m. 4 ($f\#^1, g\#^1, a\#^1$).

The last phrase, mm. 10–13, opens with an almost exact restatement of
the pitches of the opening, and continues in two descending patterns of
smaller range ($f\#^1 - g\#$ and $g^1 - b\flat$), again joined into one line. The piece
closes with ascending half-step motion, the only cadence to create such a
definite termination. The three phrases, with their interior shapes of three

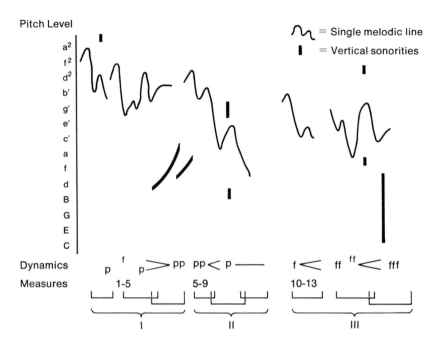

**FIGURE 1-7.** Schoenberg: *Sechs kleine Klavierstücke,* Op. 19 (1911), IV; Melodic contour, texture, dynamics, and sectionalization.

descending patterns, provide an overall three-part descent for the entire piece.

In addition to the pitch retention already mentioned, where Schoenberg is reusing melodic lines, there is also strong intervallic retention, particularly by emphasis on the major seventh and the tritone. Measure 1 outlines the major seventh a²–b♭¹, and the punctuating interval of m. 2 is the tritone. These intervals continue to occur at every phrase beginning and ending. The cadence chord of m. 4 contains an important major seventh, and the beginning of phrase 2 (m. 6) is constructed around tritones in two registers (f♯¹ — c² superimposed on a diminished triad). The two cadence chords in mm. 8 and 12 both contain all interval classes, spaced so as to emphasize the major seventh on the bottom and the tritone on top.

In contrast to the unity in the pitch elements and in the shape of the melodic lines, the three phrases are presented with differing "characters." The first is basically soft and utilizes dotted patterns and sixteenth-note groupings; the second is soft, with slower note values ( ♩, ♫, ♬ ). The last phrase is loud, *martellato*, and employs fast note values which slow to two rhythmically similar measures (mm. 11–12; cf. m. 6) and a final cadence note. Each phrase thus consists of similar pitch material, contour, and texture (a monophonic line punctuated by two chords), with variation effected by changes in dynamics and rhythmic patterns—changes which are consistent throughout one phrase.

In this piece there is also an underlying rhythmic structure which shapes the music in time. Each phrase begins with an upbeat moving to a weak accent which continues to the most accented portion of the phrase, an accent created mainly by the textural thickening. Fast note values at the beginning of each phrase slow to progressively longer values. Such an intricate structure, though apparently very simple, requires more than a casual glance at the music.[10] The subtlety of the operations, even though on a small scale, provides rewarding returns from a deeper penetration of the music.

In speaking of his Orchestral Variations, Op. 31, Schoenberg said:

> I employ constant variations, hardly ever repeat anything unaltered, jump quickly to the remoter stages of development, and I take for granted that the educated listener is able to discover the intervening stages for himself.[11]

This idea of constant variation applies to Schoenberg's other work too, as well as to many works in the twentieth century. Variational processes make demands on the listener, which return, to the perceptive musician, new insights into the processes of continuity and contrast.

## STRATIFIED AND INTERPOLATED FORMS

The ideas of development and variation have long been a part of the process of composition in Western music. These procedures are still important in twentieth-century music and form the basis for the growth of many organic formal entities. In addition to these techniques, twentieth-century composers have also employed a more segmented approach to materials, which can lead to integrated musical works when combined with return factors. These segments may consist of small bits of material, as in many of Stravinsky's works, or of layers or blocks of material—separate sound units each of which has a recognizable combination of parameters, e.g., high, dense, and loud, or low, thin, and soft. These units can be presented superimposed, juxtaposed, or interpolated into other material to create an interruption pattern on a higher level.

---

[10]For a rhythmic analysis of this work, see *The Rhythmic Structure of Music* by Grosvenor Cooper and Leonard Meyer (Univ. of Chicago Press, 1960), pp. 174–177.

[11]Arnold Schoenberg, "The Orchestral Variations, Op. 31: A Radio Talk," *The Score* 27 (July, 1960), p. 30.

Stratification and interpolation as form-creating processes are not entirely new in Western music, but certainly twentieth-century composers have made more use of these ideas than have previous composers. An understanding of these types of forms requires a new "block" approach; instead of following the organic development of an idea, the listener must perceive separate complete units in various combinations. These units are treated in many possible ways, some emphasizing direct contrast and some incorporating transformation processes. As Varèse states, a sound block can be broken into separate parts and each part developed independently, or, conversely, parts can be gathered into a complete unit. There can be gradual changes of emphasis within the sound unit (e.g., by a gradual increase in dynamics), or between sound units, as one block is overlapped with another. These transitional procedures of dissolution, amalgamation, and gradation serve as binding elements which provide the continuity contributed in other music by more traditional connective devices.[12]

All of these procedures contribute different elements to the shaping process, and demand revised thinking from the performer and listener. Ideas can be juxtaposed or superimposed with exciting and occasionally jarring effects, much as blocks of color are put together in much modern visual art. This technique requires perception on a higher level: to grasp a large-scale pattern, if there is one, or to understand the balance between units and the interruptive effect of certain blocks. On the other hand, sounds can almost imperceptibly change into other guises, as one color can merge gradually with another. In these cases clear-cut sectionalization gives way to a gradual transformation process that may be the basis of an entire work.

Many works in the twentieth century illustrate these procedures, but particularly since 1945 composers have included these techniques in their work. The effects are sometimes disturbing and chaotic, or even static; "block" procedures are peculiarly suited to express the disjointed, brutal,

---

[12]Important, perhaps unfamiliar, terms employed in the following discussions include:

Procedures of contrast: *stratification:* layering of texture, or the independent operation of more than one parameter simultaneously; *juxtaposition:* abrupt change of elements; and *interpolation:* abrupt change of elements, with (almost immediate) continuation of the first idea.

Procedures of connection: *gradation:* gradual change within one parameter, or an overlapping of two blocks of sound; *amalgamation:* the synthesis of sound events into an inter-parametric unit where parameters act together; and *dissolution:* the separation of an inter-parametric unit into its component parts, where usually each part is developed independently.

Some of these terms have been employed by other authors. See especially Edward T. Cone's article, "Stravinsky: The Progress of a Method" in *Perspectives of New Music,* I/1 (Fall, 1962), 18–26, where he particularly mentions *stratification,* but as a successive phenomenon.

and often incomprehensible nature of much of the modern world. Yet such procedures can also be the basis for a new sense of proportion and shape in the hands of a composer skilled at balancing recurrence and contrast.

Two works which illustrate different aspects of these procedures are Music for Brass Quintet by Gunther Schuller and *Threnody: To the Victims of Hiroshima* (for 52 stringed instruments) by Krzysztof Penderecki. Although both works were written in 1960–61, they are different in medium and especially in notation. Schuller relies on traditional pitch notation and meter signatures; Penderecki incorporates "time" notation (indicating the number of seconds for each section) and many different and less standardized types of pitch and timbre indications. The brass work employs a pitch series and distinctive sonorities, some of them tertian. The string composition, however, depends more on blocks of sound and sliding or indefinite pitch than on recognizable intervals and chords. In both works, stratification and interpolation are important processes in the creation of an integrated whole.

Schuller's Music for Brass Quintet is in three movements, of which only the third falls into a very clear-cut pattern (A B A'). The three movements are loosely connected by a brief introduction and closing which frame movement II. Both the first and second movements are interesting because of the factors of amalgamation and dissolution at work; no specific letter names or sectional titles adequately describe these movements.

The first movement opens with a statement of soft, sustained material (Ex. 1-14) and is interrupted in mm. 11–12 by a fast, dense, louder unit (Ex. 1-15). These ideas appear at first to be juxtaposed, with no particular

**EXAMPLE 1-14.** Schuller: Music for Brass Quintet (1961), I, mm. 1–3. Reprinted by permission of Associated Music Publishers, Inc.

**EXAMPLE 1-15.** Schuller: Music for Brass Quintet (1961), I, mm. 11–12. Reprinted by permission of Associated Music Publishers, Inc.

interrelationship; but as the piece develops, the juxtapositions form a larger pattern of interpolations—a "planting" of dense passages in the middle of sustained material which continues before and after the disturbing block. In the first movement, the opening material, after being restated, is developed; in these developmental measures the contrasting loud unit interrupts several times, reaching a culmination in the closing measures of the movement (Ex. 1-16). This dense, loud, cacophony breaks off abruptly to contrast

**EXAMPLE 1-16.** Schuller: Music for Brass Quintet (1961), I, mm. 53–55. Reprinted by permission of Associated Music Publishers, Inc.

with the beginning of the second movement. Some of the interruptions in the first movement have the same pitch content; more importantly, the units are related by the loud dynamic level, the increased speed of the notes, and the thickened texture. These blocks, composed of specific parametric characteristics, contrast with the soft, sustained, and relatively less dense material surrounding them.

The interpolated units in the first movement are related to other interruptions in the composition; indeed, it is hard to make sense out of the music in m. 56 of the last movement (Ex. 1-17) without a comprehension of the first movement. At this spot in III a slow, sustained solo (the end of a cadenza-

**EXAMPLE 1-17.** Schuller: Music for Brass Quintet (1961), III, mm. 54–59. Reprinted by permission of Associated Music Publishers, Inc.

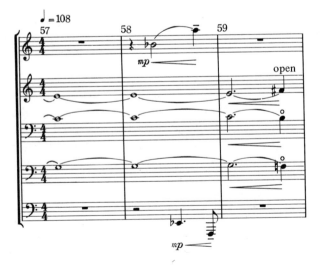

like section featuring each instrument in turn) precedes and follows a loud, fast outburst from the entire instrumental group. The sustained material moves to a return of the opening of the movement in m. 63. The interpolations occur at irregular intervals throughout the composition, increasing in frequency in the second movement and decreasing in appearances in the third. The whole work presents an interesting shape created from the contrast of two opposing units—the first continuing serenely before and after the frenzied outbursts.

The second movement is an example of amalgamation created by textural and rhythmic activity. After the short introduction, the movement begins with single notes, mostly quarters (Ex. 1-18), which gradually coalesce into a climax resembling the interpolations of the other movements (Ex. 1-19).

**EXAMPLE 1-18.** Schuller: Music for Brass Quintet (1961), II, mm. 3–13. Reprinted by permission of Associated Music Publishers, Inc.

**EXAMPLE 1-18** continued.

**EXAMPLE 1-19.** Schuller: Music for Brass Quintet (1961), II, mm. 20–21. Reprinted by permission of Associated Music Publishers, Inc.

This thickening process is repeated several times in the course of the movement, with increasingly faster note values. The movement culminates in two dense, loud sections at the end (mm. 52–58; 62–71), which break off into a soft, sustained closing chord. These amalgamations and dissolutions from a less active music into a more active climax and back again are the basis of form in the second movement; sectional delineations are not as important as the continuous thickening and thinning process. The movement is diagrammed in Fig. 1-8, which shows simultaneous and successive densities together with the general rhythmic activity of the movement. The texture is unified throughout by a number of sustained pitches and repeated-note patterns; the return to a thin texture marks the beginning of each section.

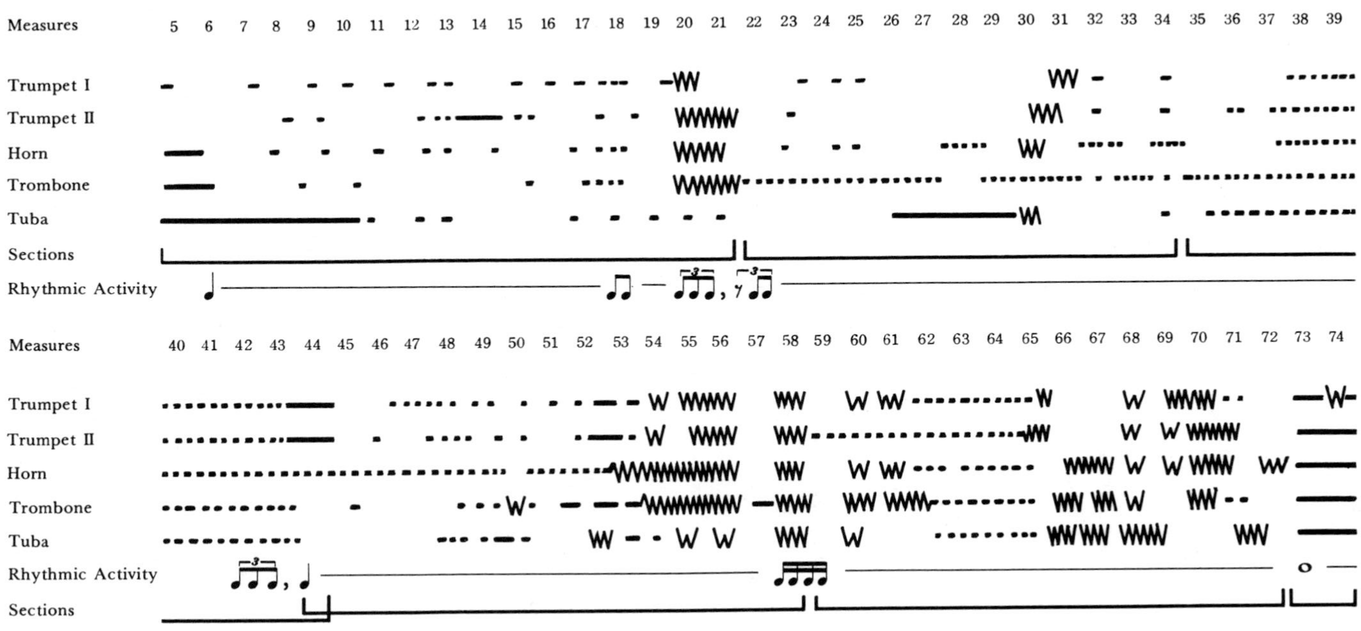

Measures 1–4 are an introduction. Texture in the rest of the movement is indicated by:

    = single notes

—— = sustained notes

WWWWW = continuous line

- - - - - = single notes

·········· = repeated notes

**FIGURE 1-8.** Schuller: Music for Brass Quintet (1961), II; Profile of horizontal density, vertical density, and rhythmic activity.

Music for Brass Quintet illustrates formal processes that are less dependent on sectional labels than on certain techniques. Each movement is shaped by contrast, often between very brief parts, and the whole is unified by a larger pattern of interpolation which develops throughout the three movements. Changes in density, both horizontal and vertical, control the second movement, as isolated pitches are synthesized into a complex which then is dissolved into its components. Increasingly faster note values and repeated notes propel this movement to a climax. The first and third movements are less propulsive, instead transforming material gradually. Only the third movement has a formal plan that could be described by traditional labels, and even this labeling would overlook the important connections with the rest of the composition.

Penderecki's *Threnody*, in contrast, is a one-movement work lasting about $8\frac{1}{2}$ minutes. Again traditional sectional labels do not adequately describe the formal processes at work, since superposition and juxtaposition of layers of material combine with transitional overlaps to produce a dynamic and impelling composition. There are several types of sound blocks—units which have certain parametric characteristics—and these blocks overlap, contrast with each other, and return in changed forms throughout the composition. The first sound block, which opens the composition, is loud, sustained, high, and dense, with all 52 strings playing the highest possible notes on their instruments, *ff*. The result is a unit of indefinite pitch; this unit changes in dynamics and timbre (vibrato is added), but the registral and textural effects are still recognizable.

A second sound block overlaps with and finally replaces the first in all instruments of the ensemble. This second unit is composed of percussive sounds and different timbral effects (playing behind the bridge, pizzicato, etc.). Again the sounds have no definite pitch and are high, but the dynamic level is lower and the resultant sound fragmented; sustained tones give way gradually to separate attacks, which are, however, connected into lines. The gradual interpenetration of the second sound unit into the first is a good example of a gradated transition from one block to the next (see Fig. 1-9, 0'–1'49'').

A new type of procedure overlaps with the second sound unit. Within one instrumental section, a note of definite pitch expands into a block of sound, bounded by specific pitch limits, and then contracts back to one note. In some cases the dynamic level also increases and decreases. This gradation within a sound unit produces a contrast to the first section of the work; instead of a uniformly thick block, a soft, thin sound in the middle register expands and contracts. The process continues to two climax points (see Fig. 1-9, 3'34'' and 4'33''), but is interrupted twice by a solid block of indefinite pitch, thick-textured like the opening of the work. These interruptions return material from the opening, restating the characteristics of pitch, texture, and duration if not of dynamics and register. The first interruption

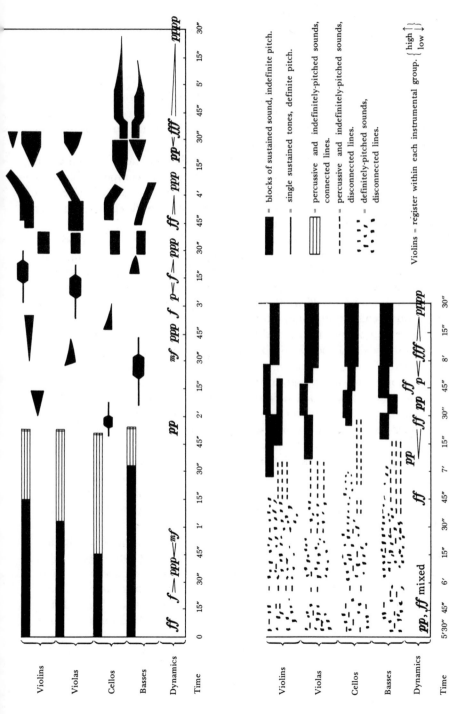

**FIGURE 1-9.** Penderecki: *Threnody* (1959–61); Sound material, register, duration, and dynamics.

is low and soft; the second is a *fff* "chord," in a middle range, which gradually decreases to a single low pitch marked *pppp*. The following five seconds of silence provide the only "rest" in the composition, perhaps the most important sectionalizing feature.

The process in this third unit (1'49"–5'26"—see Fig. 1-9) can be viewed as the growth from one note to a thicker block and a subsequent return to one sound—a process which determines the shape of the composition over an extended period of time. From this point of view, the interruptions of "chords" similar to the opening sound are the point of greatest expansion of the single note. At the same time, this whole section may also be seen as an amalgamation of individual parts into the return of the composite block of the opening, a block which recurs throughout. In either view, Penderecki has balanced a textural mass with changes in dynamics and register, creating a new section out of old materials.

The remainder of the composition (from 5'30" to 8'26") is composed of two different sorts of sound material, overlapped as at the beginning. The first unit is formed from short notes, harmonics, and percussive sounds, scattered throughout the full register of the ensemble. Although each attack has its own dynamic marking, the aural resultant is a medium-loud level. These sounds change gradually into attacks without any definite pitch, materials reminiscent of the second unit in the piece (49"–1'49"), although percussive sounds and specific timbral effects are performed in broken patterns instead of the earlier connected line. At 6'56" a block similar to the opening sound is superimposed on the activity of the ensemble. The violins play a high, dense, sustained unit that gradually dominates all the instruments. This interpenetration of two ideas is the reverse of the procedure in the opening section of the work, where a sustained block was gradually broken into separate lines. Here at the end, individual sounds are amalgamated into a composite block. Not only does this process provide a retrograde of the opening activity, but the return of thick blocks of sound creates a closure for the work. The final climax comes at 7'56", where all the instruments strike a thick *fff* chord, which decreases in volume for thirty seconds as a final cadence.

This work affects the listener from both a sonic and a formal standpoint. To some, the kinds of sound material vividly express the bombings, blasts, and sufferings in Hiroshima. Penderecki has, in addition, arranged these materials so that they have a particularly proportioned shape in time. This shape is dependent on several parameters, each of which has a slightly different design. From a textural point of view, the opening sound mass contrasts with the single notes expanding to larger blocks (1'49"), and with the separate attacks in a denser presentation throughout the ensemble (5'30"). The opening texture then returns at the end, giving a kind of A B C A pattern. Timbre and duration form a succession of sustained and separated sounds in a rondo-like fashion (A B A′ B′ A). Pitch alternates between indefinite and definite, in an A B A pattern. In each of these ternary-like designs the middle section is the longest, and can itself be broken down into phrases.

In contrast to the ternary sense of return at the end of *Threnody*, Penderecki creates a similarity between the cadences at 4'33"–5'31" and 7'57"–8'26". Each cadence is a loud chord decreasing in volume; the two places create an overlay of binary shaping for the composition. A one-minute decay concludes a 5½-minute section and a 30-second decay concludes a 3-minute section, each cadence being about one-sixth the time of the complete section. A two-part form is thus created by these cadences.

Figure 1-9 diagrams the complete work in terms of the type of sound unit, register, duration (against Penderecki's indicated time in seconds), and dynamics. The notation of the piece in many cases is similar to the figure; the complete score should be consulted after listening to the composition. Besides the more clear-cut ternary, binary, and rondo implications shown in the figure, gradual overlap is important in joining the first two and last two units. Gradation, amalgamation, and dissolution work within sections, and numerous different blocks are superimposed on each other, particularly in the middle of the composition. The listener must apprehend characteristics in each block of material and follow parametric operations separately throughout the work. In addition to superpositions of layers, interpenetrations of units, and various growth procedures, Penderecki has a sense of return and balance which creates meaningful formal shapes out of a variety of materials. *Threnody* is an effective piece and has become one of the best-known works written since 1955.

### OPEN FORMS

Much of the music composed since 1950 reveals a radical approach to structure. Western music traditionally has a beginning, a middle, and an end; a composition progresses in one direction toward certain climactic points and creates a meaningful shape in time, a shape carefully constructed by the composer. In contrast to these standard procedures, composers in the second half of the century have developed new formal techniques, which are ongoing processes rather than closed designs. These works depend not only on the composer but also on the performers and occasionally on the audience for their shape and structure.

There are all sorts of manifestations of this more open process. Different sorts of chance operations can be incorporated into the compositional act—the rolling of dice, the dropping of pins—and the results can produce either a very specific piece or one in which the performer makes choices in various parameters. Aleatory operations can occur at the performance level too, either with specifically-notated material or with more freedom of improvisation. Frequently a performer can choose his own pitch material to be stated in a certain time length, or can extend given sound units to his own temporal boundaries. Any parameter can be specified or left free by the composer, an approach that results in more participation by the performer. At times the composer chooses to control the shaping parameters (often duration, texture, or dynamics), while leaving details unspecified. In other works elements which determine the basic shape of the work are open to the judgment of the performer.

These pieces, where shape is under the control of a performer, usually provide for a formal design to be created *at* a performance—a real "open form" procedure. This process often revolves around a number of sections of music, given by the composer, which are to be arranged a different way each time the work is heard. Other approaches make use of "works-in-progress," which change (expand or contract) each time the piece is heard because the composer has "revised" the work. Theater pieces and "happenings" can also depend on openness; a scenario or suggestions for action can be the basis of an activity that may involve the audience.

The idea of a form that is not architectonically constructed within a predetermined shape is an important one in twentieth-century music. The open process is essentially new in Western music, although "compositions" such as Gregorian chant are probably the result of the juxtaposition of small units and their rearrangement in different orders at a "performance." The free-wheeling approach to form found in many newer works is based more on philosophy (particularly Oriental) and on non-Western and improvisatory musical processes than it is on the traditional structured designs of Western music. The composer is no longer a "creator" but a participant in an action that includes several human responses. An art work is not a fixed entity, which can be repeated endlessly, but an organism which changes and is reshaped with every new human contact. Such ideas were prevalent in twentieth-century arts before they became a part of musical thinking; visual artists such as Marcel Duchamp have influenced the works of, among others, John Cage and Morton Feldman, two composers who have worked with different sorts of openness in musical structure.

All these ideas raise a whole new set of questions in the approach to a musical composition. If each performance of a work is different, how can a piece be analyzed? Does the piece, indeed, really exist? Some composers have in fact denied that they are creating musical compositions; instead they describe their work as an "activity" for which they provide guidelines. It is often important for the listener to try to understand the intentions of the composer in a particular work and if possible to grasp the philosophy behind the writing. Since each composition differs, this comprehension sometimes requires reading through long sets of instructions, or devising a musical activity out of materials (e.g., several plastic sheets) given with no instructions. Books and articles on composers' thoughts, although often muddled and sometimes mystical, can provide an insight into many musical works.

Once the intent of the piece is relatively clear, one can examine the materials given by the composer and can speculate on various shaping potentials. Sometimes the materials given are extremely limited. In John Cage's *4'33"* only the time span is specified, during which any combination of instruments can do anything. This work, of course, carries out Cage's philosophy that no distinction should be made between the sounds of a composition and the other sounds of the world, a philosophy that does away with a structured "piece" in favor of free sound experiences. The materials the composer gives, however, can be much more structured. Lukas Foss, in *Echoi*, allows for improvisation within a certain time span on given pitch and dynamic materials. Other sections of the piece also specify the sound materials but leave open the time span and the number of interpolations of added music. In other compositions, changes can be made in details (micro-form) or in the largest units (macro-form), as blocks are rearranged and movements juggled.

The results of all of these procedures are mixed. If the composer does not specify certain aspects of a composition, the performers must be imaginative and musical enough to work with the materials they have in an interesting way, especially in the sensitive matter of temporal control. At times this freedom leads to an exciting, spontaneous improvisation at the time of performance, as several musical minds interact to create a new, never-to-be-repeated work. At other times, the results are chaotic or dull. Some of Feldman's works, which have a limited range of sound material, create a static atmosphere in which no progression of events is noticeable. Composers often explain such works by references to a metaphysical method of composition, which cannot be elaborated or systematized, and thus not analyzed.[13]

These less-confined approaches to form have created a radically new approach to music that tends to parallel the aesthetic of a society accustomed to non-structure, constantly-new stimuli, disposable goods, and more individual involvement. In the hands of sensitive musicians, these shaping processes can result in interesting and artistic designs, which often incorporate aspects of return or recurrence. The designs are perhaps more interesting because they *can* change, much as a mobile can present different proportions when viewed from several angles, although the constructing material remains constant. One of these musical examples of open form is *Available Forms 1* by Earle Brown, written in July, 1961 for a chamber ensemble of eighteen players. This piece consists of six pages of score, each page having four or five separate "events" on it (a total of twenty-seven events). The conductor can begin with any event and can continue in any manner he chooses, repeating or eliminating sections at will, creating any sort of arrangement until he chooses to stop. The event chosen by the conductor is indicated to the performers, who then produce the material Brown has specified. The conductor must

---

[13]See Morton Feldman, *Notes* on Mainstream recording 5007.

respect most of Brown's instructions for the micro-forms, while creating his own macro-form, although he may choose to superimpose events or occasionally change dynamic levels. The tempo of each block is specified by the conductor, too, although the events have an approximate built-in length. The performers have limited freedom within each section, as they can sometimes choose methods of attack and time placement of sounds.

Within these twenty-seven events Brown has created connections between sections of material which are evident in almost every performance of the work, and which can be emphasized by a conductor if he wishes. The events are rather limited in type. As Brown says,

> There is intentionally not too much material in this piece in order for the musicians to *hear* their position in context. It has proven to be practical in that the performers have enough time in rehearsals to become familiar with the sound of the event and of their relationship within it. It is, of course, ambiguous and never the same twice. The ambiguity does not distress the performers; it involves them creatively and creates a feeling of intensity and engagement in the performance felt by the musicians, the conductor, the audience, and me. What I have tried to achieve with this score—the composed events as "plastic" material and the given conditions of control, ambiguity, and uncontrol—is an intensification of the sense of being *involved* in the uncertain but urgent process of the work defining itself from moment to moment during performance. I "composed" the ambiguity for the sake of the flexibility (of resulting orchestral rhythm and "discovered" nuance of timbre) throughout the entire score and from performance to performance.[14]

The material includes several sections of sustained chords, usually soft and in the middle register. These chords are heard as pedal points varying in density; in fact the notes around $b\flat^1$ and $c^2$ are consistently prominent in many performances and act almost as a "tonic" if repeated enough. These chords are referential points whenever they return. In contrast to the sustained sounds, a number of sections involve separate notes (usually staccato) in all the instruments, producing a dense effect of random pitches scattered throughout the ensemble. These sections can be either soft or loud, and tend to blur specific instrumental colors.

A third type of material features more recognizable timbres, as a smaller group of instruments plays separate notes, lines, arpeggios, or chords. Particularly prominent are loud bursts in the marimba, xylophone, or piano; arpeggiated chords in various pitched percussion instruments; and wind and brass solos. Other sections indicate flutter tonguing or "unstable timbre and frequency" in the instruments, which in some performances become slow lyric melodies and in others veiled impressionistic effects. However, Brown does not exploit the multitude of coloristic possibilities available; only certain sounds and textures are incorporated into the specified events.

By creating similarities among certain of the twenty-seven events, Brown

---

[14]Earle Brown, "Performance Note" to *Available Forms 1.*

determines something of the larger form. It is hard to choose events so that there is not some alternation between the static pedals of the chords and the more active outbursts either of the whole ensemble or of isolated instruments. Textures also vary from thick sustained or active sounds to a thin layer of solo instruments. The conductor can superimpose events on the chords or can return the sustained sounds in a rondo-like pattern, using different sonorities each time. The timing of events, the pauses, and the overall durational proportions are completely within the conductor's control, and the continuity and large temporal shaping of the work depend on a sensitive perception and an interaction with the particular ensemble, audience, and occasion. Obviously such a work has no specific form that can be analyzed and diagrammed; it is only a number of *potential* shapes that can be realized under certain conditions.

Brown discusses his purpose in this piece in some detail in a prefatory note:

> A performance is a "process" which intentionally transforms the disparate independent entities into one particular integral identity . . . which is this particular work performed by this particular conductor and orchestra at this particular moment. The audible result (an available form) is the product of many independent intentions and in itself integral, inherent, and relevant, but, from a logical point of view, un-intentional in regard to its momentary particular form. . . . It is a conception of sound, organized events, and ensemble, as "plastic" material capable of being molded, modified, and "formed" in various ways. The conductor's function is analogous to that of a painter who has a canvas (time) and colors (timbre) and the possibility of working with the medium. In the case of "Available Forms 1," time is implied in the events, the timbre is given but variable (through dynamics), the micro-forms are composed, and the combinatorial possibilities are conditional in some but not all cases. With all of the conditioning there is still a high degree of "plasticity" inherent in the work, and this plasticity is an indispensable element which engages the performers, the conductor, the audience, and myself in the immediacy and life of the work.[15]

*Available Forms 1* is only one manifestation of the many possibilities for open forms, aleatory, and improvisation. The performer in such works must be imaginative and resourceful enough not only to fulfill the technical demands but also to rise to the level of a co-creator. To the listener "open form" pieces often sound no different from those composed by strict serial or computer methods; in either case the auditor must separate the various sound materials being employed and must concentrate on the shaping of these materials. In some cases interesting patterns of balance, return, and contrast emerge; in others the novelty of the sound components alone is sufficient, at least initially, to hold the attention. In the worst examples, dull sounds combine with chaotic or static presentations to produce a jumble of meaning-

---

[15]Earle Brown, "Prefatory Note" to *Available Forms 1.*

less noise. The listener should judge these pieces as he does any other work to determine if materials are stated for too long or too short a time, if contrast in some parameter functions to create variety, if a referential element produces unity.

Musical form is an elusive property of composition. Composers in the twentieth century have depended for their shaping procedures on traditional designs, on numerous developmental and variational processes, on stratification and interruption, or on a less structured approach based on extramusical considerations or on the interaction of personalities. All of these ideas present their own problems for the performer, listener, and analyst. In each case one must identify the sound material, remembering that any event in any parameter can have any function, and must try to find patterns in the interactions of the material. In some cases parameters function together to create clear-cut sections; in other works each parameter follows a separate shaping procedure. In a number of compositions sectionalization is not as important as a process of continuous growth, either in motivic development or in gradations of texture or dynamics. There are so many possibilities that it is impossible to enumerate them all; each work must be examined on its own terms. However, the constants of recurrence, contrast, and variation bind together the most traditional and the most "avant-garde" works of the twentieth century. Every work has some contrast and some element of recurrence. The problem is to find the important shaping parameters and to describe the patterns created, although not necessarily by a specific labeling.

Even though there are many different formal procedures in the twentieth century, resulting in all sorts of unique shapes, aesthetic judgment can still suggest that some works are more or less interesting on the basis of their formal structure. A number of twentieth-century works are static, not incorporating enough contrast; others are chaotic, presenting too much material in no recognizable pattern. After much listening and examination, it is possible to find an exciting variety of twentieth-century musical works in which the best of traditional procedures merge with innovative processes to create meaningful and interesting temporal shapes.

## SUGGESTIONS FOR FURTHER STUDY

*Selected Books and Articles*

Brown, Earle, "Form in New Music," *Source* 1/1 (January, 1967), 49–51. Part of this article appears as part of Brown's contribution to *Darmstädter Beiträge zur Neuen Musik* X (1965) (see reference below). Both articles discuss Brown's approach to form as both a "method" and a "non-method" and give insights into many of his compositions.

Cope, David, *New Directions in Music*. Dubuque: Wm. C. Brown, 1971. 140 pages. Discussion of the main trends in music since around 1945: electronic music, multimedia, improvisations, etc. Many descriptions of pieces and processes; little analysis or analytical method. Good source of composers and compositions.

*Darmstädter Beiträge zur Neuen Musik. Form in der Neuen Musik.* Mainz: B. Schott's Söhne, 1966. 75 pages. Edited by Ernst Thomas. Articles on form in recent music by Adorno, Ligeti, Haubenstock-Ramati, Dahlhaus, Kagel, and Brown. In German and English.

*die Reihe.* 7: *Form-Space.* Bryn Mawr: Theodore Presser, 1965 (translation of the original Universal German edition of 1960). An issue devoted to several articles on form and its relationship to space. Of general interest are the articles on form by Ligeti and Wolff.

Eschman, Karl, *Changing Forms in Modern Music,* 2nd ed. Boston: E.C. Schirmer, 1968. 213 pages. Discusses new aesthetics of form and contemporary manifestations of variations, sonatas, fugues, etc. Several detailed analyses, particularly of music before 1945.

Meyer, Leonard, *Music, the Arts, and Ideas.* Chicago: University of Chicago Press, 1967. 342 pages. A philosophical study of cultural patterns in the twentieth century and predictions for the future. Part III has a particular relevence to discussions of form and its role in new music. Extensive bibliography.

*The Modern Composer and his World,* edited by John Beckwith and Udo Kasemets. Toronto: University of Toronto Press, 1961. 170 pages. Includes articles about form in music by Vagn Holmboe and Luciano Berio (pp. 134–145).

Tyndall, Robert, *Musical Form.* Boston: Allyn and Bacon, 1964. 215 pages. Of the many books on the "standard forms" (sonata, fugue, variations, etc.), this one incorporates a number of analyses of twentieth-century works, particularly Bartók and Stravinsky.

*Compositions for Further Study*

1. The fifth movement of Berg's *Lyric* Suite (1926) is a sectional form in a familiar pattern. Listen to it and determine the form.
2. Stravinsky's *Rite of Spring* (1913) can be studied in small sections. Observe the processes of sectionalization, return, and layering that Stravinsky employs.
3. Study Bartók's String Quartets No. 4 (1928) and No. 6 (1939). How do they compare with the Fifth Quartet (1934), discussed in this chapter?
4. Compare Schoenberg's Variations for Orchestra, Op. 31 (1928) and Dallapiccola's Variations for Orchestra (1954) with Webern's Variations for Orchestra, Op. 30 (1940), discussed in this chapter.
5. Study any of Webern's early works, for example Five Pieces for String Quartet, Op. 5 (1909), Six Pieces for Orchestra, Op. 6 (1909), or Five Pieces for Orchestra, Op. 10 (1913). What creates form in these pieces? How do they compare with the piece from Schoenberg's *Sechs kleine Klavierstücke,* Op. 19?
6. Pfeiffer's *9 Images* (1968) and Mimaroglu's Preludes for Magnetic Tape are short electronic or tape pieces that can be studied only aurally. They are recorded on Victrola VICS-1371 and Turnabout TV 34177 respectively. What processes of form are evident in these short pieces?
7. Study the formal processes and philosophy evident in John Cage's *Variations I* (1958), *II* (1961) and *III* (1963); Earle Brown's *Hodograph I* (1959); Luciano Berio's *Sinfonia* (1968) and Morton Feldman's *Durations* (1960–61). Study the scores, the composers' writings, and the recorded performances.

chapter two

# Timbre and Texture in Twentieth-Century Music

RICHARD P. DELONE

## INTRODUCTION

Probably no facet of contemporary composition lends itself to assessment and discussion as easily as does the element of texture, which involves the interacting parameters of pitch and duration and their deployments in the various parts of a composition. Texture affords a basis for appraising and recalling music that avoids the traditional biases of key and chord.

If a great deal of traditional music seems to represent the realization of certain established compositional principles or forms such as variations or ternary form, fugue or sonata design, it seems that much recent music, especially some of the music written since the Second World War, fulfills in sound certain a priori textural designs and patterns, artistically arranged to present a satisfactory succession of events rather than to adhere to accepted and proven forms. This tendency is reflected on the one hand by composers' reliance on serial procedures, on the other by the introduction into their works of improvisation or chance-determined procedures which by their very nature tend to minimize the significance of pre-existent formal bases, if not rule them out completely in some cases.

In setting out to deal with texture in twentieth-century music it seems essential to acknowledge an element of music that has far too often been treated as a surface detail, incidental and even irrelevant insofar as form and organization are concerned: namely, *timbre.* How often has study of the timbral layout of a Beethoven symphony or Mahler orchestral song been given more than cursory attention in analytical discussion? What vocabulary exists for the adequate treatment of the subject of timbral mixtures and the influence of timbral changes on musical design? Yet it appears that the manipulation of timbres is of paramount importance for many current composers such as Boulez, Cage, Berio, and Carter. And we have only to turn to works of many earlier composers such as Berlioz, Mahler, and Debussy for ample evidence of the significance of timbre in music before our time. In this book timbre is regarded as an important facet of texture along with the parameters of pitch, duration, and loudness, each of which interacts with timbre. It should be apparent that musical textures represent the coordinated activity and interaction of all four parameters of music. The invention of a musical texture is composition itself.

Texture is comparable to other aspects of musical organization in that it is perceptible on both large and small scales; texture is comprised of both gross and detailed elements, as are rhythmic organization, the treatment of pitch, dynamics, orchestration, and other aspects of style. It is not an overstatement to say that most twentieth-century composers seem to have lavished more care and attention on textural details than, for the sake of comparison, composers of the Baroque era or before. By the same token, delineation of form through texture rather than through tonality and/or melodic themes has taken on an unprecedented significance in a great deal of twentieth-century composition.

The preceding statement is perhaps most easily verified when applied comparatively to timbre and dynamics. Example 2-1 is a segment of Bach's

**EXAMPLE 2-1.** Bach: *Well-Tempered Clavier,* Book II, Prelude in A minor.

**EXAMPLE 2-1** continued.

*A minor* Prelude from Book Two of the *Well-Tempered Clavier*; Example 2-2 is taken from an early twentieth-century set of pieces for string quartet by Webern. Note that Bach's prelude shows no dynamic indications of the composer's, nor is there any variation in the number of parts. The excerpt is unified by the consistent employment of a main voice and accompanying counterpoint. In contrast, the Webern movement reveals a great variety of textural detail. Every measure involves some modification of dynamics, and the piece is clearly sectionalized by changes of texture from melody supported by accompanying chords to two-part counterpoint. The effect of formal return projected by the piece is clearly a product of the *textural* recurrence (melody and chords) in the final four measures. An example such as this is clear evidence of the concern for textural details so often found in music of our time.

**EXAMPLE 2-2.** Webern: Five Pieces for String Quartet, Op. 5, No. 4. Copyright 1922, Universal Edition. Used by permission of the publisher. Theodore Presser Company sole representative United States, Canada and Mexico.

**EXAMPLE 2-2** continued.

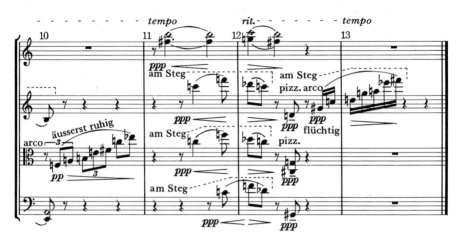

## TIMBRE

It is possible to view new treatments of timbre by twentieth-century composers as constituting one of two approaches. The first is represented by innovational treatments of traditional sound sources such as the piano, strings, the human voice, or any combinations of timbres common to traditional music. Some contemporary composers such as Shostakovich have continued to write for instruments or voices without making any new demands on them.

A second approach to the treatment of timbre in music of this century, especially music written since the end of the Second World War, involves the invention and development of a number of new, essentially experimental sound sources. The most important of these is without doubt the array of sounds produced from *electronic* sound sources.

The examples that follow provide a glimpse of some of the varying treatments of timbral detail that typify twentieth-century composition in general. The timbral deployments and sources noted here involve both traditional and innovative sound sources.

Webern's Six Pieces for Orchestra, Op. 6, are indicative of the predilection for timbral details common to many composers working just after the turn of the twentieth century. The third movement is only eleven measures long. In that brief span the composer presents an ingeniously arranged juxtaposition and combination of orchestral colors varying from the muted trumpet sonority of m. 1 supporting an almost imperceptible glimmer of solo viola line (muted) to a single strand of reiterated harp pitches that create the solo

**cadence** of the movement. Linear combinations such as the counterpoint between muted horn and flute-glockenspiel at m. 5 and harmonic combinations such as the tetrachord sounded in string harmonics in m. 4 are presented as unique formal events. The movement's succession of timbral articulations constitutes its main focal point of interest.

**EXAMPLE 2-3(a).** Webern: Six Orchestral Pieces, III (complete). © 1956, Universal Edition. Used by permission of the publisher. Theodore Presser Company sole representative United States, Canada and Mexico.

**EXAMPLE 2-3(a)** continued.

Gyorgy Ligeti's *Lux Aeterna* was composed sixty or so years after the Webern movement. Although the two works were written for different media, both utilize staggered soloistic entries rather than uniform attacks. The textural effect of the Ligeti piece results from the imaginative ways in which textural density is increased by building harmonic tension through emphasis on dissonant intervals, especially seconds.

**EXAMPLE 2-3(b).** Ligeti: *Lux Aeterna* for chorus, mm. 1–15, 34–37. Copyright © 1968 by Henry Litolff's Verlag. Reprint permission granted by C. F. Peters Corporation, New York.

\* Sing totally without accents; barlines have no rhythmic significance and should not be emphasised.

**EXAMPLE  2-3(b)**  continued.

* This texture is maintained until all voices have entered, arriving at the cadence in measure 37.

**EXAMPLE 2-3(b)** continued.

* Here t and s are not articulated.

** This passage may be sung by several basses with particulary good falsetto registers, or by 3 soli. If necessary the falsetto high B may be taken over by a tenor. If there are only 4 tenors in the choir, the first tenor should stop at the end of bar 36—with morendo—and then take over the falsetto B. In this case the first tenor's F-sharp in bars 39-40-41 is sung by an alto; the E in bar 41 is again sung by the first tenor.

Six instruments and a solo tenor comprise the timbral resources in the second movement, "Surge, aquilo," of Stravinsky's *Canticum Sacrum*. The instruments—flute, English horn, harp, and three solo contrabasses—are deployed so as to create a variety of linear and harmonic elements in accompaniment for the tenor solo. Stravinsky's unerring capacity to create fresh and novel instrumental colors can be noted in the unusual use of string bass harmonics combined in four- and five-note chords with the harp. Flute entrances are frequently highlighted by the use of harmonics or fluttertonguing, effects found in numerous recent scores. The variety of articulation, register, and style found in the brief English horn part reflects the composer's interest in exploiting fully the timbral resources of the instrumentation used. The movement is an interesting study in the creation of an engaging sequence of events from very limited and instrumental resources, an approach that has become especially common in chamber music.

**EXAMPLE 2-3(c).** Stravinsky: *Canticum Sacrum,* II, "Surge, aquilo" (complete). Copyright 1956 by Boosey & Hawkes, Inc. Reprinted by permission.

**EXAMPLE 2-3(c)** continued.

The influence of jazz-oriented techniques and novel timbral effects has had considerable impact on many twentieth-century composers' instrumentation. The next piece, by Tom Mason, reveals a virtuosic approach to the alto saxophone, and the piano part too, reveals a number of innovative sonorities and articulations.

The saxophone part makes considerable use of harmonics, fluttertonguing, and multiphonics (multiple sounds), among other demanding modes of articulation. These sounds, rather than occurring as arbitrary or contrived "special effects," constitute an integrated and convincing aspect of the piece's structure. The expansion of the saxophone's upper register is a consequence of the influence of recent jazz artists such as Charlie Parker, Paul Desmond, and others. The rapid register shifts, complex linear patterns and rhythmic fluidity of much of the piano and saxophone writing in this work clearly echo jazz improvisation.

**EXAMPLE 2-3(d).** Tom Mason: *Canzone da Sonar,* for alto saxophone and piano, pp. 1–2. © Copyright 1974 by Southern Music Company, San Antonio, Texas. International copyright secured. Used by permission.

to Fred Hemke

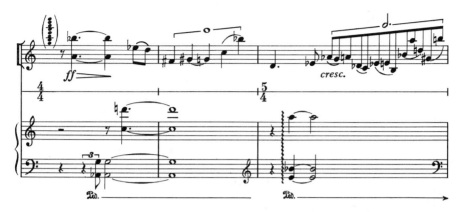

**EXAMPLE 2-3(d)** continued.

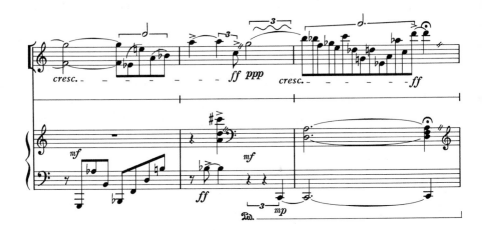

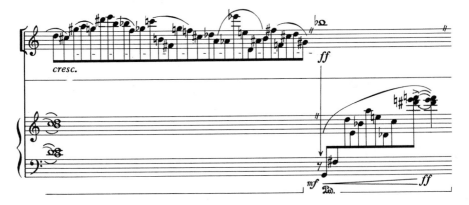

A number of pieces written during the past twenty or so years have experimented with combining traditional and electronic sounds. Kenneth Gaburo's *Antiphony IV* is such a work. It is composed for traditional instruments consisting of piccolo, bass trombone, string bass, and vocal sounds which undergo electro-mechanical modifications. The piece also incorporates electronically generated sounds; these are represented in the score (Ex. 2-3e) by geometric

**EXAMPLE 2-3(e).** Ken Gaburo: *Antiphony IV* (page 3). Used by permission of Kenneth Gaburo.

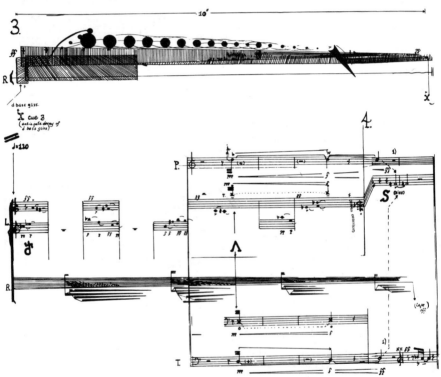

designs depicting phrase shapes, durations and dynamic levels. The piece also calls for a two-channel tape. One channel is reserved for electronically produced sounds while the other amplifies the modified vocal sounds; these are shown in the score by phonetic symbols representing the phonemes (classes of speech sounds) found in a poem by the composer's wife, Virginia Hommel.

The signs or letters in the preceding score-page (Ex. 2-3e) denote the following:

$$
\begin{aligned}
R &= \text{right speaker} \\
X &= \text{cue for the right speaker} \\
P. &= \text{piccolo} \\
L. &= \text{left speaker} \\
S &= \text{phoneme} \\
\text{ʒ} &= \text{phoneme} \\
\Lambda &= \text{phoneme} \\
T. &= \text{trombone} \\
i &= \text{phoneme} \\
B &= \text{double bass}
\end{aligned}
$$

Composers have always shown interest in expanding their available sound sources. Prior to the First World War such devices as wind machines, bird calls, and an early twentieth-century electrical tone generator called a dynamophone represented some of the many efforts to enlarge the gamut of musical and non-musical sound sources. In most instances such efforts occurred in conjunction with programmatic compositions and attempts at musical pictorialism by composers such as Richard Strauss, Respighi, and others. The period since the close of the Second World War has been one of unprecedented exploration and development of new timbres, with the important consequence that the student of music can no longer prepare for a lifetime of music-making by assimilating only the techniques, devices, forms, and crafts of pre-twentieth-century music.

One area of exploration involves a whole repertoire of *unprecedented new sounds*, some involving pitches, some entirely percussive, some involving noise, but all produced with *traditional* instruments. Examples of these include the following:

*New Sound Sources Associated with Traditional Instruments:*

(PITCHED)
*Sprechstimme* (speech-singing)
prepared piano sounds
unusual woodwind harmonics (flute in particular)
trumpet half-valve playing
humming and blowing (two pitches result)
multiple stops in general

|                |                                                              |
|----------------|--------------------------------------------------------------|
| (PITCHED)      | exaggerated brass head-shakes                                |
|                | woodwind glissandi                                           |
|                | string microtones (vertical and linear)                     |
|                | vocal glissandi                                              |
|                | horn "rips"                                                  |
|                | exaggerated tremolo                                          |
|                | blowing into a disengaged mouthpiece or reed                 |
|                | pedal tones (brass)                                          |
| (NON-PITCHED)  | speech chorus (shouting, screaming, groaning, etc.)          |
|                | activating keys or valves without blowing                    |
|                | tapping or rubbing the soundboard (strings)                  |
|                | etc.                                                         |

Along with attempts to enlarge the sound spectrum through novel treatments of traditional instruments, there is an equally significant and perhaps more systematic trend in the development of a vast potential of sounds that have in common their production or reproduction, modification or distortion, amplification or interruption by electronic devices. The essential components of the latter are the tape recorder, synthesizer and loudspeaker system. Computers have recently been introduced into techniques of sound determination and generation as well by composers such as Yannis Xenakis.

As in the case of traditional instruments, electronic media have come to be associated with the production and recording of both precise pitches and noise. In some uses the one is mistaken for the other, a consequence of our relative unfamiliarity with the sounds themselves, coupled with their tremendous capability of registration, dynamic levels, density of activity, and potential for textural complexity of electronic sound production and tape recording.

There are a number of sound-types associated with electronic composition; they fall into the following general groups:

Group I  Taped natural sounds (human sounds, such as humming or shouting, and non-human sounds, such as tapping, street sounds, metallic clatterings, etc.). The term *musique concrete* is often associated with works produced by the manipulations of these sounds.

Group II  Taped sounds such as those produced in the studio by a synthesizer or by digital sound synthesis via the computer.

Group III  Live sounds performed by an electronic sound source, such as a Synket, or by amplified flute or electronic piano.

Among the innumerable contemporary musicians contributing to the mounting repertoire of electronic works and works combining both traditional instruments and/or voices with the use of taped sounds are Pierre Schaeffer, whose compositions such as *Symphonie pour un homme seul* consist in the main of taped montages of sounds drawn mostly from groups I and II, and Karlheinz Stockhausen, whose *Gesang der Jünglinge* utilizes both sung sounds, produced by a boy soprano, and electronically synthesized sounds. Scores are generally not used for works of these groups. Indeed, the primary (usually the only) source for study of most electronic works lies in the tape itself.

Many of the most provocative composers of our time have devoted at least part of their efforts to electronic music in some form; among them are Messiaen, Xenakis, Berio, Nono, Babbitt, Cage, Křenek, Eaton, Mayuzumi, and many more. While it remains to be seen to what extent this vast component for the invention of new sounds will become a permanent part of the compositional scene, it is clear that perhaps no other musical development in this century has so altered the entire spectrum of musical sound and texture.

## SPACING AND REGISTRATION

Details of spacing and registration appear generally to be of secondary importance to the delineation of form and differentiation of style in most traditional music, as opposed to the works of many twentieth-century composers such as Debussy, Webern, Stravinsky, and others. Stravinsky's distinctive presentation of an E minor triad at the outset of his *Symphony of Psalms* is indicative of the attention to spatial detail lavished on their works by many current composers. Such an approach to compositional detail, consistently maintained, has often resulted in that special, unique "sound" that we attribute to certain composers or compositions.

Related to registral considerations is the notion of a kind of pitch center of gravity that seems often to typify the distribution of sonority in a particular work or style. For instance, the center of gravity of Mozart's G minor Symphony is higher than Beethoven's *Eroica*; Berlioz' center of gravity sounds higher than Wagner's, and Hindemith's is lower than Debussy's. Obviously such sweeping statements are almost useless without reference to specific contexts; such references will follow shortly. To generalize, it might be said that the center of gravity of a work or movement is roughly analogous to the midpoint of the total tessitura of a piece or section thereof. Imagine the high-low midpoint of the particular oboe range exploited in a symphonic movement; imagine further the registral midpoint exploited by each orchestral instrument and instrumental choir of such a work. A pitch thus identified could be called a center of gravity or pitch center (not to be confused with tonic). Admittedly, without the interval counting and range scanning needed to make an accurate assessment of the pitch center of gravity for a given work, reference to it is partly subjective, since individuals listen differently. Some of us are more attentive to "highs" than others, while some musicians, for obvious reasons such as training and individual specialities as performers, are more attentive and listen more receptively to "lows." Again, it is clear that many factors interact and combine to create the illusion of a unique "sound" or palette of sounds associated with different works or composers; in all likelihood, registration contributes to the listener's recall and interpretation of sonority. The listener's perception of characteristic sonority is largely a consequence of the particular textural layouts and devices used to articulate musical ideas; such articulation is composition.

### PREDISPOSITION TOWARDS DETAIL IN TWENTIETH-CENTURY TEXTURE AND DESIGN

Formal continuity and change in traditional music have always been affected by texture. Form delineation in most traditional works is commonly a product of coinciding changes in the organization of two or more elements such as tonality, texture, theme, or dynamics. In much twentieth-century music, by contrast, texture has assumed a *dominant* position in the delineation of form and the creation of continuity.

The two excerpts shown below, despite disparity of style, are roughly comparable in that both reveal formal continuity and formal change based to a great extent on textural patterns.

In Ex. 2-4, by Mahler, written in 1883, the texture consists primarily of a melody in the voice and a piano accompaniment that is composed of a tonic pedal octave or fifth supporting modified reiterations of a two-measure motive. Reiterations of the two-measure motive both reinforce and elaborate the vocal line. Couplings in thirds in the upper voices of the accompaniment, as well as the articulated bass pedal point, produce textural continuity, as

**EXAMPLE 2-4.** Mahler: *Songs of a Wayfarer,* I, mm. 1–21. Reprinted by permission of Josef Weinberger Limited.

Langsam

Wenn mein Schatz Hoch-zeit macht,

molto moderato

Allegro

Andante

fröh - li - che Hoch - zeit macht,

Andante

Andante

Allegro

hab' ich mei - nen trau - ri - gen Tag!

rit.

does the composer's adherence to the same overall range of the accompaniment, i.e., about three octaves. The only real deviation from the prevailing texture of the passage occurs at m. 14 with the addition of parts and a countermelody in the tenor register. Other factors such as subtle changes in dynamics, tempo, and meter clearly produce variety and heighten interest within the framework of textural continuity. The musical materials of the song, despite an unusual rhythmic organization (unusual in the context of nineteenth-century rhythmic practice in general) are essentially traditional.

The excerpt in Ex. 2-5 was written about twenty-eight years after the passage just cited. Compared texturally with Ex. 2-4, it reveals a considerably more contrapuntal layout than the Mahler excerpt as well as a far richer and more dense harmonic language. In particular, however, Berg's keyboard "accompaniment" projects a more varied pattern; after m. 2, no two measures are alike, although they are strongly related through motivic and rhythmic growth and expansion. Also, unlike the Mahler excerpt, Berg's accompaniment rarely duplicates notes sounded by the voice. Measures 1–6 form one textural section (in this case a phrase) of the song, marked by continuity of rhythm. The deployment of parts reveals changes in registration, number of parts (1 to 7), spacing (relatively close upper voices above a pedal fifth in mm. 1–3 contrasted with a wide spread without supporting pedal in m. 4). There is a continuing intensification of the contrapuntal competition between the voice and accompaniment. One might sum up the comparison of these two works by describing the Mahler song as melody and accompaniment, while Berg's represents more of a musical-poetic drama, portrayed as a conflict between voice and piano. The variety and textural complexity found in this song by Berg is clearly indicative of the occupation with textural detail found in a great deal of twentieth-century music, especially music of the Viennese School and their successors.

**EXAMPLE 2-5.** Berg: Op. 2 No. 4. Copyright 1928, Universal Edition. Used by permission of the publisher. Theodore Presser Company sole representative United States, Canada, and Mexico.

Wie - sen, Horch! ____ Horch ____ es flö-tet die

*schr zart*

Nach - ti - gall. ____ Ich will sin -

*poco* *pp sehr zart und flüchtig l.h.* *r.h.* *meno*

*frei* *langsameres Tempo*

- - - gen: Dro - ben hoch im dü-stern Bergforst, es

*mp* *p* *schwach betoni*

*poco rit.* - - - -

schmilzt und glit-zert kal-ter Schnee, ein Mäd-chen in grau-em Klei-de lehnt an feuch-tem

*8va*

*sehr ausdrucksvoll*

*spitz* *mf spitz, Zeit lassen* *p*

Perhaps more indicative of recent music is the solo cadence represented by the following example in which closure (m. 14) is accomplished by reducing the texture to one voice.

EXAMPLE 2-6. Schoenberg: *Pierrot Lunaire*, "Mondestrunken," mm. 1–16. Copyright 1914 by Wien Universal. Renewed 1941 by Arnold Schoenberg. Used by permission of Belmont Music Publishers. Los Angeles, California 90049.

**EXAMPLE 2-6** continued.

Such a close is essentially a product of textural manipulation accompanied by rhythmic deceleration. Tonic definition and harmonic progression play no part in this and similar cadential techniques. Such cadences are essentially rhythmic and melodic, and are usually quite consistent with the treatment of material found in the works for which they provide temporary or permanent closure. Such works are not based on tonality and logically avoid tonal cadence patterns.

Related to the textural ending cited above is the technique of cadential textural thickening. In the final measure of Ex. 2-7, form definition takes place through the statement of a six-voice chord. A rhythmic ritardando also emphasizes a feeling of temporary closure. The chord heard here has no functional or tonal significance whatsoever, but provides a basis for closure that is essentially rhythmic, timbral, and textural.

**EXAMPLE 2-7.** Webern: Concerto, Op. 24, I, mm. 63–69. Copyright 1948, Universal Edition. Used by permission of the publisher. Theodore Presser Company sole representative United States, Canada and Mexico.

## STRATIFICATION

A process associated with a great deal of recent composition, perhaps most notably the instrumental works of Stravinsky, is called *stratification*. The term is found in the writings of Edward Cone, who defines stratification as . . . the separation in musical space of ideas—or better, of musical areas—juxtaposed in time; the interruption is the mark of this separation".[1] Although it is not difficult to relate such a process to music of earlier times, especially some Baroque concerti grossi, stratification is a particularly important tool for creating musical shape and design in works in which less attention is paid to traditional techniques involving key change, thematic discourse, and sectionalization marked and punctuated by familiar harmonic formulas. Many of the works cited in this book reveal considerable use of stratification, often in uniquely imaginative ways. Among some of the composers in whose works one may observe this process are Elliott Carter, Gunther Schuller, and Earle Brown.

Stratification is predicated on contrasts of timbre and multitimbral combinations, registration, levels of intensity and textural density. It may amount to a striking contrast of sound in which changes in virtually every parameter coincide, as in the following example from Stravinsky's Symphony in Three Movements (Ex. 2-8). Here the initial stratum is composed of woodwind and solo horn sounds spanning nearly three octaves. The shift at No. 7 is highlighted by a dynamic accent, a complete timbral change and a subsequent change of registration supplied by the piano sonorities heard two measures after No. 7. Although this particular illustration of stratification juxtaposes two highly contrasted layers of instrumental sound, unification between the two layers results from the retention of the common element of the interval of the *third,* stated both harmonically and melodically in both strata.

Textural considerations can provide a common means for assessing music of virtually any style or genre, and can provide a basis for comparison of quite different works and styles—even periods—that transcends considerations of pitch detail and form in the historical sense. It should be clear that many composers such as Debussy and Webern have lavished attention on textural detail, using primarily textural deployments and techniques to create bases for form and definition of design, whereas in traditional music textural deployments more often articulate form *in conjunction with* other factors such as key change, thematic contrast, and tempo change.

---

[1]For a fuller discussion of this see Edward Cone, "The Progress of a Method," *Perspectives of New Music,* 1/1 (1962), p. 24.

**EXAMPLE 2-8.** Stravinsky: Symphony in Three Movements, I, 4 mm. before No. 6 to 3 mm. after No. 7. Copyright 1946 by B. Schott & Co. Ltd. Copyright renewed 1974. Used with permission. All rights reserved.

**EXAMPLE 2-8** continued.

## TEXTURAL BASES: MONOPHONY, HOMOPHONY, AND POLYPHONY

### Monophony

It is important to distinguish between the monophony, for example, of a one-voice composition for unaccompanied clarinet and that of a solo section of a work for several instruments; the latter is a polyphonic work containing sections of monophony. Furthermore, it is important to note that one-part writing may in some instances create an illusion of more than one voice through rapid changes of register or dynamics, chord outlining, and other processes. At the same time, activity shifted between two or more instruments with each sounding alternately alone, although by strict definition a type of monophony, is also a type of polyphony, since more than one voice participates.

Although these distinctions may seem moot, they are related to the discussion that follows, because in some instances the use of descriptive terms such as those noted here is arbitrary. For purposes of definition, passages, movements, or sections thereof in which notes sound alone, despite instrumental doubling, will be regarded as *monophonic*; obviously such passages may involve several instruments or voices. On the other hand, passages in which different notes sound together will be called *polyphonic*. Pitches therein may be definite or indefinite, and the pitches may be produced by conventional, electronic, or other sources.

**EXAMPLE 2-9.** Carter: Eight Etudes and a Fantasy for woodwind quartet, VII, mm. 1–15. Reprinted by permission of Associated Music Publishers, Inc.

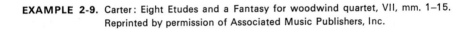

**EXAMPLE 2-9** continued.

A passage such as the one shown above involves a kind of monophony, since it consists of statements of only one pitch at a time. However, its activity is a product of timbral, dynamic, and rhythmic differentiation, not pitch. In this way, one may speak of polytimbral or polyrhythmic textures without specific reference to pitch. Passages such as this are indicative of some twentieth-century composers' reliance on single linear or pitch elements to provide a basis for polyphonic textures predicated largely on factors *other than combined pitches*. One of the most significant trends of twentieth-century music can be observed in contemporary composers' extensive use of unaccompanied melody and motives, figures, and patterns, unsupported by functional or coloristic chords.

One can point to several explanations for such emphasis on monophony by some twentieth-century composers: first, composers have largely abandoned harmony and tonality as rational bases for melody, with the result that line has become relatively free of the constraints of supporting chords; second, a renewal of interest in early music and the "discovery" of oriental music has brought about a consequent interest in line and contrapuntal processes; and third, the expanding capabilities of individual performers as well as the advancement of traditional and newly-invented sound sources have kindled an interest in unique timbres and instrumental effects that are best perceived in solo or exposed settings. The example that follows is from Book I of Debussy's *Preludes*, completed in 1910. Several of the pieces reflect an interest in unaccompanied melody and figuration divorced from tonal-harmonic limitations. The kinds of melody that occur in the example are quite varied and include motivic segments based on rhythmic repetition and sequence (mm. 1–6), implied chord outline (mm. 8–12), and toccata-like figuration (mm. 14–15).

**EXAMPLE 2-10.** Debussy: *Preludes,* Book I, No. 11, "La Danse de Puck." Copyright 1910, Durand et Cie. Used by permission of the publisher. Elkan-Vogel, Inc. sole representative United States, Canada and Mexico.

Capricieux et leger ($\flat$ = 138)

**EXAMPLE 2-10** continued.

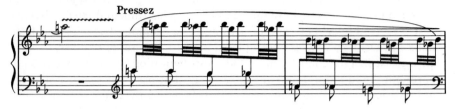

An unadorned presentation of a subject opens the fugue from Bartók's Music for Strings, Percussion and Celesta. This piece illustrates an interest, asserted by many composers working in the 1930s and '40s, in textural layouts based mostly on *linear* events and combinations.

**EXAMPLE 2-11.** Bartók: Music for Strings, mm. 1–15. Copyright 1937 by Universal Edition; Renewed 1964. Copyright & Renewal assigned to Boosey & Hawkes, Inc., for the U.S.A. Reprinted by permission of Boosey & Hawkes, Inc., and

The simple division of one line into two parts constitutes the basis of Hindemith's hocket-like deployment of parts in Ex. 2-12; precedents for this type of monophony in pre-Baroque composition are numerous. Obviously this is a more intricate treatment of one line than that shown in the previous example; it produces an illusion of polyphony, primarily because of the constant shifts of register and voicing.

**EXAMPLE 2-12.** Hindemith: *Madrigals*, No. 9, mm. 88–95. Copyright 1958 by B. Schott's Soehne. Used with permission. All rights reserved.

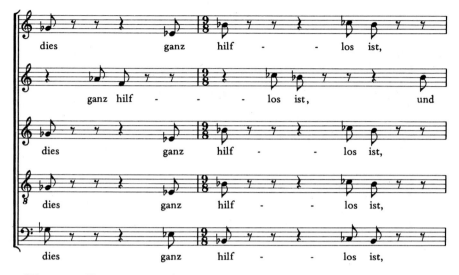

The prevailing texture of Ex. 2-13 is monophonic, in spite of vertical interval occurrences in m. 9 (p5), m. 17 (m9), mm. 18–19 (M2, p4, M3, Tritone, and m2). The instrumental parts represent the timbral and registral elaboration of a tone row; entrances and articulations are staggered so as to bring out characteristic intervallic qualities of the row, especially those of minor seconds, minor ninths, major sixths, and minor thirds. The texture is constructed primarily on one linear element that is realized in rapidly shifting registers, as in mm. 7–10. Changes in dynamics and the juxtaposition of strings and trombones produce an illusion of polyphony and combined sonority which does not in fact occur except where cited. The result is a predominantly melodic effect, enhanced by instrumental contrast, registral and dynamic changes.

**EXAMPLE 2-13.** Stravinsky: *Agon: Four Duos,* mm. 1–19. Copyright 1957 by Boosey & Hawkes, Inc. Reprinted by permission.

**EXAMPLE 2-13** continued.

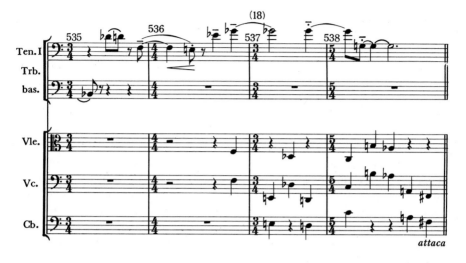

The treatment of the piano in the next passage is somewhat comparable to that of the instruments in Ex. 2-15. Here the composer is emphasizing melodic intervals of the minor second and major seventh. Occasionally vertical occurrences are heard, but in the main the passage is comprised of linear patterns that are differentiated by registral and dynamic contrast. The apparent two-part texture is as much a product of two-note patterns spanning different registers as it is a product of simultaneously sounding parts. Obviously, elements such as tempo, medium, and individual interpretation figure significantly in the listener's textural perception of such a passage.

**EXAMPLE 2-14.** Webern: Variations for Piano, Op. 27, III, mm. 1–12. Copyright 1937, Universal Edition. Used by permission of the publisher. Theodore Presser Company sole representative United States, Canada and Mexico.

**EXAMPLE 2-14** continued.

A logical consequence of serialism can be seen in the kind of telescoping of linear fragments that occurs in the third variation of Webern's Opus 30. If this piece were realized on the keyboard, it might be described as essentially monophonic, since despite occasional motivic dovetailing and overlapping there are no chords in the variation. However, the orchestration, changes of register, dynamic gradations, phrasings, and other factors produce a feeling of polyphony and counterpoint as intricate and rewarding in detail as a complex fugue might be. Comprehension of this kind of textural detail is as demanding for the listener as for the player. The textural compactness and linear conciseness represented by passages such as this has become a matter of absorbing concern to many current composers such as Berio, Stockhausen, and Boulez, and typifies the relative abandonment of approaches to texture associated with traditional tonal music; moreover, each of the six variations comprising this work displays a distinctly different texture.

**EXAMPLE 2-15.** Webern : Variations for Orchestra, Op. 30, Var. III. © 1956, Universal Edition. Used by permission of the publisher. Theodore Presser Company sole representative United States, Canada and Mexico.

**EXAMPLE 2-15** continued.

## Homophony

It is important to distinguish between two general categories of *homophony*: a main voice supported by a rhythmically distinct but subordinate accompaniment, and chordal homophony in which all voices use more or less the same rhythm with the highest part predominating (in some instances a voice other than the highest will emerge as primary). These basic distinctions apply equally well to contemporary music, although these generalities are subject to certain qualifications.

As the triadic harmonic materials that largely predetermined and limited relations between main voice and accompaniment in traditional music no longer serve such functions, some of the triad-oriented accompanimental figures such as the Alberti bass have largely disappeared from the compositional scene. Example 2-16 reflects the abandonment of key-oriented harmonic accompaniments in many twentieth-century pieces.

**EXAMPLE 2-16.** Schoenberg: *Pierrot Lunaire,* "Eine blasse Wäscherin." Copyright 1914 by Wien Universal. Renewed 1941 by Arnold Schoenberg. Used by permission of Belmont Music Publishers, Los Angeles, California 90049.

**EXAMPLE 2-16** continued.

Although both rhythm and pitch contribute to textural organization, rhythm often provides a more objective initial basis for textural analysis, as certain predispositions about pitch that are not pertinent to rhythm are built into us via early training (e.g., tonal relations in a key, membership in a triad, registration, dynamics). Rhythm, in the broadest sense, is duration, which is neither loud or soft, high or low, nor tonic or dominant.

In Ex. 2-16, one can easily grasp the essential two-part *rhythmic* basis of the passage created by the vocal recitation and uniform rhythm of the accompanying instruments. The treatment of the parts, which involves considerable crossing, produces a voice-leading that is readily apparent from study of the simplified piano arrangement of the score.

The traditional device of accompanying a main voice with repeated chords creates the homophony in Ex. 2-17. Note that a clear distinction exists between the pitch materials of the main voice and the harmonic background: the selection of melodically stated pitches commonly avoids duplication of accompanying chordal pitches, whereas in traditional music melodic and chordal pitches are regarded as interdependent and are both usually drawn from the same tonal basis.

**EXAMPLE 2-17.** Webern: Variations, for Orchestra, Op. 30, Var. I. © 1956, Universal Edition. Used by permission of the publisher. Theodore Presser Company sole representative United States, Canada and Mexico.

The function of repeated chords in passages such as the preceding one by Webern is essentially rhythmic and coloristic; no significant feeling of tonality or harmonic-melodic reciprocity is heard or intended. Note that the composer carefully avoids duplicating chordal and melodic pitches, although restatements of notes in different voices do occur. The texture is homophonic, revealing a distinct rhythmic independence of main voice and accompaniment. Note further that the composer has maintained many traditional principles of part-writing.

**EXAMPLE 2-18.** Schoenberg: String Quartet No. 4, Op. 37, I, mm. 1–6. Copyright 1939 by G. Schirmer, Inc. Used by permission.

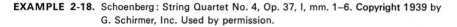

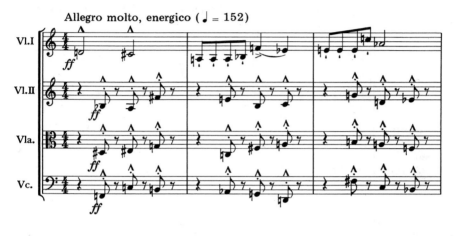

*Accompanimental Techniques*

Most of the textural arrangements used to create accompaniments in contemporary homophonic textures are derived from techniques of eighteenth- or nineteenth-century music; it is often in the pitch and rhythmic materials rather than their textural organization that stylistic differences are most observable. A simple illustration of the preceding statement can be found in the example that follows. The composer creates a background for the horn solo begun in m. 4 through very simple and essentially traditional means;

a reiterated pedal (E) in the basses, an upper-neighbor elaboration of the fifth in the cellos, a rhythmically displaced appoggiatura in the violas, and a repeated, syncopated perfect fourth in the violins. One can easily imagine such an accompaniment in a nineteenth-century orchestra or chamber work.

**EXAMPLE 2-19.** Honegger: *Pastorale d'Été*, mm. 1–7. Copyright Editions Maurice Senart, 1922. Reprinted with the kind permission of Editions Salabert, Paris.

**EXAMPLE 2-19** continued.

Figuration and chord outlining involving traditional patterns and accompaniments adapted to more complex harmonic materials are common ingredients of homophonic texture in twentieth-century music. In the example that follows, tertian chords are arpeggiated in quintuplets to supply an accompaniment for the hymntune variant stated by the violin. Again, it is in the pitch materials used and in their particular rhythmic arrangement that the passage is unique, not in the textural arrangement itself.

**EXAMPLE 2-20.** Ives: Sonata No. 4 for violin and piano, II, ms. p. 9. Reprinted by permission of Associated Music Publishers, Inc.

Lightly articulated chords, placed so as to avoid convergence on metric accents with the solo oboe and thereby maintaining some rhythmic independence, accompany the theme statement by the oboe in Ex. 2-21. A similar accompaniment, thickened texturally and animated rhythmically, is employed to support the keyboard statement of the theme that begins at m. 9.

**EXAMPLE 2-21.** Schuller: Oboe Sonata, III, mm. 1–15. Copyright 1960 by McGinnis & Marx.

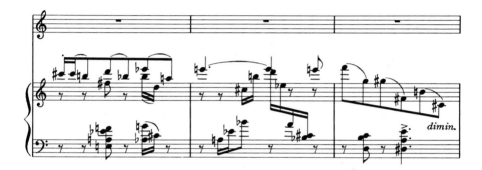

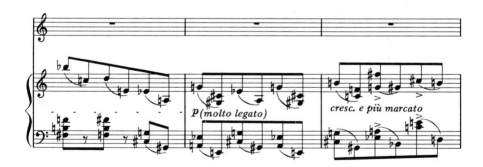

Motivic figuration alternating with chords constitutes the basis for the piano accompaniment of the song in Ex. 2-22. Although the relation of the voice and piano would appear to be that of melody and accompaniment in the Schubertian sense, the composer has unified the voice and piano (through the use of a tone row) by emphasizing particular intervallic materials through both linear and harmonic means. Although the result may be analogous to the organization of traditional Lieder through the adherence of voice and accompaniment to the same basic harmonic progression and key, the materials for creating such unity in this work are clearly non-tonal and non-triadic. It should be apparent that the treatment of the keyboard contributes to the delineation of mood of the text by Hildegard Jone in a way quite comparable to Schubert's technique of mood delineation through the keyboard.

**EXAMPLE 2-22.** Webern: *Drei Lieder,* "Wie bin ich froh" (No. I), Op. 25, mm. 1–5. © 1956, Universal Edition. Used by permission of the publisher. Theodore Presser sole representative United States, Canada and Mexico.

OSTINATI. Perhaps the most typically twentieth-century accompanimental device has been the ostinato. Obviously ostinati are by no means limited to homophonic textures; in fact, since ostinati are often melodic in construction, their use is equally appropriate to contrapuntal textures.

Many composers such as Stravinsky, Bartók, and Hindemith have employed repetitive rhythmic-harmonic schemes as accompaniments. These patterns are often called *harmonic* ostinati in contrast to recurring phrases or figures of an essentially melodic cast. For study purposes it is useful to distinguish between melodic and chordal ostinati.

The appeal of ostinato technique to twentieth-century composers from Debussy to current avant-garde composers lies in part in the need for unity created by the virtual abandonment of functional chord progressions to shape phrases and define tonality. Secondly, many composers, particularly those associated with neoclassicism, have found the use of ostinato devices of the passacaglia type quite compatible with their stylistic and aesthetic values; many composers of the 1930s and '40s turned to ostinato techniques almost as receptively as had Baroque and Renaissance composers.

Recurrence, in contrast to occurrence, is crucial to the recognition of any ostinato. Ostinati consist of one or more parts that provide repetitive bases for other more varied types of activity. The repetition of such patterns often involves some intervallic or rhythmic modification, but the essential features of the pattern must be easily recognized if it is to retain its identity. Rhythmic changes in the form of (1) displacement or (2) truncation or extension are most typical of ostinati treatments.

The ostinato in Ex. 2-23 consists of the figure in the string bass, mm. 1–9 of the excerpt; it projects a march-like rhythm and implies a simple alternation of tonic and dominant (with added ninth). The rhythmic action of the ostinato is absolutely unswerving in this instance, although the accents produced by rhythmic configuration in the other instruments are metrically shifted.

**EXAMPLE 2-23.** Stravinsky: *L'Histoire du Soldat.* Used by permission of J. & W. Chester Ltd., London

Ostinati are typically observed as recurring, accompanimental melodies, constructed in such a way as to provide a more or less neutral melodic framework against which more diversified activity may occur. The prime requisites for such ostinati lie in both simplicity of construction and symmetry of recurrence, so that such figures soon recede into the background through their lack of melodic sufficiency and capability to sustain interest.

The ostinato stated in the second bassoon in the segment in Ex. 2-24 illustrates effectively the considerations noted above. It serves as an accompanying melody or counterpoint while defining the tonality and maintaining a steady rhythmic pulse for the projection of more engaging activity in the first bassoon and clarinet.

**EXAMPLE 2-24.** Stravinsky: Octet, Finale, mm. 1–20. Copyright 1924 by Edition Russe de Musique; Renewed 1952. Copyright and Renewal assigned to Boosey & Hawkes, Inc. Revised Version Copyright 1952 by Boosey & Hawkes, Inc. Reprinted by permission.

**EXAMPLE 2-24** continued.

The successive pitches of a melodic ostinato are given harmonic significance as well in the passage shown next from *The Revelation of Saint John the Divine* by Argento. Note also that the opening of the vocal solo reflects the seconds and thirds of the ostinato. The intervallic properties of an ostinato frequently influence those of surrounding voices or melodies; the opposite is also true.

**EXAMPLE 2-25.** Argento: *The Revelation of Saint John the Divine,* I, mm. 1–17. Copyright 1968 by Boosey & Hawkes, Inc. Reprinted by permission.

**EXAMPLE 2-25** continued.

Note further that the composer has unified the opening eight measures by limiting voice and instruments to the same eight-pitch set (E, F, G, A, B♭, C, D♭, and E♭). The remaining four pitches of the available twelve are introduced in mm. 10–12, and the opening eight pitches of the ostinato are given further emphasis melodically and harmonically in mm. 13–16. In passages such as this, certain characteristic elements of an ostinato—in this case pitches—are marked for recognition and subsequent development; mm. 13–16 of the accompaniment, though not an explicit statement of the original three-measure ostinato, are clearly derived from it.

Somewhat analogous to the preceding is the fact that many writers regard serial technique as a further manifestation of the principle of ostinato technique, since serial technique is based on the principle of recurrence (both literal and permuted) of a basic set of pitches, rhythms, timbres, or dynamics roughly comparable to an ostinato.

A further facet of ostinato technique can be seen in the divided deployment of the ostinato statements. The staggering of ostinato statements between instruments of contrasting timbres contributes to the interest that the figure may create; in the example shown here, an eight-note figure alternates between second violin and viola in different octaves as a background for the main voice, which enters in m. 5.

**EXAMPLE 2-26.** Schoenberg: String Quartet No. 3, Op. 30, I, mm. 1–8. Copyright 1927 by Wien Universal Edition. Renewed 1954 by Gertrude Schoenberg. Used by permission of Belmont Music Publishers, Los Angeles, California 90049.

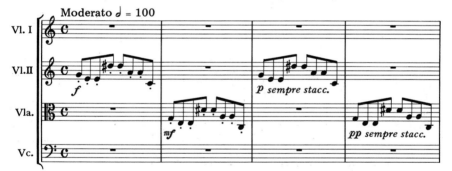

In and of themselves melodic ostinati seldom reveal significant or diverting pitch contours. Twentieth-century composers have treated rhythmic, dynamic, and registral aspects of the ostinato more flexibly than pitch.

Melodic ostinati generally create counterpoint, as was noted earlier. The function of the ostinato in Ex. 2-27 is to provide an accompaniment, in this case a rudimentary counterpoint, for the main voice and supporting chords. Despite its repetitiveness this ostinato remains to some degree rhythmically independent of the main voice by virtue of its displaced accents, emphasized here with octave doublings. The accented notes here serve as emphasized tonic pedals as well.

**EXAMPLE 2-27.** Hindemith: Second Piano Sonata, I, mm. 95–100. Copyright 1936 by B. Schott's Soehne. Copyright renewed 1964. Used with permission. All rights reserved.

In music of the past twenty-five or so years, *literal* recurrence of an ostinato often is not found, though recurrence involving at least one or more musical elements does occur. Such works often reveal the use of quasi-ostinati, or passages in which ostinato-like organization exists despite the absence of literal repetition of melodic figures or progressions. Their components reveal a generally ostinato-like organization, despite the fact that there is no rhythmically symmetrical recurrence of any of the pitch groups or motives. In Ex. 2-28 devices such as diminution, truncation, fragmentation, rhythmic restatement, imitation, and extension occur, and the impact of the passage is one of considerable unity. The accompaniment of the main voices (the trumpets) is created by a complex of contrapuntally organized voices, each of whose organizations reflects ostinato technique.

**EXAMPLE 2-28.** Stravinsky: *Agon,* Interlude, pp. 61–64. Copyright 1957 by Boosey & Hawkes, Inc. Reprinted by permission.

**EXAMPLE 2-28** continued.

**EXAMPLE 2-28** continued.

A colorful succession of triads forms the basis of the harmonic ostinato that occurs as an accompaniment to a movement from Hindemith's *Kleine Kammermusik*. Three statements of the ostinato plus one measure which supports the melodic cadence in the oboe appear in the example; each segment of the figure is two measures long. Each repetition is exact; neither rhythm, pitch, nor voice-leading is modified in this use of ostinato.

**EXAMPLE 2-29.** Hindemith: *Kleine Kammermusik,* III. Copyright 1930 by B. Schott's Soehne. Copyright renewed 1957. Used with permission. All rights reserved.

**EXAMPLE 2-29** continued.

Ostinato and quasi-ostinato treatments of linear and vertical elements permeate the structure of Bartók's Fourth String Quartet. The excerpt shown here is indicative of the composer's use of ostinati to accomplish several different functions. Two-measure units constitute the basis for repetition of the C-G fifths, with dynamics and the subtle placement of the ornamenting A♭ grace-notes delineating the two-measure lengths. While the conflicting augmented thirds in the cello are not symmetrically arranged and do not constitute an ostinato, they do form a textural associate of the figure, a secondary component, so to speak.

The figure cited here serves several functions aside from providing a colorful accompaniment for the motive introduced in m. 4 in the violins; C, the movement's tonic as well as the root of the viola's C-G fifth, underpins the passage's apparent bitonal setting (C and C♯). Furthermore, the rhythmic symmetry of the figure provides a stable referential basis against which the listener may assess the interjections of the cello and the displaced accents of the upper strings; the syncopations in the violins are emphasized frequently by both dynamic accents, bowing, and octave doublings.

**EXAMPLE 2-30.** Bartók: String Quartet No. 4, V, mm. 8–30. Copyright 1929 by Universal Edition; Renewed 1948. Copyright assigned to Boosey & Hawkes, Inc., for the U.S.A. Reprinted by permission of Boosey & Hawkes, Inc., and Universal Edition.

**EXAMPLE 2-30** continued.

Ostinato techniques projecting both linear or harmonic materials, or both, must be regarded as an essential part of accompaniment techniques in homophonic or contrapuntal textures in twentieth-century music. Stemming as it does from music of the distant past, ostinato technique more reflects an approach to composition that extends tradition than reflects innovation. It seems fruitless to try to redefine ostinato in such a way as to include novel and explorative accompanying devices associated with a great deal of current music; it is better to let more progressive and radically novel compositional devices stand and be defined on their own.

PEDALS   Pedal points, or organ points, have occurred in various guises since the earliest phases of part-music; like traditional music, twentieth-century music reveals many forms of pedal point, only a few of which are noted here. Although pedal point usually takes the form of a sustained bass note above which various kinds of activity are projected, it is important to note that pedal effects occur sometimes as sustained or articulated notes in virtually *any* part of the texture; they are common in both homophonic and contrapuntal music, and may occur in one voice or be a product of activity involving two or more voices. In some instances, particularly in recent music, complete chords or massed blocks of sound serve as "pedals" against which other textural layers are projected. Far from disposing with pedal point because of its past associations with tonic or dominant grounds in tonal music, twentieth-century composers have unveiled many novel and imaginative pedal techniques.

In Ex. 2-31 B occurs as a repeated pedal in the bass. Through the convergence of both the soprano and the keyboard bass on B, a feeling of tonality is achieved; B is also emphasized in the upper voice of the accompaniment. Dissonance occurs in this passage as a simple consequence of movement above and below the pedal B. Uses such as this are clearly extensions of traditional practice.

**EXAMPLE 2-31.** Britten: *Winter Words,* V, "Choirmaster's Burial" mm. 46–56. Copyright 1954 by Boosey & Co. Ltd. Reprinted by permission of Boosey & Hawkes, Inc.

**EXAMPLE 2-31** continued.

Stravinsky's use of a pedal dyad (a minor ninth) represents a novel extension of pedal technique, introduced at m. 122 of the passage from *Threni* shown in Ex. 2-32. Although this dyad has structural importance in the work as a whole, it has no tonic reference. The role of pedals such as these is coloristic and supportive but not tonally functional. It is in the latter sense that it differs most from that noted in Ex. 2-31.

**EXAMPLE 2-32.** Stravinsky: *Threni*, De Elegia Prima, Diphona II. Copyright 1959 by Boosey & Co. Ltd. Reprinted by permission of Boosey & Hawkes, Inc.

**EXAMPLE 2-32** continued.

The note G, sounded in the flute and horn of the orchestral accompaniment, serves as a pedal *under* which changing harmonies and a gradually thinned texture effect a close to Marie's Lullaby in Act I, Scene 3, of Berg's *Wozzeck*. Although the pitch has no unambiguous functional meaning, it provides a referential element to which the listener may relate the moving chords and solo voice-line. Note that g¹ is introduced as a chord member at m. 396 of the score so that its continuation as a pedal has been carefully prepared.

**EXAMPLE 2-33.** Berg: *Wozzeck,* Act I, Scene 3, Marie's Lullaby, mm. 396–416. Copyright 1931, Universal Edition. Used by permission of the publisher. Theodore Presser Company sole representative United States, Canada and Mexico.

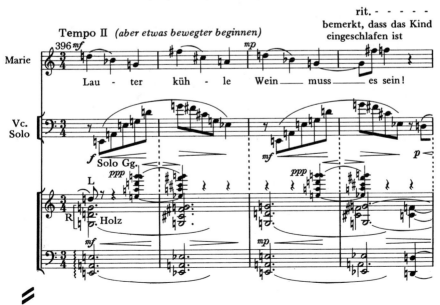

**EXAMPLE 2-33** continued.

Pedals, in the form of single reiterated pitches, dyads, or chords, often suggest tonal references in pieces in which key in the traditional sense has no significance. Pedal pitches can represent structural goals and beginning points, and perhaps most importantly, simple expedients for piling up dissonance and heightening tension; such pedal passages often create an expectation for release quite analogous to traditional patterns of tension and release based on prolonged dominants, sequences of seventh chords, or successions of secondary dominants or diminished seventh chords.

Example 2-34 contains an extended segment from the first movement of Bartók's Fourth String Quartet. The excerpt begins with the last eight measures of the exposition (of a sonata form) and continues with eighteen measures of the ensuing development. Two significant pedals occur within this excerpt; the first is found in mm. 4–17 and the second from m. 18 to the close of the example.

**EXAMPLE 2-34.** Bartók, String Quartet No. 4, I, mm. 41–65. Copyright 1929 by Universal Edition; Renewed 1948. Copyright assigned to Boosey & Hawkes, Inc., for the U.S.A. Reprinted by permission of Boosey & Hawkes, Inc., and Universal Edition.

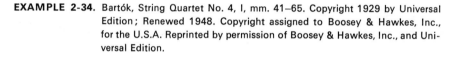

**EXAMPLE 2-34** continued.

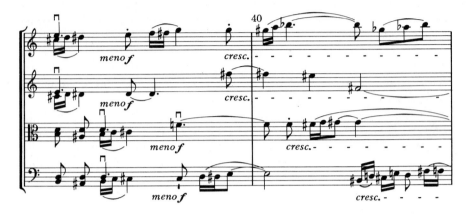

**EXAMPLE 2-34** continued.

The note E is projected cadentially in m. 43 of the example; the cadence is prepared through converging step motion and staggered articulations of unisons on e¹ and e. Careful study of the succeeding fourteen measures will reveal that E is retained as an almost constant common pitch in the stretto that follows through occurrences as a sustained member of the D-E dyad that closes the exposition at m. 49 and as a common or pedal pitch that passes from voice to voice throughout the beginning of the development (mm. 49–57). Through this retention of E as a pedal pitch, rearticulated and revoiced, the composer provides a subtle reference for the surrounding counterpoint and at the same time links the development logically with the end of the exposition.

Beginning with m. 54 the first violin begins a motion towards g²; E is still emphasized in the second violin and viola. A new section, characterized initially by the introduction of a kind of written-out shake begins at m. 58. The pitch G, previewed by the activity of the first violin and supported by d¹ in the cello, replaces E as a new focal point. Through simple reiteration (mm. 58–62) and by appearance in both the second violin and viola, g¹ is sounded as an articulated pedal for three more measures. Obviously the knowledgeable treatment of such pedals (or common tones) presents a task for the performer that less subtle, traditional pedal usage seldom demands; by the same token, *aural* awareness of such pedal usage demands a very perceptive listener.

Passages such as this often imply compositional influences of and links with the past not necessarily evident at first hearing. In any context pedals, or subtle extensions or derivatives of traditional pedal techniques, reflect a very simple but basic facet of compositional technique which involves, in its simplest form, the projection of a dynamic element against a static one. Far from abandoning pedal effects, contemporary composers have explored new and novel ways of modifying and developing innovative pedal devices.

### Contrapuntal Textures and Procedures

Mastery of counterpoint, the technique of combining melodies, has long been viewed as the equivalent of mastery of the craft of composition. Twentieth-century composition has been typified by an attitude on the part of many composers of detached objectivity and the deëmphasis of such nineteenth-century preoccupations as mood portrayal and musical imagery. If nineteenth-century composers seem to us to have been somewhat embarrassingly concerned with subjective matters, twentieth-century composers, as a group, appear to have been more concerned with purely musical matters such as form, style, continuity, and musical rationality.

The wholesale adoption of contrapuntal techniques and forms by a great many twentieth-century composers can be observed in such works as Hindemith's *Ludus Tonalis*; Schoenberg's *Pierrot Lunaire*; Webern's Symphony Op. 21; Stravinsky's *Symphony of Psalms*, second movement; Bartók's Music for Strings, Percussion, and Celesta, first movement; Carter's Piano Sonata; Stockhausen's *Kontra-Punkte*; Boulez' Third Sonata; and numerous other works, all of which incorporate canons, fugues, or highly contrapuntal movements or sections. More important, most twentieth-century compositions reveal approaches to musical texture more akin to principles of counterpoint than the chord-dominated homophony of a great deal of eighteenth- and nineteenth-century composition. Counterpoint and the general projection of melody against melody, rhythm against rhythm, and textural layer against layer characterize most clearly the fundamental difference of approach to style and organization between nineteenth- and twentieth-century composers.

### Two-Voice Framework and Two-Part Writing

The most apparent and often professed source of many twentieth-century composers' approach to counterpoint is the works of J. S. Bach and his Netherlands predecessors. While the structural dominance of an outer-voice framework can be observed in many twentieth-century pieces, the influence of harmonic function, also an inevitable feature of Bach's music, is *not* generally observed in twentieth-century counterpoint except in some tonal composers' continuation of derivative cadential patterns based on traditional root-progressions. In the passage that follows from Stravinsky's ballet *Orpheus*, there is a reliance on outer voices coupled with the cadential assertion of a strongly defined B♭ tonality. Both outer parts are rhythmically independent and melodically sufficient, with contrary motion predominating.

**EXAMPLE 2-35.** Stravinsky: *Orpheus,* Interlude before Bacchantes dance. Copyright 1948 by Boosey & Hawkes, Inc.

**EXAMPLE 2-35** continued.

A structural framework created by the outer voices is found in the "Musette" from Schoenberg's Suite, Op. 25. The lowest voice, a pedal, serves as a ground for the entire dance, while the outer parts create a framework for the activity of parts in much the same way as do many earlier works.

**EXAMPLE 2-36.** Schoenberg: Suite for Piano, Op. 25, "Musette," mm. 1–10. Copyright 1925 by Wien Universal Edition. Renewed 1952 by Gertrude Schoenberg. Used by permission of Belmont Music Publishers, Los Angeles, California 90049.

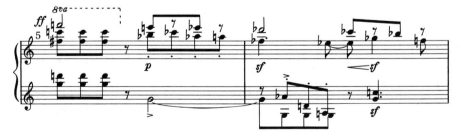

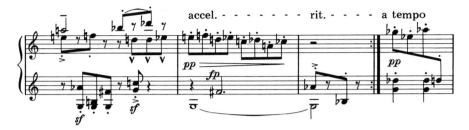

The renaissance of contrapuntal procedures in twentieth-century music can be divided into two main approaches, the one embracing works in which the outer voices provide a structural framework for the texture as a whole, the other including works with an essentially linear and contrapuntal approach but which lack the outervoice polarity referred to above. Pieces in the latter group generally make little use of tonality or traditional formal bases and instrumentation, and are as a rule far more innovative in materials and organization than those noted previously. Composers such as Boulez, Stockhausen, Nono, Berio, Cage, and, to a large extent, Webern fall into this group of composers oriented to non-tonal contrapuntal exploration.

### Two-Part Composition

Two combined melodies generally interact in one of the following ways: as a main voice and contrapuntal accompaniment or associate; by sharing the roles of leader and follower on a divided or staggered basis somewhat similar to a musical conversation; or on an equal and competitive basis. In the last context, perhaps more common in twentieth-century music than in earlier contrapuntal works, two equally significant but independent parts compete simultaneously; the result is a composite activity that poses a challenge for the performer and listener alike.

Since the essence of counterpoint is combined melody, any analysis must take account of such melodic factors as durations, meter and accents, contour, range, and tonal relations. Since combined melodies produce harmonic relations, factors such as harmonic intervals, consonance and dissonance (where pertinent), and other aspects of simultaneity are also important.

Another consideration, one which has achieved a position of paramount importance in contemporary music, is the question of timbral combinations. Two contrapuntally organized voices tend to blend better if performed on a single keyboard instrument than if the parts are assigned to dissimilar timbres, e.g., horn and cello, violin and trombone, or soprano voice and synthesizer. The approach to composition taken by many current composers considers timbre at least as important as rhythm and pitch; it does not always illuminate a composition to treat voices in analytical abstractions as timbrally neutral as some analysts have approached traditional works.

Two-voice compositions and sections are far more common in the twentieth century than was true in the nineteenth. This fact may be attributed to many of the considerations with which we have already dealt, in particular the liberation of melody from the constraints of tonal-harmonic conventions. Collections of pieces such as Bartók's *Mikrokosmos*, Hindemith's *Ludus Tonalis*, Shostakovich's Piano Preludes and many others are indicative of the renewed interest in two-part writing.

In Ex. 2-37 two voices unfold in counterpoint. The two parts are rhythmically independent; they also lie in distinct ranges and move as far apart as three octaves. Rhythmic displacement, contrary motion, and contrasting string articulations contribute to their contrapuntal independence. Timbral differentiation of the voices, however, is minimal.

**EXAMPLE 2-37.** Hindemith: String Trio, Op. 34, I, mm. 1–6. Copyright 1924 by B. Schott's Soehne. Copyright renewed 1952. Used with permission. All rights reserved.

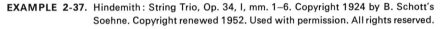

The rhythmic activity is divided on a more or less *equal basis* between the two voices in a kind of musical dialogue, the formal relation maintained is canonic, and the two strings avoid rhythmic duplication until the cadence. Although little real timbral difference exists between the two parts, they are clearly contrasted tonally, since each part employs pitches not used by the other. The four-note pattern in the upper voice centers on D, while the lower voice's tonic is G♯, with a resultant emphasis on the tritone.

**EXAMPLE 2-38.** Bartók: 44 String Duets, No. 33, "Song of the Harvest," mm. 6–15. Copyright 1933 by Universal Edition, Ltd.; Renewed 1960. Copyright and Renewal assigned to Boosey & Hawkes, Inc. Reprinted by permission of Boosey & Hawkes, Inc., and Universal Edition.

Two equally active parts, in canon at the sixth, constitute the texture of Ex. 2-39. Although the voices are rhythmically independent, their ranges overlap, as in m. 5. Since they lack significant timbral contrast, individuality of the parts is of less consequence than composite rhythmic-tonal effect.

**EXAMPLE 2-39.** Stravinsky: *Threni*, De Elegia Tertia, 1. Querimonia, 174–175. Copyright 1959 by Boosey & Co. Ltd. Reprinted by permission of Boosey & Hawkes, Inc.

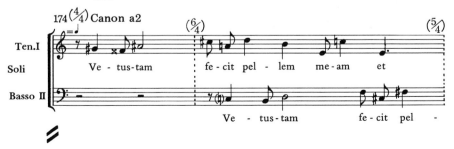

**EXAMPLE 2-39** continued.

Two-part texture often can be viewed as a distillation of chords of three, four, or more notes, elaborated rhythmically. Obviously the recognition of such elaboration is much surer when the chordal basis itself is unequivocally clear, as in much traditional music.

The Interludium by Hindemith in Ex. 2-40 consists of a main voice and accompaniment. The two parts contrast rhythmically through the prevailing 2:1 proportion, and both reveal elements of linear as well as harmonic conception, with an abundance of step progressions and clearly defined contours.

The suggestion of chord outline as a basis for the elaboration of either or both of the voices is of course open to question, since no unmistakable basis for chord recognition such as the triad or seventh chord can be discerned in the passage. However, since it is unlikely that such a passage (or any passage) can be heard in stylistic isolation, and since past experience conditions the hearer to associate successive skips with chord outline, particularly when they fall within a recurring rhythmic unit, it seems likely that the passage will project an illusion of chord structure.

**EXAMPLE 2-40.** Hindemith: *Ludus Tonalis,* Interludium, p. 20, mm. 1–4. Copyright 1942 by B. Schott's Soehne. Copyright renewed 1970. Used with permission. All rights reserved.

Two-voice mirror counterpoint forms the basis for the following keyboard passage by Bartók, although the texture is not limited strictly to two parts. The rhythmic basis involves an imitative dialogue. By sustaining opening notes of the various motivic entrances, the composer adds the dimension of vertical sonority to the basic two-part counterpoint.

**EXAMPLE 2-41.** Bartók: Piano Concerto No. 2, I, mm. 44–48. Copyright 1933 by Universal Edition; Renewed 1960. Copyright and Renewal assigned to Boosey & Hawkes, Inc., for the U.S.A. Reprinted by permission of Boosey & Hawkes, Inc., and Universal Edition.

Later in the same composition, similar motivic materials are juxtaposed in rhythmic alternation between two markedly contrasting timbres. The somewhat nasal blend of clarinets and oboes voiced in octaves, played off against double octaves in the keyboard, forms the basis for two-part counterpoint accompanied by a horn pedal, timpani, and a low string ostinato.

**EXAMPLE 2-42.** Ibid., III, mm. 79–93. Copyright 1933 by Universal Edition; Renewed 1960. Copyright and Renewal assigned to Boosey & Hawkes, Inc., for the U.S.A. Reprinted by permission of Boosey & Hawkes, Inc., and Universal Edition.

**EXAMPLE 2-42** continued.

Practically all of the resources of parametric contrast are brought into play to vary the essential two-part counterpoint in Ex. 2-43. The capability of timbral, dynamic, and registral contrast to highlight and shade various aspects of two linear four-note pitch groups is well documented in the excerpt. In contrast to Ex. 2-42, no supporting or accompanying voices occur. The interest and variety of the passage is based entirely on the orchestral elaboration of a lean, two-part texture, shown in a piano arrangement and in score.

**EXAMPLE 2-43.** Webern: Variations for Orchestra, Var. III, mm. 1–16. © 1956, Universal Edition. Used by permission of the publisher. Theodore Presser Company sole representative United States, Canada and Mexico.

**EXAMPLE 2-43(a).** Piano Version

**EXAMPLE 2-43(b).** Score

**EXAMPLE 2-43(b)** continued.

The two-part segment of a work for woodwinds that appears in Ex. 2-44 reveals a significantly different approach to the creation of a unified yet diversified contrapuntal texture. Unity is a result, among other things, of the canonic relation between clarinet and bassoon. Given this basic interdependence of parts, the composer fashions a complex contrapuntal combination through the use of linear materials that in themselves are sharply contrasted, and which, as a result, produce an equally diverse combination of imitative parts.

The statement in the clarinet begins with a two-measure phrase based on a simple, metrical rhythm and projecting a melodic contour suggesting chord outlines; the second unit introduces a septuplet figure in largely step motion, closing with the rhythmic figure that ended the first unit. The tiny crescendo at the close of the second unit suggests further continuation. An angular figure, whose phrasing displaces the $\frac{4}{4}$ meter, begins the final unit; a further rhythmic displacement coupled with a dynamic crescendo, heightens the drive to a climax and a sudden registral change that signals the end of the statement, coupled with the entry of the bassoon. The bassoon entry is highlighted by its placement four octaves below the clarinet.

The rhythmic independence of the two parts is effected through the simultaneous use of widely dissimilar durations (mm. 11–14), irregularly spaced accents (mm. 9–11), the avoidance of convergence on metric accents, and generally contrasted paces in the two voices (mm. 10–12). Other factors that contribute to the individuality of parts are the use of different levels of intensity, contrasted articulations, and directional patterns involving either oblique or contrary motion. The parts have in common the fact that neither exhibits a strong tonic; the harmonic intervals neither elicit a feeling of tonality nor reveal traditionally observed patterns of dissonance treatment.

Although this example is a product of a markedly different musical style from that of the Webern example cited previously, both excerpts reveal the use of contrasted rhythms, dynamics, registers, articulations, and timbres to produce a highly intricate and elaborate two-voice texture. The passages also have in common the adherence to a limited set of materials. In the case of the Webern example the limitation is that of two slightly contrasted pitch-sets of four notes each; in the case of the Carter excerpt the limitation consists in maintaining a canonic relation (actually part of a three-voice fugato) while at the same time exploring tonal patterns and relations which, though they contain elements that seem to reflect traditional tonality in melodic outline, do not really conform to traditional tonality. Taken as a pair, these two examples give a sampling of some of the highly disparate techniques associated with twentieth-century contrapuntal textures.

**EXAMPLE 2-44.** Carter: Eight Etudes and a Fantasy for woodwind quartet, Fantasy, mm. 1–16. Reprinted by permission of Associated Music Publishers, Inc.

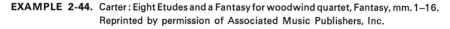

**EXAMPLE 2-44** continued.

### Contrapuntal Aspects of Fuller Textures

In dealing with fuller textures it is important to note again that in many instances three or more parts evolve from a basic two-part design. The fact that a composition's structure may be geared to two fundamental voices, as shown previously, does not prohibit the inclusion of other parts or voices of an essentially duplicating, reinforcing, or coloristic role.

In Ex. 2-45 the lower voice is elaborated harmonically through the addition of lower-voice coupling. The rhythmic combination of main voice and accompaniment is in no way altered.

**EXAMPLE 2-45.** Bartók: *Mikrokosmos,* Vol. 6, No. 150. Copyright 1940 by Hawkes & Son (London) Ltd.; Renewed 1967. Reprinted by permission of Boosey & Hawkes, Inc.

In contrast to the preceding excerpt, the passage in Example 2-46 consists of three distinct and independent lines. The upper two lines, because of their rhythmic diversity and displaced accents, compete on a more or less equal footing, one line often taking up the slack of the other's longer durations. The lowest voice, on the other hand, lacks both the rhythmic and contoural variety of the others; it moves in almost continuous eighth-note motion. As a result, the lowest part recedes into the background as an accompanimental counterpoint. The fact that the lowest voice is not differentiated timbrally from the upper keyboard part further minimizes its individuality.

Like the Piston example (Ex. 2-46), the passage from Stravinsky's *Agon* (Ex. 2-47) consists of three-part counterpoint. In this case, however, the rhythmic and timbral deployments of a small instrumental ensemble, coupled with the composer's unerring scoring and exploitation of the virtuosic capabilities of the solo violin, are brought to bear in such a way as to produce the illusion

**EXAMPLE 2-46.** Piston: Sonatine for Violin and Harpsichord, I, mm. 1–14. Copyright 1948 by Boosey & Hawkes, Inc. Reprinted by permission.

Allegro vivo ($\quad$ = 126-132)

of a far richer textural palette. The listener is confronted with so many diverse arrangements of three basic voices that it is likely he will get an impression of a greater number of parts than those actually heard at any given point in the score.

The three basic parts of the counterpoint consist of the bass line, which is distributed between piano and two trombones; the ostinato-like motivic development in the solo violin, which is treated in parallel sixths; and the heterophonic fashioning of two flute parts from one that results in a composite single voice that alternates with the mandolin.

**EXAMPLE 2-47.** Stravinsky: *Agon*, Coda, mm. 193–207. Copyright 1957 by Boosey & Hawkes, Inc. Reprinted by permission.

Three discrete rhythmic modes, that is, patterns of durations, constitute the basis for three strata of activity in the following passage from Messiaen's *L'Ange aux parfums*. Both of the upper lines are harmonically thickened through essentially triadic sonority, treated in parallel or similar motion. The lower line, a projection of whole steps, is divorced from any functional or tonal definition. It should be clear that both rhythm and relative textural density contribute to the linear independence of the parts. The texture is an adaptation of three-voice writing. It might also be said that in passages such as these the various textural strands are given individuality by the particular kinds of intervallic or harmonic structures associated with them. In the previous example, for instance, the two upper "lines" of triadic planing are differentiated by their special harmonic materials, the one projecting triads, the other treated in major-minor seventh chords. The bass line, while devoid of any harmonic materials, implies a whole-tone scale.

**EXAMPLE 2-48.** Messiaen: *L'Ange aux parfums* for organ. Extract from "Les Corps Glorieux." Reprinted with permission of Alphonse Leduc & Cie, Owners and publishers, Paris.

Contrapuntal elements are integrated with harmonic, timbral, and dynamic ones in the closing section of a choral work by Schoenberg, shown in Ex. 2-49. Lines appear both as single strands and as harmonically thickened layers of activity; one voice is differentiated through the use of rhythmically independent *Sprechstimme*. The number of parts varies from as many as six ensemble parts to as few as two solo lines. Concerto-like contrasts between large and small groups are also found, as at m. 4.

The textural components of this section of the work consist in part of the following:

choral speech: m. 1 (of the example)
two-voice counterpoint: m. 19
solo soprano accompanied by tutti chorus: mm. 9–19
four-part imitative counterpoint mm. 2–3
dialogue involving two-voice couplings: mm. 4–5$\frac{1}{2}$
three-part texture of two-voice couplings and choral speech: mm. 9–10
solo and chordal punctuations in juxtaposition: m. 11

two upper parts in counterpoint (imitative) supported by three- and four-part chords: (m. 15–19)

dynamic and textural crescendo from two to six parts, moving from contrapuntal to chordal deployment: (m. 19)

**EXAMPLE 2-49.** Schoenberg: *Mima'amakim (Out of the Depths,* Psalm 130), Op. 50b, mm. 28–44. Used by permission of the Copyright Owners, Israeli Music Publications Limited, P.O. Box 6011, Tel Aviv, Israel.

**EXAMPLE 2-49** continued.

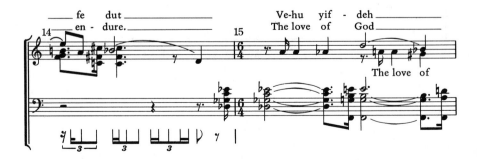

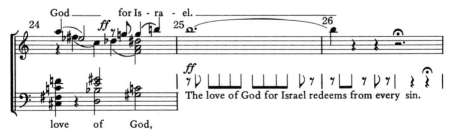

**EXAMPLE 2-49** continued.

Ve - hu   yif - deh   et Yis-ra - el. _____
The love   of God   for Is - ra - el. _____

Despite the limitations of the voice, the composer has fashioned an extended choral work by capitalizing on a rich variety of textures. The rhythmic
designs and contrasts, together with changes in number of parts, registration
and dynamics, are as significant structurally as pitch details. The piece reveals
an overall homogeneity of intervals and pitch succession which is largely due
to the serial technique involved.

Another approach to contrapuntal texture is demonstrated by the following
excerpt from Mel Powell's *Filigree Setting for String Quartet* (Ex. 2-50).

Although only ten or so years separate their dates of composition, the
Schoenberg and Powell pieces differ widely in both selection and deployment
of materials. Despite the presence of a notated metric scheme (which is hardly
audible, but is a practical expedient to rehearsal and performance coordina-
tion), the parts in the Powell work are arranged so as to completely evade
uniform accents, either agogic or metric. Attacks are always staggered, as in
mm. 1–5, to heighten individual entrances. Furthermore, essentially rhythmic

**EXAMPLE 2-50.** Mel Powell: *Filigree* for String Quartet, mm. 11–21. Copyright by G.
Schirmer, Inc. Used by permission.

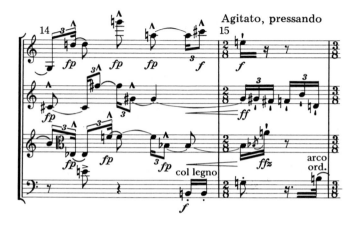

imitative relations (as in m. 1 between the two violins) are constantly modified in such a way as to avoid symmetry or exact restatements. The harmonic sonorities that occur appear to be secondary to the projection of linear details, if not a mere consequence of them, especially because the parts seldom articulate notes simultaneously, and at no point in the excerpt do as many as three voices articulate together. This treatment of harmonic materials and their articulation contrasts strongly with the passage from Schoenberg, which involves considerable play on vertical sonority in the form of chords ranging from three to six notes.

The preoccupation of current composers with conciseness and succinct contrapuntal developments is commonly attributed, among other sources, to the influence of passages such as the one that follows, by Webern (Ex. 2-51). In this brief segment of a movement spanning nineteen 2/4 measures at approximately 50 quarter-beats per minute, as many as six melodically sufficient voices participate in the contrapuntal texture. For example, in m. 9 five sets of rhythmically coupled instruments are organized in counterpoint against the strand of motivic melody in the first violins. Virtually every part of the orchestra contributes to the contrapuntal fabric. Motivic fragments are related through common intervallic materials, the most noteworthy of these being the semitone and the major and minor third. Each wisp of linear detail and its succeeding variants is perceptible through its uniqueness of rhythmic shape. In m. 9, for example, no two motivic figures articulate together after the first eighth of the measure.

In this discussion of contrapuntal textures we have dealt primarily with processes and illustrations more typical of the twentieth century, some of which have their roots in earlier music. It is important to reemphasize that although the current century has witnessed much change and many stylistic developments, schools, vogues, and fads, a large group of twentieth-century

**EXAMPLE 2-51.** Webern: Six Orchestral Pieces, I, Op. 6, mm. 1–14. © 1956, Universal
Edition. Used by permission of the publisher. Theodore Presser Company
sole representative United States Canada and Mexico.

**EXAMPLE 2-51** continued.

composers including Hindemith, Prokofiev, Sibelius, Copland, Piston, Shostakovich, Hanson, Harris, Britten, Milhaud, Schuman, Bloch, and many more have written counterpoint without departing significantly from traditionally acknowledged techniques and devices. The contrapuntal techniques commonly employed seldom if ever exceed in inventiveness or craft the techniques found in the works of J. S. Bach. This in itself is neither good nor bad; the understanding of much if not most of twentieth-century music is not predicated on the appreciation of new or novel contrapuntal processes, but rather on the raw materials—pitch, rhythm, and timbre—of which the works are composed.

## TIMBRE

So far, rhythm has been regarded as a primary basis for understanding contrapuntal textures. However, timbral and dynamic factors are also extremely important in the creation of contrapuntal voices. In some works, especially those of composers such as Penderecki and Varèse, timbre has assumed a dominant role over other parameters through a stratification of timbral sonority that might be regarded as *contratimbral* organization (as distinct from the traditionally assumed role of discrete pitches in determining textural strands of *counterpoint*). Contratimbral or polytimbral texture involves the combination and succession of various separate and composite timbres. Often such timbres include non-pitched sounds, sounds of indeterminate pitch, percussive sounds, electronic or recorded sounds, or combinations of any of these.

Example 2-52 shows three excerpts from Penderecki's *Threnody: To the Victims of Hiroshima,* for 52 stringed instruments. This work explores contratimbral string effects using both precise and indefinite pitches. The legend provided by the composer for the players' realization of notational symbols for the unusual string effects employed in the work is also reproduced here.

Example 2-52(a) reveals twenty-four violins in a combined crescendo of sustained pitches each of which represents the "highest note of the instrument (indefinite pitch)," indicated at the point of inception on the previous score page. Obviously twenty-four players so directed will produce a composite indeterminate pitch, since each of the twenty-four may theoretically arrive at a different highest pitch. This timbre is to be produced without vibrato, in contrast to the wide vibrato of the sound in the group representing Violins 6–10. These two timbral layers or masses are superposed above the collective and staggered entrances of ten celli, each group of which presents a series of string effects involving both percussive and bowed articulations. This textural unit is in a sense polytimbral, since four streams of *modes of attack* are introduced at different points in time and sustained for approximately fifteen seconds. The basses join the ten violins mentioned earlier to form a kind of web, enveloping the celli. Motion is achieved both by the series of dissimilar events in the celli and by the crescendo of the surrounding strings. Also, the conflict of high, indiscriminate pitches produces the illusion of constant vacillation, although from a different viewpoint this facet of the texture is essentially static.

The succeeding textural event amounts to a fifteen-second intensification of the preceding one through a widening of the vibrati of the upper violins, an increase in the number of instruments in the middle layer of mixed bowed and struck sounds, and a transformation of the wide vibrato in the low strings into a very rapid one, marked ⋜. At this point in the score the upper and lower strings actually exchange articulations.

**EXAMPLE 2-52.** (a), (b) ,and (c) and legend. Penderecki: *Threnody*; score pages 6, 12, and 13. Copyright 1969 by Polskie Wydawn Muzyczne. Used by permission of Polskie Wydawn Muzyczne and Belwin Mills Publishing Corp.

## ABBREVIATIONS AND SYMBOLS

| | |
|---|---|
| ordinario | ord. |
| sul ponticello | s. p. |
| sul tasto | s. t. |
| col legno | c. l. |
| legno battuto | l. batt. |

| | |
|---|---|
| raised by $^1/_4$ tone | ╁ |
| raised by $^3/_4$ tone | ╫ |
| lowered by $^1/_4$ tone | ♭ |
| lowered by $^3/_4$ tone | ⅃ |
| highest note of the instrument (indefinite pitch) | ▲ |
| play between bridge and tailpiece | ↑ |
| arpeggio on 4 strings behind the bridge | ⼦ |
| play on tailpiece (arco) | ╼ |
| play on bridge | ⬥ |
| percussion effect: strike the upper sounding board of the violin with the nut or the finger-tips | ╤ |
| several irregular changes of bow | ⊓ V |
| molto vibrato | ⩘⩘⩘ |
| very slow vibrato with a $^1/_4$ tone frequency difference produced by sliding the finger | ⌇⌇⌇ |
| very rapid not rhythmicized tremolo | ⋜ |

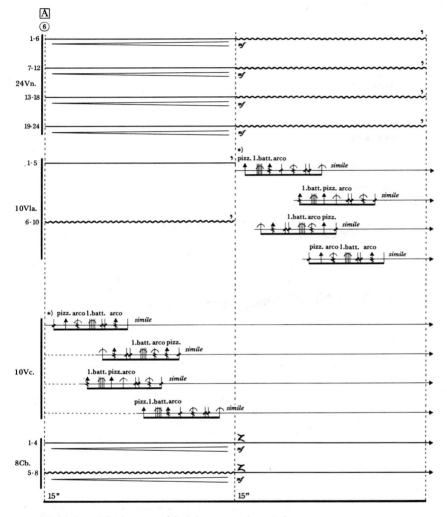

* Each instrumentalist chooses one of the 4 given groups and executes it
  (within a fixed spaceoof time) as rapidly as possible.

**EXAMPLE 2-52** continued.

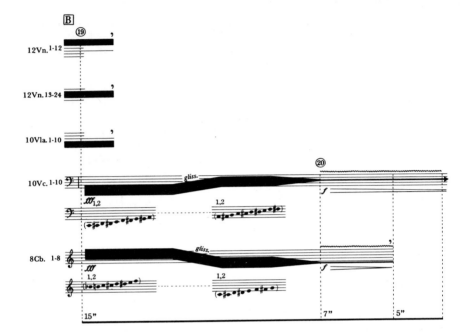

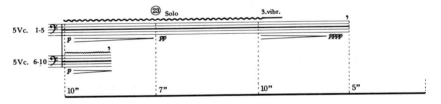

Example 2-52(b) shows two score pages spanning nos. 19 through 24. At no. 19 three groups of upper strings (violins and violas) project one massive sound layer composed of semitones and quartertones superimposed over a wide range. Theoretically, each instrument sounds a discrete pitch, although the result is essentially one of massive noise. Note that an oblique relation suggesting collective part independence is created by the contrary-motion glissandi heard in the low strings. Subsequent to this event the sound is reduced over a 44-second span to a whisper of non-vibrato solo cello, focused on D. The contrast of this isolated, cadential definite pitch is most expressive in the context of the piece and its obvious symbolic meanings. This textural cadence concludes the opening section of the movement.

Twelve separate string voices unfold the timbral polyphony in Ex. 2-52(c). Both indefinite pitches, as in violins 13 and 14, and precisely tuned pitches, as in violins 15 and 16, played on the bridge, are combined and alternated with percussive treatments of lower strings. At the end of the excerpt two alternate tone-clusters, one composed of quarter-tones, are stated. Sound-masses such as these, clearly differentiated by their respective densities and dynamic levels, can form separate composite parts or layers with an inter-relationship analogous to that of single lines of counterpoint, and can easily be viewed as extensions of the device of line thickening noted earlier. Such sound-masses assume a static quality not necessarily projected by less imposing kinds of clusters. Although no electronic sound production or performance occurs in this work, many of the effects heard resemble sounds associated with electronic sources.

An important phase of recent twentieth-century composition is that of aleatory. In some of their works composers such as John Cage, Earle Brown, and Gunther Schuller provide the performer with a sketch only, from which a unique texture, different in each performance, may result from the invention, whim, and artistry of the performers. *Available Forms* I by Earle Brown is such a work, written in 1961 for a large chamber ensemble. The fact that the piece calls for twenty-two individual instruments, with no doublings of any part, implies considerable emphasis on timbral display and combinations of solo and grouped instruments. Page 4 (of six) is shown in Ex. 2-53. It is segmented into units (called *events*) marked off by heavy lines. The sequence of events is in no way determined by the order on the page; the conductor determines the succession of events and so indicates to the performers by holding up one to five fingers. The realization of the non-rhythmicized note patterns on page 4 is a product of the performer's inventiveness. Upon a downbeat from the conductor (a beat that implies performance pace and intensity by its speed of thrust), the participants realize the various figures assigned to them by the composer at the dynamic level indicated. In event I, nine instruments representing all instrumental families except the brasses unfold their respective patterns. The resultant "chance polyphony" displays

**EXAMPLE 2-53.** Earle Brown: *Available Forms I*, p. 4. Reprinted by permission of Associated Music Publishers, Inc.

both harmonic and linear elements. Although certain factors such as pre-scribed range, specific pitches, selection of instruments, and approximate time-span affect the texture, the precise details of the texture are chance happenings. Obviously, as in the case of jazz improvisation, figured bass realization or the vocal improvisation associated with some early forms of opera, the musical result is to a great extent based on the capabilities of individual players.

Event 2 contrasts with event 1 in that it is completely static, consisting of a four-part sonority, a conjunct tetrachord containing the notes B, C, D, and Eb, voiced for a unique color combination with the bassoon in a strikingly high register. Event 3 allows the four participants to articulate their sonorities as either arpeggiated or simultaneously sounded chords. The effect, of course, is almost entirely chordal and it produces a composite timbre whose indi-vidual components do not stand out.

A trio of winds presents improvised counterpoint in event 4. (The x's indi-cate that the performer is to continue playing the same series until a stop is indicated by the conductor.) The selection of pitches, directional patterns, and registration afford part-independence; rhythmic independence of parts, however, is essentially a product of chance, an "available form." The main determinant of the improvised counterpoint of event 5 is the use of a con-toural graph, as in the trombone, as a guide to pitch selection. Trombone, viola, and bass are free to select pitches and invent rhythms based on the graph provided and adhering to the dynamic levels marked; two timpani present ascending glissandi after intoning their respective pitches; the bass clarinet is assigned specific pitches in a descending, wavy contour. The score offers great potential for textural complexity and contrapuntal interest; there can be little doubt that this potential poses an important challenge to contemporary players and composers, especially those who regard traditional contrapuntal techniques as irrelevant.

### TEXTURE AND FORM

Two compositions representing distinctive styles of twentieth-century music are cited in the succeeding pages. The purpose of the discussion is twofold: to show the interrelatedness of textural layout and formal design, and to compare some of the stylistic textures and devices associated with twentieth-century music.

Stravinsky's *Threni* reveals that composer's typically economical and effec-tive deployment of instrumental resources. The various formal divisions reflect the divisions of the text, which is taken from the Lamentations of Jeremiah. But more importantly than the textual divisions and various serial operations, formal design is delineated by textural layout, contrast, and recurrence. The end of a row statement, for example, is highlighted by a significant textural change.

The first elegy is in a rondo form that begins after a brief introduction, *Incipit Lamentation Jeremiae Prophetae*; this introduction consists of an orchestral statement based on the row and its inversion stated together, followed by a soli-duet between sopranos and altos, unfolding several row permutations and motivic materials of subsequent significance in the work proper.

An outline of the main sectional components (e.g., A and B of the first elegy, mm. 19–65 of the score), coupled with a brief description of the main textural components of the various sections is given in Ex. 2-54. Capsule excerpts from each section follow the outline, though if possible, the score should be consulted in conjunction with several listenings. This movement is noteworthy for its interaction of linear and harmonic materials. Although one passage may be evolved contrapuntally (e.g., the tenor canons at m. 66) and another may call for far less elaborate treatments of parts (the parlando and pedal dyad at mm. 27–41), the piece's partitions reveal, for the most part, a reciprocity of vertical and linear elements. Furthermore, a preference for certain characteristic melodic and harmonic materials implying tonality creates referential bases throughout; such elements, typically Stravinskian, are inevitably projected and marked for recognition by the most skillful and adept handling of textural detail, instrumentation, and dynamics.

It should be clear from a comprehensive study of the work that an understanding of the manipulation of the textural elements is essential. The section is organized in the alternating form of a rondo, A B A B A. The statements of Hebrew letters Aleph, Beth, Caph, and Resh form a common, ritornello-like link between the main sections A and B.

| Section | Measures | Sub-sections | Measures | Text | Texture |
|---------|----------|--------------|----------|------|---------|
| A | 19–61 | a | 19–26 | aleph | 4 voices . . . chordal orch. |
| | | b | 27 to 41 | Quomodo | chorus *parlando* pedal dyad |
| | | c | 42 to 61 | *"* | contrapuntal texture *tenor-bugle* in imitation motivic *countermelody in alti* orch. tremolo ostinato in vlns. and celli |
| B | 62–65 | a′ | 62 to 65 | Beth | 4 imitative voices over chordal accomp. |
| | | d | 66 to 67 | Florans | Tenor canon, unaccomp counterpoint, two-part. |

The alternation of chordal and contrapuntal textures is basic to the organization of the piece, as is the juxtaposition of choral singing with choral parlando. Sustained dyads and trichords are juxtaposed with the ostinato-

**EXAMPLE 2-54.** Stravinsky: *Threni,* De Elegia Prima, mm. 19–67. Copyright 1959 by Boosey & Co. Ltd. Reprinted by permission of Boosey & Hawkes, Inc.

**EXAMPLE 2-54** continued.

*Sounds 8va bassa notes of Cb.

**EXAMPLE 2-54** continued.

like development of a three-note tremolo string figure. The latter provides an accompaniment for the three-part counterpoint in mm. 42–56. The unique two-voice canon produced by the tenor and bugle in mm. 43–61 is differentiated from the two-part counterpoint associated with Section B that follows by the timbral contrast of tenor-bugle against two tenor voices. As noted earlier, the ritornello-like treatments of statements of the Hebrew letters in four-part choral style, accompanied by orchestral punctuations, help produce unity and create an intrasectional link.

Note that the piece is unified in part by the placement of major sevenths or minor ninths, which act as basic referential intervals in the work (derived from the opening semitone of the row), in different pairs of instruments or voices, as at m. 23 in the low strings, at m. 26 in the first clarinet and bass clarinet, and at m. 35 between the first horn and the coupled sarrusophone and piano.

Spacing and registration figure significantly in the textural layout of the piece. The *Quomodo* passage is accompanied by dark, low-voiced sonority in mm. 27–41. The formal change at m. 42 is heightened by the shifting of all activity to soprano and alto instruments and to voices lying generally above $c^1$. The wide separation of bugle and tenor in m. 57–61 contrasts with the overlapping part-writing of two tenors at mm. 66–67. The treatment of various recurring voicings and discrete groups in this work and in many other recent compositions suggests a far greater reliance on the form-shaping capabilities of textural elements, especially timbre, than in traditional music. It seems apparent that in some works a characteristic treatment of sonority in certain timbral associations may well provide a referential element and unifying basis for recall analogous to that of other parameters in traditional music.

A final illustration is from Elliott Carter's Double Concerto, a work which represents an excellent source for the study of texture. It is composed for two competing chamber orchestras, each containing an assortment of winds, brass, percussion, strings, and solo keyboard instruments (in the first orchestra, harpsichord, in the second, piano). The positioning of the players on the stage is important to the subsequent alternation and superposition of groups, just as is true, for instance, in the case of Bach's Second *Brandenburg* Concerto.

The composer's division of the work into the following formal plan, Introduction, Cadenza for Piano and Coda, implies that the exploitation of textural arrangements as well as considerations of tempo, mood and timbre constitute an important aspect of the work.

Hierarchic levels[2] of the organization of musical texture constitute possibly the most fundamental form determinant in this non-serial composition, many of whose motivic and harmonic materials clearly suggest a key. A textural

---

[2]Leonard Meyer, *Music, the Arts and Ideas* (Chicago: University of Chicago Press, 1967), pp. 294–316.

hierarchy can be understood to function in this and many other contemporary works in the sense that textural organization occurs on large scales (the span of one prevailing deployment of parts for any one of the sections) on smaller scales (the duration of a sub-section or phrase), and on the level of detail (the particular voicing, spacing, and timbral disposition given to a chord, motive, figure, or pattern).

Although the preceding statement may be interpreted as applicable to virtually any work, it is doubtful that this is the case, since many works, especially those of contemporary serial and avant-garde composers, lack the differentiation of formal units above the level of detail, or certainly above the level of the phrase. It is in its formal organization, particularly in the approach to musical texture as a primary form determinant, that this work reveals its essential connection with tradition, more so, for instance, than in the character of the melodic, rhythmic, and harmonic materials constituting the substance of its style. The passage in Ex. 2-55 is drawn from the coda of the piece.

The prevailing texture of the Coda is one in which the two orchestras are heard both combined and alternating in an intricate counterpoint involving both melodic figures, percussive sounds in rhythmic counterpoint, contrapuntal and polytimbral combinations, and polydynamic shadings of virtually all of these elements. At the level of the phrase it is clear that the alternation of activity between orchestras plays an important part. This sort of textural play can be seen, for example, in mm. 647–652 of the score, shown in Ex. 2-55.

Within the various orchestral statements heard beginning at m. 647 there is a rich assortment of motivic, rhythmic, and harmonic material. In m. 647 the composer has marked both the Percussion 3 and Oboe-Clarinet coupling as principal parts; the result might be described as consisting of a primary level of competing counterpoint backed by a secondary or accompanying level composed of both motivic counterpoint (as in the bassoon and horn), rhythmic counterpoint (as in the percussion group), and rhythmically elaborated harmonic sonority (as in the piano). Obviously the perceptibility of such complex and masking strands of activity may be called into question, at least on the basis of a single hearing.

The latter consideration is even more relevant when the question of the level of details of voice-leading, spacing, and instrumentation are considered; there can be no question that the composer has lavished great care and concern for detail on the construction of such a passage. Unless such details are to be regarded as incidental to the gross effect of such passages (an idea which seems improbable) it can be assumed that an understanding of the composition is in part based on the realization and comprehension of such details.

The oboe and clarinet, although similar in contour and rhythm, as in m. 647, are clearly differentiated by the kinds of melodic intervals assigned to them, essentially fifths and fourths in the oboe and mainly thirds, sixths, and seconds (or their octave displacements) in the clarinet. The spacing of the oboe-clarinet pair is close and they frequently overlap, adding to their inter-dependence as a unit. This active wind counterpoint contrasts drastically with the pianissimo chord in the winds of the first orchestra whose voicing is quite homogeneous, as is the string-harpsichord sonority in orchestra I heard in m. 648. This treatment of sonority clearly contrasts with the array of detached single pitches and dyads that occurs in the piano in m. 650. Here again, the homogeneous spacing of string sonority, involving a projection of stacked sixths in m. 651 of orchestra 2, is contrasted with the subsequently stated symmetrical chord in the harpsichord. This activity occurs in conjunc-tion with a contrapuntal coupling of the viola and contrabass differentiated by both rhythmic placement and uniqueness of melodic materials. The effect is both cumulative and disparate.

Measures 653–658 reveal a stunning array of sonority, timbre, and in particular group and individual instrumental spacings. Extremely dense chords, featuring massed seconds, occur in the harpsichord ranging over four octaves in the lower range. The four winds of the first orchestra reach a four-note chord in m. 654 with a distinctively wide spacing, a spacing which is prepared by the preceding motivic play that acts an an upbeat to m. 654. Viola and cello, in their own separate register, underscore the wind section with a chord of stacked ninths.

The material assigned the four winds of orchestra 2, beginning at m. 653, is similar in intervallic content to that heard in the winds of orch. I, and the two units are rhythmically interdependent. Their interdependence is height-ened through the use of common vertical intervals; compare the sonorities that they sustain and elaborate in mm. 654–656:

This passage is typical of the textural complexity and compositional preci-sion common to a great deal of recent music. Despite its demands on the player and listener, passages such as this reflect contemporary composers' search for innovative sonority and individuality of style, often coupled with techniques of organization clearly reflecting if not literally patterned after traditions of the recent or distant past.

**EXAMPLE 2-55.** Carter: Double Concerto for Piano and Harpsichord with Two Chamber Orchestras, mm. 647–658. Reprinted by permission of Associated Music Publishers, Inc.

**EXAMPLE 2-55** continued.

**EXAMPLE 2-55** continued.

**EXAMPLE 2-55** continued.

## SUGGESTED LISTENING AND SCORE-STUDY

Stravinsky, *Rite of Spring; Symphony of Psalms; Threni*
Bartók, String Quartet No. 4
Webern, Op. 5; Op. 6; Op. 29; Op. 30
Schoenberg, *Pierrot Lunaire*, Op. 19
Hindemith, *Band* Symphony
Berg, *Lyric* Suite
Carter, String Quartet No. 2; Double Concerto
Ives. *The Unanswered Question;* Fourth Symphony
Cage, Sonatas and Interludes for Prepared Piano
Stockhausen, *Gesang der Jünglinge*
Messiaen, *Oiseaux exotiques*
Boulez, *Le Marteau sans maître*
Penderecki, *Threnody*
Berio, *Circles*
Xenakis, *Diamorphosen*
Argento, *The Revelations of St. John the Divine*
Brown, *Available Forms I*
Schuller, Concerto for Jazz Quartet and Orchestra
Heiden, Partita for Orchestra

chapter three

# Rhythm in
# Twentieth-Century Music

ALLEN WINOLD

Of all the aspects of music, rhythm is one of the easiest to discern and most elusive to discuss. Even the untrained listener is aware of the importance of rhythm as a shaping force in music, and he can often perceive and remember significant rhythmic characteristics of a particular composition. But the description of these characteristics is all too often vague, superficial, and incomplete, even when undertaken by the trained musician. If this is true for traditional western art music of the past, it is even more valid for music of the twentieth century.

Several reasons may be adduced for this problem. Individual differences in performance and perception may influence greatly the rhythmic characteristics of a composition, making it difficult to analyze rhythm convincingly and unconditionally from consideration of the printed score alone. Whereas traditional pitch notation is fixed and absolute and one can, within reasonable limits, expect that the pitches written will be those played and heard, traditional rhythmic notation is relative and subject to subtle or significant variations in duration, accentuation, and grouping. Not only is rhythmic notation inadequate as a basis for analysis, it may actually lead to errors or oversimplifications in description of the sounding rhythmic events. The relation of rhythmic symbols to rhythmic sounds will be a central topic in this chapter.

Another difficulty in rhythmic analysis is the absence of a generally accepted, comprehensive theory of rhythm applicable to music of various periods and styles including music of the twentieth century. There is no lack of efforts in this direction, and some of the most significant works are listed in the bibliography at the end of this chapter. Though these and other works have contributed to our understanding of rhythm, no single one has the general acceptance and comprehensiveness which would qualify it as the theoretical basis for the consideration of rhythm in twentieth-century music in this chapter. It would be impossible in this brief essay to present in detail such a theoretical basis, but it is implied in the discussion of twentieth-century rhythm which follows. It is clearly indebted to ideas from the writers mentioned in the bibliography and to other theorists.

## THE NATURE OF RHYTHM

When we consider that the root meaning of the word "rhythm" is flow, as in the flow of a river, we are reminded of one of the greatest pitfalls in any consideration of rhythm in music. We can never stop the flow of a river to examine and describe it, for then we no longer have a flow, but only still water. So, too, the experience of rhythm in music must always be that of sounds moving in time. If we arrest this motion, we no longer have rhythm, but only isolated sounds in space or inanimate notes on paper.

The study of rhythm is the study of the flow in time of sounds and silences. If this seems to be a definition of music itself, it may serve to remind us that the study of rhythm involves some consideration of all the aspects of music. Duration is the special province of rhythm, but the ordering and organization of temporal units is the vital core of rhythmic analysis, and here pitch, harmony, texture, dynamics, and timbre may play as significant a shaping role as the durations themselves.

How do we perceive rhythm? Gestalt psychologists tell us that any act of perception involves background and foreground elements. In a painting these elements are often easy to identify—a foreground figure of a man against a background of a neutrally colored wall, a foreground figure of a tree against a background of a sky. In music, we frequently find an analogous situation, such as that illustrated in Ex. 3-1.

Texturally, the background is the accompaniment in the lower instruments and the foreground is the melody in the first violin. In terms of rhythm, the background is the metric structure and the foreground is made up of durational patterns projected against it. Metric structure involves both meter (the organization of beats or pulses into groups) and tempo (the speed of the beats or pulses), but it is a broader term than either. It includes all

**EXAMPLE 3-1.** Prokofiev: String Quartet No. 1 (1930), I, mm. 1–3. Copyright 1943 by International Music Company, New York.

those rhythmic aspects which provide a background of temporal regularity or structure. Other terms which have been used to represent the twofold division of metric structure and durational patterns are "regularity and differentiation" (Cooper) and "regulative rhythm and configurative rhythm" (Haenselmann).

Sometimes background and foreground may be subject to different interpretations. Figure 3-1 is a classic example of this in visual perception. We

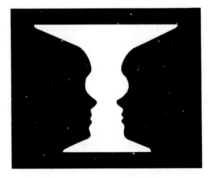

**FIGURE 3-1**

may regard the white space in the middle as background and perceive two faces on the sides as foreground, or we may reverse this and regard the black space on the sides as background and perceive a vase in the middle as foreground. Example 3-2 represents an analogous situation in music. We may regard the first violin and cello as a metric background of simple triple meter ($\frac{3}{4}$) and perceive the middle instruments as a conflicting or syncopated pattern in the foreground, or we may reverse this and regard the middle instruments as a metric background of compound duple meter ($\frac{6}{8}$) and perceive the first violin and cello as a syncopated pattern in the foregound. Ravel's notation suggests a third possibility, the alternation of simple triple meter and compound duple meter.

**EXAMPLE 3-2.** Ravel: String Quartet, II, mm. 1–5. Copyright 1951 by International Music Company, New York.

In other instances in both visual and aural arts, it is difficult or impossible to separate background and foreground. Indeed, we may anticipate our later discussion to say that fusion or lack of differentiation of background metric structure and foreground durational patterns is one characteristic direction in which twentieth-century rhythmic practice has moved.

A unique aspect of the question of background and foreground in musical rhythm is the fact that sometimes the same sound events provide us simultaneously with information on the background and the foreground, or, stated more accurately, they present a foreground of durational patterns and imply a background of metric structure. The melodic line of Ex. 3-1 sounded alone could still imply the metric structure. The interacting lines of a polyphonic texture may imply the metric structure even if no single line expresses the metric structure as obviously as the lower parts do in Ex. 3-1.

The basic questions of rhythmic analysis involve consideration of the background of metric structure, the foreground of durational patterns, and the interactions between them. In the sections which follow, we shall explore each of these as they relate to music of the twentieth century, beginning with examples which are closest to earlier practices and moving to examples which depart from these practices.

## METRIC STRUCTURE

Let us begin by examining a piece of twentieth-century music in which the metric structure shows clear allegiance to earlier practice. In traditional terms this example would be analyzed as being in $\frac{2}{4}$ meter or simple duple meter in a moderately fast (*mässig schnell*) tempo.

**EXAMPLE 3-3.** Hindemith: Piano Sonata No. 2 (1936), I, mm. 1–26. Copyright 1936 by B. Schott's Soehne. Copyright renewed 1964. Used with permission. All rights reserved.

Mässig schnell ( ♩ = 108)

Analysis using terms such as these would prove inadequate as a basis for discussing twentieth-century rhythmic practice for at least two reasons. First, it is based to a large extent on notational considerations and, second, it is not presented in terms that would readily allow us to compare this metric structure with other, more complicated metric structures. To ameliorate this, let us attempt to describe the metric structure in more general terms.

As we listen to the beginning of this excerpt we are aware of pulses sounding on different levels. Pulses are recurring short stimuli which we perceive as points in time. They may be enunciated as the beginnings of sounds or of measured silences, or implied by the performer or listener on the basis of context or past experience. To say that pulses are heard on different levels is to say that they are heard at different rates of speed. The repeated G's in the left hand of Ex. 3-3 enunciate pulses on the half-note level; the four left-hand notes of each measure enunciate pulses on the eighth-note level and imply pulses on the quarter-note level.

Usually pulses on one particular level are heard as the basic unit of movement or timekeeping. Pulses on this level are called *beats* and the level itself is called the *beat level*. Levels faster or slower than the beat level are heard in relation to it and may be termed division levels and multiple levels respectively. In Ex. 3-3, Hindemith suggests the quarter note as the basic unit or beat in that he has indicated its speed with a metronomic marking.

Pulses differ from one another in terms of their strength or accentuation. In Ex. 3-3, the pulses at the beginning of each measure are heard as strong or accentuated pulses because of agogic accent (length accent) and pitch accent. Other factors which might tend to make a pulse strong or accentuated are dynamic accent (loudness accent) or the fact that it occurs at a point of significant change in harmony, texture, tone color, or melodic direction.

It is through accentuation that pulses are organized into basic two-pulse (strong-weak) or three-pulse (strong-weak-weak) groups. Any pulse group larger than three pulses may be considered as a combination of the basic two-pulse and three-pulse groups; a four-pulse group would be 2 + 2, a five-pulse group would be 3 + 2 or 2 + 3; a six-pulse group would be 3 + 3 or 2 + 2 + 2, etc. In Ex. 3-3, the quarter notes on the beat level as well as the eighth notes on the first division level are organized into two-pulse or duple groups. Sixteenth notes on the second division level are also organized into two-pulse groups or into four-pulse groups (2 + 2).

Accentuation and grouping on the beat and division levels are implied to an extent by the meter signature. On the multiple levels, however, especially on the level of the measure or slower, the meter signature gives us no information about accentuation and grouping. To determine these, the analyst must consider all aspects of the music and weigh various considerations against each other. One general principle that may be applied here is that literal or varied repetition tends to establish the identity of a group. In Ex. 3-3, the fact that mm. 4–6 represent a varied repetition of mm. 1–3 tends to establish groupings of three measures. Similarly, we find two-measure groupings in mm. 7–8 and 9–10.

We might even carry this type of analysis on to higher or multiple levels, using such criteria as change of texture, harmony, pitch direction, dynamics, and tone color as well as repetition to determine accentuation and grouping. Example 3-4 represents a complete analysis of the metric structure of Ex. 3-3. Pulse groups are bracketed ⌐⎯⎯⌐ , strong pulses are marked ⎯⎯ , weak pulses are marked ⌣ . *Simile* (*sim.*) is used to indicate the continuation of the pattern.

**EXAMPLE 3-4.**

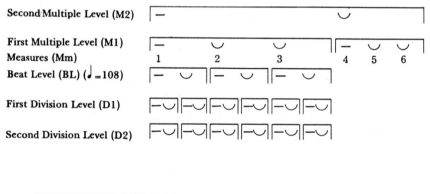

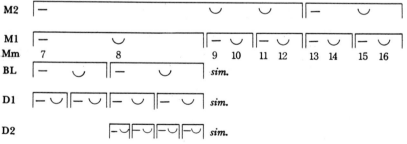

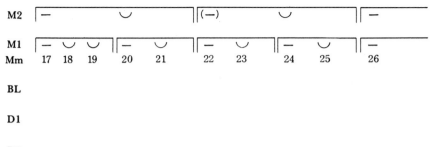

The analysis of metric structure on higher or multiple levels is subject to varying interpretations. Edward Cone has suggested that "the typical musical phrase consists of an initial downbeat ( ╱ ), a period of motion ( ∪ ), and a point of arrival marked by a cadential downbeat ( ╲ )."[1] According to this, measures 1–3 might be analyzed as follows: ╱ ∪ ╲ . On the other hand, Cooper and Meyer insist that all rhythmic grouping must involve the relation of a single strong pulse to one or two weak pulses.

It might be argued that analysis of metric structure on higher levels, especially when dealing with measures or groups of measures, is no longer the province of rhythm but rather of form. This, however, can serve to remind us that in one sense form *is* rhythm on a larger scale and that the borderline between the two is not clear cut. To illustrate this, we might rewrite the first part of Ex. 3-3 as shown below in Ex. 3-5.

**EXAMPLE 3-5.** Hindemith: Piano Sonata No. 2, I, mm. 1–4, rewritten.

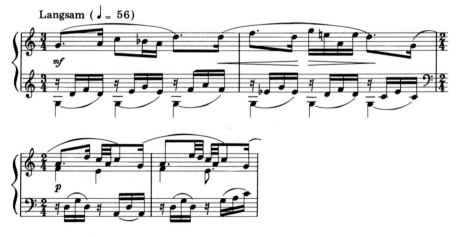

[1]Edward Cone, *Musical Form and Musical Performance* (New York: W. W. Norton Co., Inc., 1968), p. 27.

Notice that the *sounding* metric structure of Ex. 3-5 is basically the same as the original Hindemith example even though the notation is different. We have said "basically the same" rather than "identical" for it cannot be denied that there are subtle nuances which are expressed by the particular type of note value used, choice of metric signature, placement of barline, and length of measure. These have been developed in the course of music history and have become thoroughly embedded in our traditional thinking about rhythm, so that we would probably be startled to see a chorale notated in $\frac{4}{64}$ or a waltz notated in $\frac{6}{2}$, even though theoretically this would be possible.

While we should not minimize the importance of notational conventions, we cannot make them the sole basis for an analysis of rhythm. That is why we have attempted in this section to develop a more general set of terms to describe metric structure. We shall return later in this chapter to further consideration of the interaction between written notation and sounding metric structure.

### Common Practice Metric Structures

Our analysis of the Hindemith example has given us some basic concepts and terms which we may now use to describe what might be called "common practice" metric structure in a manner analogous to "common practice" harmony. In both cases, the terms refer to practices which are generally identified with music of the late seventeenth, eighteenth, and early nineteenth centuries, but which may also be found in music of earlier and later periods.

The purpose of describing common practice metric structures is simply to provide a relatively familiar and comprehensible set of norms with which deviants in contemporary practice may be compared and contrasted (with the understanding that such comparison in no way implies anything about the value of a particular practice). The twin fallacies of regarding contemporary practice either as a corruption of the perfection of earlier practice or as an improvement on the primitivism of earlier practice have both been long exposed and need not detain us further here.

With these conditions understood, we may proceed to describe common practice metric structures in general terms as follows:

1. Pulses are clearly enunciated or implied on all levels, and they are *isochronal* or equal-timed; that is, they are heard at regularly recurring intervals of time. Pulses on the fastest or division levels rarely approach extremely fast rates of speed.

2. Pulse groups on the beat level, the first division level, and the first multiple level may be in either two-pulse or three-pulse groups. On faster and slower levels they tend to be in two-pulse groups.

3. Pulse groups on the beat level, all division levels, and usually the first multiple level are unvaried; that is, once two-pulse or three-pulse groups are established on particular levels they are maintained throughout the composition or section.

4. Pulse groups on various levels are *synchronous;* that is, all pulses on slower levels coincide in time with strong pulses on faster levels.

5. Metric structures tend to remain consistent in tempo throughout a composition or section.

6. In terms of notational practice, it is customary for composers to choose a beat value and measure length which enable them to write whole compositions or sections without changing meter signature.

### Unusual Metric Structures With Regularly Varied Pulse Groups

We have said that common practice metric structure is characterized by the fact that pulse groups on the beat and division levels tend to remain constant and unvaried once established. Already in the eighteenth and nineteenth centuries isolated exceptions to this appeared in such works as the mad scene from Handel's *Orlando* or Brahms' Variations on a Hungarian Song. In the twentieth century we find many examples of regularly varied pulse groups on the beat or division levels, that is, pulse groups that vary in a regularly recurring pattern such as $3 + 2$, $3 + 2$, $3 + 2$ or $2 + 3 + 2$, $2 + 3 + 2$, $2 + 3 + 2$. These may be expressed in notation in several different ways. One of the most frequently used devices is the complex or unusual meter signature, that is, a meter signature with a top figure other than 2, 3, 4, 6, 8, 9, or 12, as used in common practice meter signatures.

Quintuple meter ($\frac{5}{4}$, $\frac{5}{8}$, etc.), septuple meter ($\frac{7}{4}$, $\frac{7}{8}$, etc.) and other similar meters are used with such frequency in some twentieth-century styles that it may seem inappropriate to refer to them as unusual. The metric structure of a work in quintuple meter may be relatively simple, making the term "complex" meter also somewhat inappropriate. Both of these terms, however, seem more accurate than terms like "asymmetrical" meter or "irregular" meter. An organization such as $\frac{7}{8}$ ♩♪ ♩♪♩ ♩♪ is certainly symmetrical, and if it is repeated often it would sound regular or consistent. Ultimately, metric structure is best described through detailed analysis of pulse groupings on various levels rather than through attempts to represent the organization with a single term.

In Ex. 3-6 the meter signature refers to the first division level of the metric structure indicating that the eighth notes on this level are to be grouped into regularly recurring three-pulse groups. However, the dotted quarters on the beat level are heard in alternating groups of threes and twos as indicated by the dotted line.

**EXAMPLE 3-6.** Debussy: *Trois Nocturnes* (1899), II ("Fêtes"). Copyright 1914, Durand et Cie. Used by permission of the publisher. Elkan-Vogel, Inc. sole representative United States, Canada and Mexico.

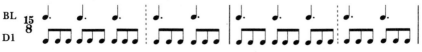

In Ex. 3-7, Bartók has actually specified the pulse groupings in the signature. Notice that pulses on the second division level ♪ are equal-timed and grouped into 3 + 2 + 2 + 3 as indicated in the signature. Pulses on the first division level are not equal-timed but are instead first ♩. ♩ in a two-pulse group and then ♩ ♩. in a different two-pulse group. On the beat level pulses are equal-timed ♩♪♩♪ and organized into regularly recurring two-pulse groups. The ability to understand a complex metric structure such as this in terms of its various levels is of great value in both performance and listening.

**EXAMPLE 3-7.** Bartók: String Quartet No. 5, (1934), Scherzo (Trio), m. 9. Copyright 1936 by Universal Edition; Renewed 1963. Copyright and Renewal assigned to Boosey & Hawkes, Inc., for the U.S.A. Reprinted by permission. Permission granted by Universal Edition A.G., Vienna, for all countries of the world except USA.

We shall not attempt to illustrate all of the possible complex or unusual signatures used in twentieth-century music. The main point is that any signature must be translated into a metric structure on various levels to be thoroughly understood. A seemingly bizarre signature such as that used by Chávez in Ex. 3-8 can be understood by analyzing it as shown.

**EXAMPLE 3-8.** Chávez: Sonata No. 3 (1928), IV, m. 1. Copyright 1933 by Mills Music, Inc., Copyright renewed. Used with permission. All rights reserved.

Another method of notating changing pulse groups is the use of changing meters or multimeter. Sometimes, as in Ex. 3-9, two meter signatures are written at the beginning of the composition, and the alternation between them in the course of the piece is made clear by the dynamic accentuation and pitch patterns of the music.

In other cases each change of meter is written at the beginning of each measure. It is also possible to express varied pulse groups in the notational

**EXAMPLE 3-9.** Bernstein: *West Side Story* (1959), "America," mm. 1–2. Copyright 1957 by Leonard Bernstein and Stephen Sondheim. Used by permission.

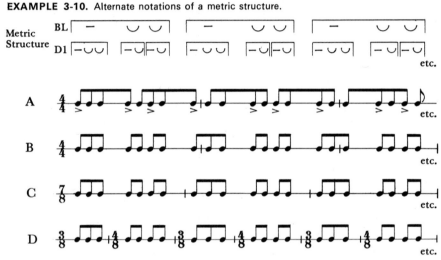

framework of a common practice meter by the use of unusual beaming, or by the placement of dynamic or pitch accent. Example 3-10 shows how the same basic metric structure could be notated in these ways as well as by means of unusual meter signatures or change of meter.

**EXAMPLE 3-10.** Alternate notations of a metric structure.

Although A and B in Ex. 3-10 might be called syncopated patterns rather than unusual meters, they could produce the aural effect of an unusual metric structure $(3 + 2 + 2)$, especially if carried on for a long time in all parts of the musical texture. C and D would be called unusual meter and multimeter respectively, but would result in basically the same metric structure. The choice of notation depends upon the composer's attitude toward the implications of barlines, accents, changes of signatures, beaming etc. Stravinsky, for example, says, "The bar line is much, much more than a mere accent, and I don't believe that it can be simulated by an accent, at least not in my music."[2] Though the metric structure would be basically the same for all four examples, the different notations imply differences in the

---

[2]Igor Stravinsky and Robert Croft, *Conversations With Igor Stravinsky* (Garden City, N.Y.: Doubleday and Company, Inc., 1959), p. 21.

character of the metric structure and could suggest varying interpretations to the performer.

The examples of unusual metric structure that we have discussed in this section have several points in common. In all of them, pulses on at least one level are isochronal or equal-timed. When these are grouped in varying two-pulse or three-pulse groups this will naturally result in pulses on the next slowest level that are non-isochronal or unequal-timed. Moreover, in all of these unusual metric structures there is a regular pattern or periodic recurrence of the varied pulse groups. In the Bartók excerpt (Ex. 3-7), for example, the 3 + 2 + 2 + 3 ordering of pulse groups on the eighth-note level is maintained throughout a section of this composition, thus establishing a degree of consistency, regularity, or predictability. Unusual metric structures of this type are probably closest to common practice metric structures in the sense of security or continuity they give the listener or performer.

### Unusual Metric Structures With Irregularly Varied Pulse Groups

It is also possible to have unusual metric structures in which the changes in pulse groups are more random or irregular, with no consistent pattern or periodic recurrence of the varied pulse groups. The listener or performer is conscious of equal-timed pulses on the beat or a division level but he cannot anticipate from one moment to the next how they will be grouped. Notationally this type of metric structure may be expressed through frequent changes cf meter signature, through changes in beaming, or through irregular accentuation. Example 3-11 is a well-known example of this technique. The irregularly varied pulse groupings, together with the articulation, harmony, and orchestration vividly portray the frenzy of a sacrificial dance.

**EXAMPLE 3-11.** Stravinsky: *The Rite of Spring* (1913), Sacrificial Dance, mm. 1–12. Copyright 1921 by Edition Russe de Musique. Copyright assigned 1947 to Boosey & Hawkes for all countries of the world. Reprinted by permission.

In Ex. 3-12 Copland has used a combination of unusual beaming, accents, and change of meter to create irregularly varied pulse groups.

**EXAMPLE 3-12.** Copland: *Appalachian Spring* (1943–45), No. 13, rhythm only. Copyright 1945 by Aaron Copland; Renewed 1972. Reprinted by permission of Aaron Copland, Copyright Owner, and Boosey & Hawkes, Inc., Sole Publishers and Licensees.

Although there are moments in both Ex. 3-11 and Ex. 3-12 when a pulse grouping is repeated several times, the grouping changes before a full sense of regularity and predictability can be established.

Frequently composers using unusual metric structures with irregularly varied pulse groups will notate them without any meter signature at all. In this case a given note value is to be maintained as a steady equal-timed pulse throughout. The organization of this pulse into groups is suggested by the varying lengths of the measures, the beaming, and other musical factors. Example 3-13 illustrates this technique and brings to our attention another critical point in the analysis of metric structure.

**EXAMPLE 3-13.** Hindemith: String Quartet No. 3, Op. 22 (1923), II, mm. 1–8. Copyright 1923 by B. Schott's Soehne. Copyright renewed 1951. Used with permission. All rights reserved.

Schnelle Achtel, Sehr energisch ($\flat$ = 176—184)

The opening measure of this example consists of five reiterated C sharps in all instruments. There is nothing in the music to indicate whether these are to be played and heard as 3 + 2 or as 2 + 3. Though we may choose one or the other division as a preliminary organization to assist in the initial stage of study of this work, ultimately we should attempt to perform and hear this measure as five equal pulses. Indeed it is probably more consistent with the spirit of the entire movement that the listener have a sense of relentlessly ongoing pulse rather than of constantly shifting pulse groupings.

In any work, the level on which changes of pulse groups occur is of special significance. If they occur on a slow beat level or a multiple level, the beats

themselves will remain isochronal and the general sense of regularity will not
be markedly disturbed. However, if they occur on a division level this will
result in non-isochronal or unequal-timed beats and will bring about a
stronger sense of irregularity or disruption in the metric structure. To understand this, compare the Hindemith Sonata excerpt in either the notation of
Ex. 3-3 or Ex. 3-5 with Ex. 3-14, in which the music is rewritten with varied
pulse groups on the first division level. The non-isochronal beats of Ex. 3-14
produce a sense of metric irregularity that is stronger than in either of the
two previous versions.

**EXAMPLE 3-14.** Hindemith: Piano Sonata No. 2, I, rewritten.

## Unusual Metric Structures With Nonsynchronous Pulse Groups

In our discussion of common practice metric structures we have noted
that pulse groups on different levels are *synchronous*, that is, all pulses on
slower levels coincide in time with strong pulses on faster levels. In Ex. 3-1,
for example, the quarter-note and half-note pulses coincided in time or were
synchronized with the strong pulses on the eighth-note level.

It is possible to have a metric structure with *nonsynchronous* pulse groups,
and there are several ways of achieving this type of metric structure. One is
to maintain identical pulses in all parts but to organize them into different
groupings in different parts. In Ex. 3-15 the eighth-note and quarter-note
pulses in the contrabass are organized into unvaried, regularly recurring
duple groupings throughout. At the beginning of the excerpt the cornet and
trombone are also organized into the same grouping, and so the metric

structure at this point is synchronous and not unlike a common practice metric structure. Beginning at m. 14, however, the brass parts are organized into inconsistently varied pulse groups which no longer coincide with the pulse groups of the contrabass part. At this point the metric structure becomes nonsynchronous. On the analysis below the music, points of synchronization between the two parts are indicated with a solid line and points of nonsynchronization are indicated with a dotted line.

**EXAMPLE 3-15.** Stravinsky: *L'Histoire du Soldat* (1918), "The Soldier's March," mm. 1–19. Used by permission of J. & W. Chester, Ltd., London.

Stravinsky has chosen to change meter signatures in both parts to follow
the varied pulse groupings of the brass in mm. 14–17, using beaming to
indicate the ongoing duple grouping of the contrabass. It would have been
possible to reverse this as demonstrated in Ex. 3-16, maintaining the meter
signature appropriate for the contrabass structure and using beaming in the
brass parts to indicate the varied groupings.

**EXAMPLE 3-16.** Ibid., rewritten.

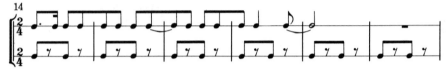

It would also have been possible to use different meter signatures in each
part to indicate the different groupings, as shown in Ex. 3-17.

**EXAMPLE 3-17.** Ibid., rewritten.

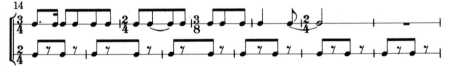

Once again we have seen that basically the same metric structure may be
notated in a variety of ways, and once again we should point out that the
choice of notational method will affect the character or flavor of the metric
structure even though it may not change its basic objective structure.

A subtle example of nonsynchronous metric structure is given in Ex. 3-18.

**EXAMPLE 3-18.** Webern: Cantata No. 1, Op. 29 (1940), III, mm. 27–28. © 1954, Universal
Edition. Used by permission of the publisher. Theodore Presser Company
sole representative United States, Canada and Mexico.

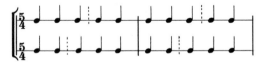

Webern has used a dotted line in the middle of the $\frac{5}{4}$ measure to indicate
that the grouping for some parts is two-pulse followed by three-pulse, and
the reverse in other parts. This division results from textual accentuation as
well as from purely musical considerations. It might be claimed that factors
of pitch and instrumentation tend to make one pulse grouping more prominent than the other and lead to the claim that Webern's distinctions are not

really audible. However, careful listening to this passage can lead to an appreciation of the two different pulse groupings sounded independently in an effective counterpoint of accentuation. The situation might also be described in terms of ambiguity of background and foreground, as discussed in the introduction to this chapter.

Another method of achieving nonsynchronous relations between the parts of a musical texture is to have both different pulse groupings and different pulse rates in the different parts. In Ex. 3-19(a) the cello and viola begin with synchronous relations with both parts moving in triple groupings, but by the third measure of the example the cello has changed from triple to duple groupings with slightly slower pulses. The first pulse of each group in the cello part does coincide with the first pulse of each group in the viola part, but the second pulse of the cello grouping does not coincide with any pulse in the viola part.

**EXAMPLE 3-19.** Bartók: String Quartet No. 2 (1920), II, 3 mm. after no. 41. Copyright 1920 by Universal Edition; Renewed 1956. Copyright assigned to Boosey & Hawkes, Inc., for the U.S.A. Reprinted by permission. Permission granted by Universal Edition A.G., Vienna, for all countries of the world except USA.

The notational form chosen by Bartók here, the simultaneous use of two different meter signatures, is sometimes called polymeter. The passage could, however, have been written in at least two other manners, as shown above. Example 3-19(b) involves irregular division of the beat, and Ex. 3-19(c) involves a somewhat unusual rhythmic pattern, but both examples would produce basically the same nonsynchronous metric structure as the original notation in Ex. 3-19(a).

Again the choice of notation is not an arbitrary one, since it colors the player's interpretation and probably the listener's perception. But to take the notational manner as the sole criterion for description and analysis would be to miss the basic structural significance of this metric structure. Example 3-19(b) is just as clearly nonsynchronous or "polymetric" in its *sounding* metric structure as Ex. 3-19(a), even though only one meter signature is used.

With nonsynchronous metric structures such as this it is possible to indicate an "implied" pulse which is in effect the least common denominator of the different pulse groups. In simple cases such as two against three (as in Ex. 3-19) or three against four, this implied pulse may actually serve as a guide to hearing and performing.

With more complex relations this is impractical. The implied pulse in the Ives example (Ex. 3-20) would be 1680 pulses per quarter note ($5 \times 6 \times 7 \times 8$). Obviously this could not possibly be of any assistance, and instead the pulse groups of each part must be performed individually. The total effect of this passage is generally that of a rhythmic blur with primary points of coincidence or accentuation at each quarter note and secondary points of accentuation at the triplet half note.

Another way to achieve nonsynchronous relations is to begin various elements of a musical texture at different times and at different tempi. In Ex. 3-21, the four flutes enter in an *allegro* tempo, which bears no clear relationship to the *largo* tempo of the strings. This represents a clear example of the kind of stratified or layered texture discussed in Chapter 2.

In some aleatory (chance) works performers are free to choose both the time relation between the beginning of the first part and subsequent parts and the tempo of subsequent parts.

**EXAMPLE 3-20.** Ives: *Three Places in New England* (1903–11), "The Housatonic at Stock-
bridge," p. 85. Copyright 1935, Mercury Music, Inc. Used by permission.

**EXAMPLE 3-21.** Ives: *The Unanswered Question* (1908). Copyright 1953 by Southern Music Publishing Company, Inc. Used by permission.

### Unusual Metric Structures Involving Aspects of Pulse Rate or Tempo

In all of the types of unusual metric structures we have examined to this point we have noted a general tendency to move from the relative simplicity, consistency, and control of common practice towards complexity, inconsistency, and freedom in contemporary practice. Turning to the consideration of pulse rate or tempo we find at least in some music of the twentieth century an interesting reversal of this trend.

There is a general tendency in the history of tempo to move from the relative regularity of the eighteenth century toward the rubato of the nineteenth century. The lack of actual recordings from this period makes it necessary to base such a statement upon verbal descriptions in various treatises, forewords, and critiques or upon deductions from the intrinsic evidence in the music itself, but it is a generally accepted conclusion. It may be noted parenthetically that some present-day performers tend on one hand to overemphasize the strictness and consistency of pulse rate in Baroque music and on the other hand to underemphasize or distort aspects of the freedom and variability of pulse rate in some Romantic music.

Some twentieth-century composers have continued this trend toward increasing freedom in tempo, culminating in works in which the variability of pulse rate and pulse groupings tends to obscure metric structure completely. This will be discussed in the next section of this chapter. Other twentieth-century composers like Stravinsky have sought to reverse the trend, at least in some works, by qualifying or replacing tempo terms with metronomic markings, and by specifying, both in words written over the music and in other writings, that the pulse is to be maintained strictly without alteration or rubato. This mechanical approach to pulse, which some writers have identified with the influence of the machine in our society, continues to be an important aspect of the style of some composers.

Between these two extremes of great freedom and mechanical strictness there is a middle ground of structured change in pulse rate or tempo which has been a significant area of exploration for twentieth-century composers. In Ex. 3-22 the frequency and the specificity of tempo change go beyond that of common practice, but not so far as to destroy completely the sense of metric structure.

**EXAMPLE 3-22.** Bartók: Fourteen Bagatelles, Op. 6 (1908), XI. New Version Copyright 1950 by Boosey & Hawkes, Inc. Reprinted by permission.

Changes of tempo can often be significant indicators of structural points in music of the twentieth century. Bartók's Violin Duet No. 33 illustrates the use of alternating tempi (Lento, ♩ = 58 and Piu Mosso, ♩ = 88) to create formal divisions. On a larger scale, in Bartók's Sixth Quartet, the recurring *Mesto* sections ( ♪ = 96) are alternated with sections in contrasting tempi creating what might be called a "tempo rondo." In the first movement of the Third Quartet of Schoenberg, changes of tempo indicate such structural points as the beginning of the second theme group, the development section, and the recapitulation section. In this and other serial compositions one could almost say that the composer provides changes of tempo for the performer and listener as aids in perceiving the structure of the music. This structure might not be as apparent from other aspects of music such as the treatment of pitches, vertical sonorities, and textures, since these are all subject to continuous application of variation techniques. Literal repetition and traditional aspects of tonality are ruled out as form-delineating procedures in some contemporary music, and so changes or recurrences of tempi may act almost as a substitute.

We have discussed unusual metric structures involving changes in pulse grouping and those involving changes in pulse rate as though these were completely separate. Frequently in twentieth-century music, however, both types of change will be used together. A special example of this combined change of pulse rate and pulse grouping is the technique known as "metric modulation," usually associated with Elliott Carter and other contemporary composers. The term *modulation*, traditionally applied to the process of tonality change, is here applied to the process of change in pulse rate and/or pulse grouping. A feature of this technique is that one note value of the old tempo and meter is made equivalent to another note value in the new tempo and meter. We could call this note value a "pivot note value" in a manner analogous to a pivot chord in tonal modulation, that is, a chord which has one function in the old key and at the same time a different function in the new key. In both cases the pivot note value or the pivot chord serves to provide a degree of unity and cohesiveness which would not be present if the change were made without any relation to the previous section.

Two examples from Carter's Fantasy for woodwind quartet may serve to illustrate this technique. In both cases we have indicated only the rhythmic skeleton of the clarinet and bassoon parts since these will serve to illustrate the points under consideration.

**EXAMPLE 3-23.** Carter: Eight Etudes and a Fantasy for woodwind quartet (1950), Fantasy, mm. 16–18. Reprinted by permission of Associated Music Publishers, Inc.

In m. 16 of Ex. 3-23, triplet quarter notes are sounded in the clarinet against regular quarters in the bassoon. In m. 17 quarter notes in $\frac{6}{4}$ move at the same rate as the triplet quarter notes in the previous $\frac{4}{4}$ ♩ = ♩.. In m. 18 the quarter notes continue at the same rate but are now back in $\frac{4}{4}$ meter. Since triplet quarter notes and regular quarter notes in $\frac{4}{4}$ stand in a 3:2 ratio, the tempos of the $\frac{4}{4}$ meter in m. 18 and 16 stand in a 3:2 ratio, i.e., 126/84.

From this we can derive a formula which may be used to determine the metronome marking of the new tempo in cases of metric modulation.

$$\frac{\text{new tempo}}{\text{old tempo}} = \frac{\text{number of "pivot note values" in old metric unit}}{\text{number of "pivot note values" in new metric unit}}$$

Study the following example (Ex. 3-24) and try to determine the new tempi in mm. 32 and 35.

**EXAMPLE 3-24.** Ibid., mm. 31–36. Reprinted by permission of Associated Music Publishers, Inc.

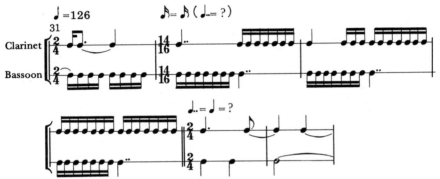

Applying the given information to our formula we have

$$\frac{\text{new tempo (x)}}{126} = \frac{4\ (\text{♪})}{7\ (\text{♪})} \qquad 7x = 504 \quad x = 72$$

Therefore the new tempo in m. 32 would be ♩.. = 72, and in m. 35 it would be ♩ = 72.

The idea of proportional change of meter and tempo is not new; indeed the 2:3 ratio of Ex. 3-23 was a common one in the sixteenth century in the relationship between sections in duple and triple meter. What is new in the twentieth century is the more complex use of this technique, and the more frequent and extensive use of the technique throughout a composition.

### Unusual Metric Structures
### With Obscured Pulse

The idea of having pulses obscured, rather than clearly enunciated or implied, is also not new. It can be found in vocal recitative, and in isolated instrumental examples in earlier music. What is new is the extensive application of this technique to a wide variety of compositional types and the means used to achieve it.

Example 3-25 illustrates a fairly traditional approach to obscured pulse. With the exception of the group of nine eighth notes in the first measure, most of the excerpt is notated in a rather traditional manner. The words, *frei in Zeitmass* (free in tempo) and *rubato*, however, indicate that the passage is to be played in a recitative-like style, and in most performances the sense of pulse would be obscured.

**EXAMPLE 3-25.** Hindemith: *Symphony "Mathis der Maler"* (1934), Versuchung des Heiligen Antonius, beginning. Copyright 1934 by B. Schott's Soehne. Copyright renewed 1962. Used with permission. All rights reserved.

In some contemporary works a sense of obscured pulse is achieved through extensive use of unusual metric structures with change of pulse rate, change of pulse groupings, and nonsynchronous relations between pulse groups on various levels. When these reach the degree of complexity of Ex. 3-26, the listener may lose the sense of pulse. Carter has provided a simplified alternate rhythmic notation; compared with this the original notation may be regarded as a written-out rubato.

**EXAMPLE 3-26.** Carter: Double Concerto (1962), m. 50. Reprinted by permission of Associated Music Publishers, Inc.

There are other examples in which the composer has used far less complex written notation than that of Ex. 3-26, but has specified that the performer should seek to avoid any implication of accentuation or grouping. *Pithoprakta* of Xenakis, for example, is notated almost entirely in $\frac{2}{2}$ meter. The composer has said, however, that barlines in his music are to be regarded somewhat like mileposts on a road, which show the traveler his location in space but have absolutely no relation to the basic features of the natural landscape. So too, barlines in *Pithoprakta* and similar works may show the performer where he is in time and in relation to other performers, but they do not relate specifically to the structure of the music. In a valid performance of works like this, the pulse groupings should be obscured so that the shape of larger aspects of the work can be perceived. Though this approach is crucial to contemporary works of this nature, the proper balance of emphasis upon grouping and accentuation on various levels is a significant factor in the interpretation of all music.

Finally we may note that obscured pulse may result from two unique and often diametrically opposed contemporary compositional procedures—automated music, including both electronic music and computer-generated music, and chance or aleatory music. The precision and control available to the composer of automated music allow him to produce durations and intensities of sounds without any relation to an ongoing sense of pulse, if he so chooses. On the other hand the freedom in rhythm given the performer in some chance music allows him to produce the same general effect of obscured pulse.

Example 3-27 illustrates the manner in which electronic composers may control precise duration. The middle line indicates the duration of each sound event; the numbers indicate centimeters of tape at a speed of 76.2 cm per second. It is unlikely that the composer intended any sense of pulse underlying these varied durations, or that any such pulse will be perceived.

Example 3-28 illustrates the freedom given the performer in a chance music composition. Here the pitch material is specified, but the durations and even the ordering of these pitches is left to the interpretation of the performer. Again it is probably not the intention of the composer that any clear sense of underlying pulse be heard, although it may be difficult for some performers to avoid introducing this.

When pulse is drastically obscured, the traditional dichotomy between a regulative background of metric structure and a configurative foreground of durational patterns is no longer valid. In this case it can be said that all of the sounding rhythmic events are heard as a foreground *gestalt* projected against a background of silence or time itself.

It must be remembered that even though the composer's intention of obscured metric structure is perfectly expressed in his notation and perfectly realized in the interpretation of the performer, it is still possible for the lis-

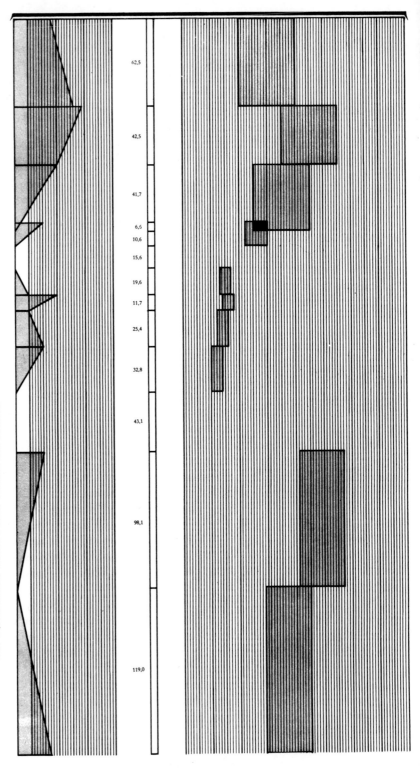

**EXAMPLE 3-27.** Stockhausen: *No. 3 Elektronische Studien, Studie II.* © 1956 Universal Edition. Used by permission of the publisher. Theodore Presser Company sole representative United States, Canada and Mexico.

**EXAMPLE 3-28.** Berio: *Tempi Concertati* (1962), pp. 50 and 52. Reprinted by permission of Associated Music Publishers, Inc.

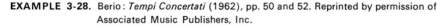

follow the lines right or left                    play in any order

tener, with his experiences and expectations of traditional metric structure, to superimpose a traditional metric structure upon the music he hears. Indeed, it can be said that one of the primary responsibilities for rhythmic training at all levels is to enable listeners to perceive, accept, and appreciate the full gamut of possibilities of metric structure accurately and appropriately, whether it be expressed in a thirteenth-century *estampie* or a twentieth-century aleatory composition.

Just as the emphasis upon regularity of pulse in some twentieth-century music has been linked to the influence of technology, the emphasis upon obscurity or irregularity of pulse in other works may be linked to the influence of socio-cultural trends which seek to reject the dominance of technology and rationality. Works like John Cage's *Music of Changes*, Karlheinz Stockhausen's *Mikrophonie I*, or Morton Feldman's *Atlantis* illustrate the enormous variety in aesthetic rationale, compositional processes, notational procedures, performance practices, and perceptual problems to be encountered in works with obscured pulse or obscured metric structure. It is difficult to make any meaningful generalizations about these works. Indeed, some composers like Stockhausen deliberately explore new practices and procedures in each new work they write. It is not unusual to find new works with an accompanying set of instructions and explanations by the composer which equal the actual composition in length. Far from being frivolous, this can serve as a needed reminder that every serious work of art must be approached as much as possible on its own terms, rather than as a mere representative of a class of works.

Though we have attempted in this section to organize the metric structures found in contemporary music into general categories it is neither possible nor advisable to force every composition into one of these categories. Individual works will frequently use a variety of metric structures, and individual metric structures may resist categorization or fall on the borderline between two categories.

## DURATIONAL PATTERNS

Let us return once more to the opening of the Hindemith Second Sonata as a fairly typical representative of common practice, and this time examine the melodic line for durational patterns.

Just as the pulse was the basic unit for consideration of the background of
metric structure, the duration, that is, the span of time from one pulse or
point in time to another, will be the basic unit for consideration of the foreground of durational patterns. In the melodic line of Ex. 3-29 Hindemith
uses a relatively small *duration complement,* or number of different durations.
These could be arranged in a *duration scale,* or an ordering of durations from
shortest to longest. This is listed below in terms of notes and in terms of
number of shortest durations (sixteenth notes) in each duration.

We might further note that the *duration range,* the difference in length between the shortest and longest durations, is relatively narrow in this example
(1 to 10). Finally we can count the number of times each single duration is
used to determine a *duration hierarchy,* an ordering of durations according to

frequency of use. It is obvious that the eighth note is the most frequently used (39 times), and thus we can say that the melody moves basically at the first division level (eighth-note level) of the metric structure. We could compare the prominent use of the eighth note in the rhythm aspect of this excerpt to the prominent use of the pitch class G in the pitch aspect. The remaining durations in order of frequency are ♪.(13), ♩(7), ♪(6), and finally the duration ♩  ♪ which is used only once at the climax of the melody.

It is obvious that we have adapted the terms *duration complement, duration scale, duration range,* and *duration hierarchy* from terms traditionally applied to pitch. This in itself is indicative of the preoccupation with pitch and the relative neglect of rhythm in traditional theory. In modern theoretical writings, however, these terms or similar ones are being used with increasing frequency. Consideration of these aspects of rhythm can give us some insight into individual works and some analytical tools for the purpose of comparative analysis.

But we cannot make the single duration the focus of our analysis any more than we could make the single pitch the focus of an analysis of melody. Our concern must rather be with the grouping of durations into patterns. We propose to use two methods of analyzing rhythm patterns. The first, which we shall call *rhythmic units*, is more objective and better suited for descriptive, comparative, *inter-opus* analysis. The second, which we shall call *rhythmic gestures*, is more subjective and better suited for prescriptive, interpretive, *intra-opus* analysis.

### Rhythmic Units

*Rhythmic units,* for our purposes, are characterized by the fact that they occupy a period of time equivalent to a given unit of the underlying metric structure. In the case of the Hindemith Sonata (Ex. 3-29) the rhythmic unit is generally the measure or the time span from one pulse to the next on the first multiple or half-note level.

Having delineated the size of rhythmic units according to their relation to the underlying metric structure, we may then describe them in several different ways. The most explicit and precise ways would be in notation or in numerical ratios. The rhythmic units of Ex. 3-29 are given below together with their frequency of occurrence.

| | | |
|---|---|---|
| ♪. ♪ | (3:1) | 12 times |
| ♩ ♫ | (2:1:1) | 6 times |
| ♫♫ | (1:1:1:1) | 3 times |
| ♬♩ ♪ | (1:1:4:2) | 2 times |
| ♪. ♬ | (6:1:1) | 1 time |
| ♩ ♫♩ | (5:1:1:1) | 1 time |

In a more general sense we may categorize rhythmic units according to the way in which the duration patterns of the rhythmic unit relate to the pulses of the metric structure. We may distinguish four basic types of patterns in rhythmic units:

1. *Metric* or even-note patterns. The durations of the pattern are identical with pulses on a given level of the metric structure. Examples would be ♩♩♩♩ in the Hindemith excerpt or ♪♪♪♪ in the Schoenberg excerpt (Ex. 3-32).

2. *Intrametric* or confirming patterns. The durations of the pattern are based upon pulse groups within the metric structure but are not identical to the pulses of the metric structure. The accents (dynamic, agogic, and pitch) of the pattern confirm or support the accentuation of the metric structure. Examples would be ♩· ♪ in the Hindemith or ♩·· ♪ in the Schoenberg.

3. *Contrametric*, nonconfirming, or syncopated patterns. The durations of the pattern are identical to or based upon the pulses of the metric structure like types 1 and 2, but unlike these, the accents of the pattern do not confirm or support the accentuation of the metric structure; instead, they momentarily disrupt or conflict with it. Our definition of syncopation is a broader one than usual, covering situations ranging from the relatively mild disruption of metric structure caused by displaced agogic accent, as in ♫♩ ♪ from the Hindemith example, through such typical examples as beginning notes on weak pulses and carrying their durations over succeeding strong pulses or substituting rests for notes on strong pulses, to the relatively strong disruption of metric structure caused by displaced dynamic accents.

4. *Extrametric* or irregular patterns. The durations of the pattern are based upon pulse groups which are outside the normal pulse groups of the metric structure and are nonsynchronous with them. A typical example would be the triplet eighth notes in m. 7 of the Schoenberg excerpt. This type of rhythmic unit is sometimes called irregular division of the beat, but it must be remembered that this phenomenon may occur on any level of the metric structure.

This manner of delineating rhythmic units according to metric units is subject to the objection that it contradicts the proper phrasing of the particular pattern. The alternative, however, of presenting each pattern according to the way it would be performed or heard would inevitably entail a high degree of interpretation. For example the 3:1:1:1 pattern $\frac{6}{8}$ ♩· ♫♪ could in various musical contexts and with various performers and listeners be regarded as 1:1:1:3 (e.g., ♫♩ |♩· ♫♩ |♩· ~ ), or as 1:1:3:1 (e.g., ♫ |♩· ♪♫ |♩· ♪ ~ ), or as 1:3:1:1 (e.g., ♪ |♩· ♫♪ |♩· ♫ ~). We shall take such interpretative distinctions into account in the discussion of rhythmic gestures which follows. For purposes of comparing the rhythmic content and style of different composers or periods of composition, however, consideration of metrically delineated rhythmic units as described above does provide us with a useful analytical technique which is relatively objective and easy to apply and which does frequently point to some clear-cut stylistic differences.

### Rhythmic Gestures

The *rhythmic gesture*, in contrast to the rhythmic unit, is not limited by the underlying metric structure; its beginning, end, and length are subject to varying interpretations based upon consideration of factors contributing to cohesiveness and separation. Strict or varied repetition of a rhythmic gesture tends to establish the identity of the gesture. The use of similar durations, dynamics, pitches, textures, timbres, etc., tends to establish the cohesiveness and unity of a rhythmic gesture; the use of strong contrast in any musical aspect tends to establish the separation of one rhythmic gesture from another. Sometimes the composer will use phrasing markings to identify rhythmic gestures.

Rhythmic gestures may be described according to their beginnings and endings. There are three basic types of beginnings—*thetic*, beginning on a strong pulse (usually the first pulse of the measure); *anacrustic*, beginning on a weak pulse (usually the upbeat of a measure); and *initial rest*, beginning after a rest or tied-over note (usually on the first beat or first division of the beat in a measure). There are also three types of endings—*strong*, ending on a strong pulse (usually the first beat of a measure); *weak*,[3] ending on a weak pulse (usually the second beat or the second division of a measure); and *upbeat*, ending on a strong or weak pulse in the upbeat of a measure. These types of beginnings and endings are shown in the analysis below.

**EXAMPLE 3-30.** Hindemith: Piano Sonata No. 2 (1936), I, mm. 1–26. Copyright 1936 by B. Schott's Soehne. Copyright renewed 1964. Used with permission. All rights reserved.

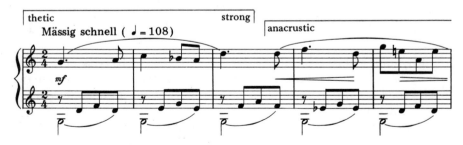

---

[3]The traditional terms "masculine" and "feminine" seem singularly inappropriate, especially in view of recent socio-cultural trends.

**EXAMPLE 3-30** continued.

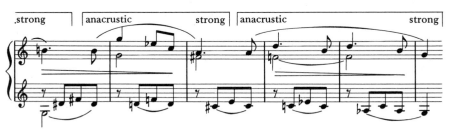

Rhythmic gestures may also be described in terms of the types of rhythmic units they contain. In Ex. 3-30 the first gesture contains intrametric patterns, the second has intrametric and metric patterns, and the third has intrametric and contrametric patterns.

More important than the description of individual rhythmic gestures is an analysis of the way one gesture is related to another. Let us begin by examining the way succesive gestures are related in the melodic line of Ex. 3-30. Notice how the rhythmic unit ♩ ♫ in the second measure of the first gesture is transformed into ♫ ♫ in m. 5, by splitting the quarter note of the first rhythmic unit into two eighth notes. A similar process may be observed in mm. 7 and 9 where the eighth note is split into two sixteenths.

Relations between rhythmic gestures in different parts of the texture are also significant. Notice, for example, how the even-note rhythmic units of the upper part of the right hand in mm. 11 and 12 are answered or imitated in the upper part of the left hand two measures later.

Finally we may consider the composite rhythm of this passage, that is the durational patterns produced by the interaction of all the sounding parts of the musical texture. In the Hindemith example the composite rhythm results in even eighth notes throughout except for mm. 8–10, where sixteenth notes are momentarily heard, and m. 26 where the cessation of the eighth-note composite rhythm on the first beat signals a structurally important cadential point.

**EXAMPLE 3-31.**

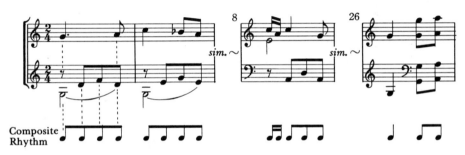

### The Cooper and Meyer Approach

The problem of delimiting and describing durational patterns is approached in a somewhat different manner by Grosvenor Cooper and Leonard Meyer in their book *The Rhythmic Structure of Music.*[4] Cooper and Meyer have classified rhythm according to accent and grouping into five basic types, named according to the *feet* of the Greek system of poetic meter.

> iamb = weak — strong  
> anapest = weak — weak — strong } end accented  
> trochee = strong — weak  
> dactyl = strong — weak — weak } beginning accented  
> amphibrach = weak — strong — weak } middle accented

Applied to relatively simple patterns, these terms may be used effectively and unambiguously. To describe more complicated examples Cooper and

[4]Chicago: University of Chicago Press, 1960.

Meyer have evolved a rather elaborate system involving analysis of rhythmic activity on several hierarchical levels and the use of overlapping groupings to cover possibly ambiguous situations. This is illustrated in their analysis of the fourth piece from Schoenberg's Op. 19.

**EXAMPLE 3-32.** Schoenberg: *Sechs kleine Klavierstücke,* Op. 19 (1911) No. 4, Copyright Universal. Analysis from Grosvenor Cooper and Leonard Meyer, *The Rhythmic Structure of Music,* p. 175. © 1960 University of Chicago Press.

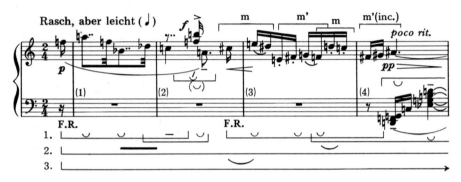

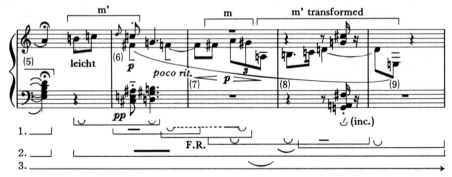

The analysis immediately below the first two measures indicates an anapest overlapping a trochee. Cooper and Meyer call this the fundamental rhythm (F.R.) of the piece and describe it as follows:

> The opening impulse is a middle-accented rhythm with a two unit anacrusis and an afterbeat bolstered by a shocking forte upbeat on the subprimary level (measure 2).[5]

They regard the third and fourth measures as a transformation of the fundamental rhythm as indicated in the analysis, and base this upon the motivic analysis (m) indicated above these measures. They reject the metrically conditioned grouping indicated in Ex. 3-33.

**EXAMPLE 3-33.** Ibid., p. 176.

The difficulties inherent in the problem of analyzing rhythmic groupings is recognized by the authors in the following statement:

> Rhythmic grouping is a mental fact not a physical one. There are no hard and fast rules for calculating what in any particular instance the grouping is. Sensitive, well-trained musicians may differ. Indeed, it is this that makes performance an art—that makes different phrasings and different interpretations of a piece of music possible. Furthermore, grouping may at times be purposely ambiguous and must be thus understood rather than forced into a clear decisive pattern. In brief, the interpretation of music—and this is what analysis should be—is an art requirng experience, understanding, and sensitivity.[6]

It is clear from the last statement in this quotation that the primary purpose of the Cooper and Meyer approach is the consideration of problems of interpretation. The great strength of this approach is the possibility of achieving penetrating analyses of individual works through the sensitive application of valid general principles. But it is precisely the possible diversity of interpretation that makes this approach difficult to use as an analytical tool for comparing the rhythmic content and style of different composers or different periods of composition.

### Common Practice Durational Patterns

If it is difficult to characterize periods of rhythmic practice in terms of metric structure, it is even more difficult to characterize them in terms of

---

[5]*Ibid.*, p. 174.
[6]*Ibid.*, p. 9.

durational patterns. Differences between individual composers or works may be as significant in this respect as differences between periods of composition. Nevertheless, it is possible to make some qualified statements about the use of durational patterns in the period of common practice and then to contrast these with aspects of contemporary practice.

The following characteristics are typical of common practice durational patterns:

1. The duration complement and range is generally small or moderate. In terms of duration hierarchy, one duration will usually predominate and be heard as the basic unit of movement in a particular composition. Though extremely long durations (sustained pedal notes, for example) may be heard in some compositions, the use of extremely short durations is rare except in such specialized cases as trills, tremolos, or other ornaments, or in some rapid passages of virtuoso display pieces.

2. Rhythmic units are usually based on metric or intrametric patterns, but certain contrametric or extrametric patterns may be hallmarks of individual composers or styles within common practice. Examples of this would be the use of contrametric or syncopated patterns associated with suspensions, or the frequent use of triplets in themes of a composer like Anton Bruckner. Triplets and other extrametric patterns are usually heard on division levels.

3. Rhythmic gestures are typically made up of a limited number of rhythmic units; sometimes they may be based on a single rhythmic unit or on a pair of alternating units.

4. Thetic, anacrustic, and initial rest gestures are used, but there is some tendency to favor an anacrustic analysis. Strong endings would probably hold a statistical edge, but with some composers, like Mozart, the weak ending may be a significant stylistic feature. Upbeat endings are rare.

5. Exact or varied repetition of rhythmic gestures and return to a rhythmic gesture after a contrasting gesture are typical of common practice. Though complete reliance upon one rhythmic gesture throughout an entire composition is possible, as for example in the C-major prelude of the first book of the *Well-Tempered Clavier*, the other extreme of complete avoidance of repetition is rare. In general there is a balance between unity and variety in the rhythmic gestures of a given composition.

6. The composite rhythm will usually result in patterns which confirm the metric structure, frequently in metric or even-note patterns identical to pulses on a particular level.

In the sections which follow we shall consider twentieth-century rhythmic practice in terms of the relation of durational patterns to metric structure. We shall organize our discussion into four general categories: common practice durational patterns in the framework of common practice metric structures, unusual durational patterns in the framework of common practice metric structures, common practice durational patterns in the framework of unusual metric structures, and unusual durational patterns in the framework of unusual metric structures.

### Common Practice Durational Patterns
### in the Framework of Common Practice
### Metric Structures

Many twentieth-century works like the Hindemith sonata previously discussed illustrate the relatively conservative use of common practice durational patterns in the framework of common practice metric structures. Other examples would be Prokofiev's *Classical* Symphony, where the composer is paying homage to traditional style, or numerous examples in Bartók's *Mikrokosmos* where the composer is exploring novel aspects of pitch or harmony and has deliberately adhered to traditional rhythmic practice to avoid presenting the performer and listener with too many unusual elements at once.

Rather than exploring such works in detail we shall turn to other categories, beginning with works which follow most of the characteristics listed for common practice but depart from these in certain ways, and moving to works which differ radically from common practice.

### Unusual Durational Patterns
### in the Framework of Common Practice
### Metric Structures

Example 3-34 presents the opening measures of a work in which the rhythm is similar in many ways to common practice.

**EXAMPLE 3-34.** Babbitt: Three Compositions for Piano (1947–48), No. 1. Used by permission of Boelke-Bomart, Inc., Hillsdale, N.Y. 12529.

The durational patterns and the composite rhythm are clearly derived from and, in general, confirm the metric structure. The sixteenth note is clearly established as the most prominently used duration, and the rhythmic units, though often contrametric or syncopated, do not differ radically from those of common practice. What is unusual is the fact that no single rhythmic gesture is literally repeated, even though all are similar and obviously related. The fact that the passage is based upon a rhythmic set or series of 5:1:4:2 pulses on the sixteenth-note level need not concern us here since this technique is discussed in the final chapter of this book. One result of the application of the technique here is the sense of constant variation.

On the other hand, an insistent sense of unity results from the fact that all of the rhythmic gestures (usually a measure in length) have thetic beginnings and upbeat endings. These tend to break the work up into separate blocks of rhythmic activity, but the great variety of rhythmic relations within these blocks keeps the piece moving forward in time.

Another technique of twentieth-century rhythm is the opposite of the constant variation of rhythmic gesture discovered in Ex. 3-34: the use of *ostinato,* or the insistent repetition of a rhythmic idea. Ostinato technique is nothing new in itself; examples may be found in numerous works from all periods. What is new is the more extensive and pervasive use of the technique (it may be regarded as almost a cliché in the rhythmic practice of a composer like Stravinsky), and the frequent choice of strikingly complex rhythmic gestures as the basis for the ostinato.

Compare the following ostinato patterns.

**EXAMPLE 3-35(a).** Brahms: Symphony No. 4, IV. Copyright 1932 by E. F. Kalmus, New York.

**EXAMPLE 3-35(b).** Chopin: Polonaise in A-flat Major, Op. 53.

**EXAMPLE 3-35(c).** Hindemith: *Konzert für Orchester,* Op. 38 (1925), IV, mm. 1–2. Copyright 1925 by B. Schott's Soehne. Copyright renewed 1952. Used with permission. All rights reserved.

**EXAMPLE 3-35(d).** Berg: Violin Concerto, II. Copyright 1936, Universal Edition. Used by permission of the publisher. Theodore Presser Company sole representative United States, Canada and Mexico.

The patterns in Ex. 3-35(a) and 3-35(b) are typical of traditional ostinati; Ex. 3-35(c) shows a more complex pattern. Example 3-35(d) shows a complex syncopated ostinato pattern which Berg uses with shattering effectiveness to portray the anguish of the death of Manon Gropius in the second movement of his Violin Concerto. Similar ostinati may be found in Berg's operas and in other twentieth-century works.

Example 3-36 illustrates two interesting uses of accents in simple durational patterns in the framework of traditionally notated meter. The main difference between the rhythm of these two passages is the fact that the Beethoven accents, though they are in conflict with the meter, occur each time at the same place in the measure; the Stravinsky accents occur in an irregular, unexpected manner. In both cases, one could debate whether to call the resulting aural effect one of change in the background of metric structure or unusual accents in the foreground of durational patterns heard in conflict with metric structure.

**EXAMPLE 3-36(a).** Beethoven: String Quartet in F. Major, Op. 18 no. 1, IV, mm. 144–148.

**EXAMPLE 3-36(b).** Stravinsky, *The Rite of Spring,* "Dance of the Adolescents." Copyright 1921 by Edition Russe de Musique. Copyright assigned 1947 to Boosey & Hawkes for all countries of the world. Reprinted by permission.

Example 3-36 also illustrates the use of durational patterns, delineated by pitch and dynamic accent, which are in conflict with the written meter. The difference between this example and those of Ex. 3-36 is that in Ex. 3-37 the metric structure is clearly established in some parts of the texture and the durational patterns are heard against this in a momentary conflict. Passages of this nature are sometimes called cross-rhythms, and may also be analyzed polymetrically.

**EXAMPLE 3-37.** Stravinsky: *The Rite of Spring,* "Game of Seduction." Copyright 1921 by Edition Russe de Musique. Copyright assigned 1947 to Boosey & Hawkes for all countries of the world. Reprinted by permission.

The examples in this section have highlighted three principal themes of this chapter: the sometimes problematic relation of metric background to rhythmic foreground, the relation of notated rhythm to sounding rhythm, and the relation of common practice to twentieth-century practice. We turn now to examples which depart even more obviously from common practice in their use of durational patterns.

Though triplets, duplets, and even quintuplets, septuplets and other complex extrametric patterns may be found in earlier music, they are almost always even-note patterns and are almost always on a division level, that is, they represent irregular division of the beat. Twentieth-century practice departs from this in at least two ways. Example 3-38 illustrates durational patterns which are based on an extrametric (i.e., triplet) division of the beat, but in contrast to traditional practice the durational patterns are not basic, even-note patterns but are more complicated and sometimes even syncopated.

**EXAMPLE 3-38.** Schuller: Seven Studies on Themes of Paul Klee (1959), III, "Little Blue Devil," m. 5. © 1962, Universal Edition. Used by permission of the publisher. Theodore Presser Company sole representative United States, Canada and Mexico.

Performance of patterns of this nature requires that one first hear the momentary change of underlying pulse and then base the pattern on this as shown below the example.

Example 3-39 illustrates the use of extrametric patterns on higher or multiple levels.

**EXAMPLE 3-39.** Walton: Symphony (1936), I. By permission of Oxford University Press.

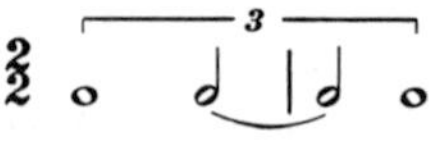

Paul Creston[7] points out that there are two other possible methods of notating this pattern in terms of extrametric or irregular division of the measure or the beat rather than in terms of higher levels.

---

[7] Paul Creston, *Principles of Rhythm* (New York: Franco Columbo, 1964), p. 113.

**EXAMPLE 3-40.**

In Ex. 3-41, the extrametric or irregular pulse groupings occur on several different levels, and the patterns based on them are complex and syncopated. Patterns of this nature are not only challenging to hear and perform; if carried on for a long period of time in various parts of the texture, they may have the aural effect of obscuring the pulse of the metric structure. In this respect, however, we should mention that in a live performance where one may watch the baton of the conductor or the movements of the performer, one may *see* beats which provide a clear *visual* background of metric structure against which the foreground of durational patterns is projected. Lacking this visual component, a recorded performance can never fully recreate the total experience of a live performance. The study of *kinesics*, which has shown us how visual gestures or "body language" can supplement or sometimes even contradict verbal language, can effectively be applied to the study of music.

In contrast to the complicated patterns of the previous examples, some twentieth-century works use patterns which look relatively simple on paper but which actually represent a radical departure from common practice in subtle but significant ways.

As an example of this let us examine the opening measures of Webern's Symphony Op. 21 in three different ways. First, we can observe the opening twelve measures in terms of the two principal linear elements, as in Ex. 3-42.

Each of these lines is distributed among various instruments (*Klangfarbenmelodie*), and each of them is treated canonically, with the imitation following at the time interval of two measures. The most noticeable rhythmic aspect of both lines is the expressive use of rests. Whereas rests in traditional music are used primarily to signal the endings of rhythmic gestures, they are here an integral part of each gesture.

None of the smallest rhythmic units (measures in this case) of these two lines would be impossible to find in common practice rhythm, but some of them, like ♩ or ♩, would probably be more likely to occur in accompanimental figuration than in a melodic line. What is striking is the degree of contrast between the two lines which Webern has achieved. The patterns in line 1 (or 2) tend to confirm the accentuation of the metric structure, since eight measures out of thirteen have notes on downbeats of measures. In contrast to this, patterns in line 3 (or 4) usually conflict with the metric structure, with only two out of thirteen measures having notes on downbeats of measures. This contrast may assist the listener in distinguishing the contrapuntal lines of the texture.

Rhythmic gestures provide another interesting point of comparison between the two principal linear elements. The upper line (line 1 or 2)

**EXAMPLE 3-41.** Ives: Symphony No. 4 (1909–1916), II, no. 39. Reprinted by permission of Associated Music Publishers, Inc.

* Solo Piano renotated in the part.

**EXAMPLE 3-42.** Webern: Symphony, Op. 21 (1929), I, mm. 1–15. Copyright 1929, Universal Edition. Used by permission of the publisher. Theodore Presser Company sole representative United States, Canada and Mexico.

begins with a four-measure gesture followed by a measure of rest. The next gesture is three measures in length and is rhythmically identical with the last three measures of the first gesture. The final rhythmic gesture is five measures in length, but could be subdivided into gestures of three and two measures. The lower line (line 3 or 4) begins with a four-measure gesture, followed by a five-measure gesture which could be analyzed as a repeat of the first gesture plus a one-bar extension. The final rhythmic gesture is four measures in length. Both lines may be analyzed, therefore, in terms of three rhythmic gestures. The second gesture in both lines is clearly derived from the first and represents a truncation in the upper line, an extension in the lower line. The third gesture in both lines is based on varied treatment of rhythmic ideas from the first gesture.

An analysis of this section based upon these lines depends upon following the use of the twelve-note set. Such an analysis gives us insight into the compositional procedure and inner meaning of the work, but it ignores the durational patterns expressed by any one instrument. It is also possible, however, to consider the rhythmic gestures of this work according to their distribution among the various instruments.

As indicated in Ex. 3-43, there are sixteen different rhythmic gestures heard in the ten individual instruments (treating the harp as two parts, a higher and a lower). Each of these gestures is imitated at a time interval of two measures by another instrument, usually of the same timbre family. In any one part there is always an interval of rest separating one gesture from the next; these rests range from one to sixteen measures in length, considering the repeat of this section. The gestures themselves range in length from a single measure with just one sounding note to five-measure durational patterns which might be analyzed as consisting of two successive rhythmic gestures. A variety of anacrustic and thetic beginnings and strong and weak endings may be heard in the gestures.

A third way of regarding this work would be to consider the composite rhythm formed by the interaction of the parts of the texture. This is indicated below the score in Ex. 3-43. Notice that the pattern ♩ ♩ ♩ dominates the beginning of the excerpt through m. 14. The opening measure could almost be considered a variant of this pattern with rests substituted for notes. From m. 15 to m. 22 the pattern of composite rhythm changes to even quarter notes, providing a clear contrast and marking a structural point in the music. The even quarter-note pulses of these measures could lead to a strong emphasis upon the metric pulse at this point, but this is counteracted to an extent by the use of four tempo changes during these measures. The change to different patterns together with the thinning out of the texture in mm. 23–24(a) prepare us for the return to the opening material in the repeat.

Aural rhythmic study of this work might well be done in the reverse order

**EXAMPLE 3-43.** Ibid., mm. 1–25.

**EXAMPLE 3-43** continued.

to that in which we have discussed it. The listener can first attend to the larger aspects of composite rhythm and tempo change. On subsequent hearings he can listen for the rhythmic gestures of the individual parts, and finally, with the aid of an analyzed score, he can attempt to follow the double canon of *Klangfarben* lines which is of course the compositional core of the work. To say, however, that a study of this work should begin and end with a study of these lines, and to regard such matters as the rhythmic gestures of individual parts and the composite rhythm of the parts as mere incidental by-products of the contrapuntal and orchestration process, is to miss part of the multi-faceted richness of this work.

Webern himself addressed himself to a similar problem in his introduction to Heinrich Ysaak's *Choralis Constantinus*. Speaking of a phrase in the *Prose* of the 14th office in this work he said.

> The manner in which the three parts are always worked into one another, in just such a way as to make the individual life of each stand out all the more clearly, this the highest art, and the euphony of the piece is indescribable . . . To the ideal of making each voice an independent highly individual entity Heinrich Ysaak dedicates every artifice of counterpoint, and it is from this ideal that the boldness of his technique springs . . . Parallel perfect consonances are often found, and hidden fifths and octaves still oftener. Ysaak employs them in order to attain special effects of sound. I can not agree with the assertion, made in the Introduction to Part I of the Choralis Constantinus, that these progressions are 'at any rate unintentional.' Nothing 'slips past' a master like Ysaak, who has such a wonderful command of his craft, and if so-called incorrect progressions of this kind are present in his music, then he certainly intended them.[8]

What Webern has said here about Ysaak's use of pitch and harmony would certainly apply to his own use of rhythm. Nothing "slips past" Webern, including such significant details as the rhythmic gestures of individual parts and the composite rhythm created by their interaction. This is what makes the analysis of his music so rewarding, if it goes beyond mechanical details of serial technique to an exploration of the sounding structure of his music.

### Common Practice Durational Patterns in a Framework of Unusual Metric Structures

We have seen in the previous section that composers frequently present new ways of treating the foreground of durational patterns against a relatively conservative background of common practice metric structure. In this

---

[8]This paragraph is taken from *Denkmäler der Tonkunst in Österreich*, volume 32, Isaac, H., Choralis Constantinus II, Akademische Druck- u. Verlagsanstalt, Graz, Austria.

section we shall explore the reverse situation, in which composers have used relatively traditional common practice durational patterns against a background of unusual metric structures. Some writers refer to these two types of contemporary rhythmic practice as divisive rhythm and additive rhythm respectively.

Actually we have already seen examples which belong to the category of common practice durational patterns in the framework of unusual metric structures (refer to Ex. 3-6, 3-7, 3-9, 3-11, 3-13, etc., to see how the durational patterns used are predominantly metric or intrametric patterns which clearly confirm the underlying metric structure). In such cases it almost seems that the composer considers the unusual metric structure to provide sufficient rhythmic interest (and incidentally performance problems), and therefore does not feel compelled to add to this the complexity of unusual durational patterns.

Instead of citing further examples along this line, we shall merely present two slightly expanded or varied applications of this principle. Example 3-44 presents an excerpt which at first glance seems not to fit in this category. The metric structure of five pulse groupings is unusual. The durational patterns written above it seem also to be more highly syncopated and irregular than those of common practice; however, careful study of this passage will show that the varied durations of the four parts are skillfully arranged so that their composite rhythm results in even eighth notes corresponding to the pulse of the metric structure.

**EXAMPLE 3-44.** Filigree Setting for String Quartet (1959), mm. 1–2. Copyright 1965 by G. Schirmer, Inc. Used by permission.

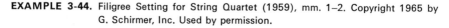

Similarly in Ex. 3-45 the durational patterns themselves are complex, but they result in a composite rhythm of even sixteenth notes in mm. 11–13. Measure 14 suggests a continuation of this principle in even triplet sixteenth notes in the first two beats of the measure.

**EXAMPLE 3-45.** Ibid., mm. 11–14. Copyright 1965 by G. Schirmer, Inc. Used by permission.

All of the works mentioned so far in this section have been based on unusual metric structures in which the pulses are enunciated but organized into varied groupings which depart from common practice. It is also possible to have relatively simple durational patterns occur in the framework of metric structures with obscured pulse, as for example the groups of even thirty-second notes in the opening of the Powell quartet cited in Ex. 3-46.

Here we have an interesting reversal of the situation discussed in Ex. 3-44 and 3-45, in which fairly complex, contrametric patterns were written so as

**EXAMPLE 3-46.** Ibid., opening. Copyright 1965 by G. Schirmer Inc. Used by permission.

to produce a composite rhythm which clearly articulated the pulses of the metric structure. In Ex. 3-46, fairly simple even-note patterns are written so as to produce a composite rhythm which obscures any sense of pulse. Powell states that the X "replaces a time signature where there are no fixed communal tempi and/or metrical units. In such cases, all parts begin simultaneously but thereafter each proceeds independently as directed." Note that in an obscured metric structure, rhythmic units must be determined by such criteria as beaming or proximity of notes in terms of pitch.

### Unusual Durational Patterns in the Framework of Unusual Metric Structures

The maximum of rhythmic complexity may be achieved by presenting a foreground of unusual durational patterns against a background of unusual metric structure. Sometimes this is heard just as a momentary point of rhythmic ambiguity separating sections of relatively stable rhythmic structure. In other instances, where complexity in both durational patterns and metric structure is continued for a long period of time, the net result may be an obliteration of differentiation between foreground and background.

In Ex. 3-47 players are not only required to play extrametric patterns such as triplets and groups of five, seven, and ten notes, but to do this in the framework of $\frac{5}{8}$ meter with tempo changes. Obviously, faithful performance of this small excerpt places enormous demands upon the performer, but the net result may actually be close to the freedom of Ex. 3-46. The difference in the two examples, however, is that the composer wishes to control the relation of one part to the other in Ex. 3-47 but is willing to leave this more to chance in Ex. 3-46.

Many of the works of Iannis Xenakis and other recent composers reach such a high degree of continued rhythmic complexity that it would be pointless to attempt to hear pulse and pattern in the traditional sense. Instead one must shift from hearing small details to hearing larger or longer moments of

**EXAMPLE 3-47.** Ibid., m. 36. Copyright 1965 by G. Schirmer, Inc. Used by permission.

rhythmic activity. These are called "clouds" of sound, and they play a role in this music similar to the role of the single duration or short rhythmic unit in traditional music. One may study these "clouds" to see how single durations and pitches are combined to produce textures of varying rhythmic and vertical density. Rhythmic density may be simply defined as the number of separate sounds per given unit of time; vertical density is discussed in Chapters 2 and 5.

Of more significance, however, is the way in which the clouds are organized into macropatterns, just as in traditional music single durations are organized into micropatterns or rhythmic units and gestures. Our perception of such complex music must generally be in terms of alternating moments of tension and release, or of activity and rest. Though this is indispensable for understanding such complex music, these considerations are of prime importance for all music.

## PRE-COMPOSITIONAL APPROACHES TO RHYTHM

Sometimes contemporary composers' use of durational patterns will be based on certain pre-compositional approaches which seem to be governed by mathematical considerations as much as aural considerations, even though the end result may be as convincing musically as if more traditional approaches had been used. Though prefigured somewhat by such earlier techniques as fourteenth-century isorhythm, the extent and complexity of precompositional approaches to rhythm is a new and important aspect of twentieth-century music. From the many possible techniques evident in contemporary compositions, we have selected three examples.

The first simply illustrates the derivation of a series of rhythmic patterns by adding one pulse to each pattern and then reversing the process. The beginning of each pattern is marked by the higher pitch.

**EXAMPLE 3-48.** Stockhausen: *Kreuzspiel* (1960), mm. 7–12. © 1960, Universal Edition. Used by permission of the publisher. Theodore Presser Company sole representative United States, Canada and Mexico.

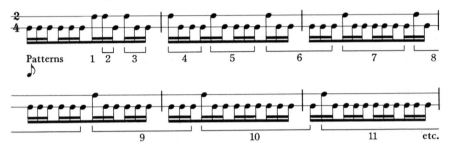

The second example is representative of the carefully worked out details in compositions of Webern. The mathematical relations are indicated in the example.

**EXAMPLE 3-49.** Webern: Concerto, Op. 24 I, mm. 1–5. Copyright 1948, Universal Edition. Used by permission of the publisher. Theodore Presser Company sole representative United States, Canada and Mexico.

Notice that the second half of the example is rhythmically a retrograde version of the first half, except that ♩ ♩ ♩ becomes ♪ ♪ ♪ ♪ .

The last example shows some of the unique rhythmic techniques of Messiaen which have had great influence on contemporary composers.

**EXAMPLE 3-50.** Messiaen: *Quatuor pour la fin de temps,* VI, "Danse de la fureur, pour les sept trompettes," letter F. Copyright 1942, Durand et Cie. Used by permission of the publisher. Elkan-Vogel, Inc. sole representative United States.

A full explanation of these techniques may be found in Messiaen's *Mon Langage Musicale.* A summary of his ideas is contained in his preface to *Quatuor pour la fin de temps,* a portion of which is translated below.

I employ here, as in most of my works, a special rhythmic language. Beyond a secret predilection for the prime numbers (5, 7, 11, etc.), the notions of measure and time are replaced here by the sense of a short value (the sixteenth note, for example) and of its free multiplications; and also by certain "rhythmic forms" which are: the added value; augmented or diminished rhythms; non-retrogradable rhythms; and the rhythmic pedal.
a) The added value. Short value added to any rhythm, whether in the form of a note, a rest or a dot.

By a note:

By a rest:

By a dot:

Ordinarily, as in the examples above, the rhythm almost always appears with the added value from the outset, without having been heard previously in its simple state.
b) Augmented or diminished rhythms. A rhythm may be followed immediately by its augmentation or diminution according to various forms, of which some

examples are here given (in each example the first measure contains the normal rhythm, the second measure its augmentation or diminution).

Addition of one third of the value:

Withdrawal of one fourth of the value:

Addition of a dot:

Withdrawal of a dot:

Classical augmentation:

Classical diminution:

Addition of twice the value:

Withdrawal of two-thirds the value:

Addition of triple the value:

Withdrawal of three-fourths the value:

One may also use inexact augmentations or diminutions. This rhythm contains three eighth notes (classical diminution of three quarter notes) plus the dot (added value) which renders the diminution inexact.

c) Non-retrogradable rhythms. Whether one reads them from right to left or left to right, the order of their values remains the same. This peculiarity exists in all rhythms divisible into two mutually retrogradable groups, the one in relation to the other, with a central "communal" value.

The following example shows a succession of non-retrogradable rhythms (each measure contains one of these rhythms).

d) The rhythmic pedal. An independent rhythm which repeats indefatigably, without concern for the rhythms which surround it.

In the years since publication of this work Messiaen has expanded this system, and he and his students have moved in the direction of serialization of rhythm. For a fuller discussion of some of these aspects of rhythm see Chapter 6.

## NEW NOTATIONAL PRACTICES

New rhythmic practices in twentieth-century music have in some instances occasioned the search for new notational techniques to represent them. The following summary has been adapted from Erhard Karkoschka, *Das Schriftbild der neuen Musik*.[9]

1.00  Alterations of traditional notation
    1.10  Simplification. This would include the substitution of beams for flags in modern vocal notation, a tendency in at least some works to avoid note values like 32nd and 64th notes, the absence of meter signatures in multi-metric works, and the practice of using, for ease in reading, one large meter signature for groups of instruments in an orchestra score instead of a meter signature for each line.
    1.20  Expansion and addition. This would include proposals by Henry Cowell for the use of shaped notes like △ and ◻ to indicate three-fold and fourfold divisions, more extensive use of beaming to indicate special expressive groupings, and greater use of metronomic markings and precise or unusual verbal tempo and character indications.
2.00  Partially new bases
    2.10  Notation of approximate durations. These would include such techniques as using black notes without heads to indicate notes to be played as fast as possible and the use of noteheads of varying lengths to indicate approximate durations as indicated in Ex. 3-51.

**EXAMPLE 3-51.**
as fast as possible

    2.20  Frame notation. (*Rahmennotation*). This means that within established boundaries the performer has some possibility of choice of speed of notes. In the following example from Stockhausen's *Zeitmasse* the players begin and end together but are urged to a variety of varying tempi within these boundaries by the varying note values and tempo indications.

---

[9]© 1966 by Moeck Verlag, Celle/FRG. Used by permission.

**EXAMPLE 3-52.** Stockhausen, *Zeitmasse*, mm. 156–158, rhythm only. © 1957, Universal Edition. Used by permission of the publisher. Theodore Presser Company sole representative United States. Canada and Mexico.

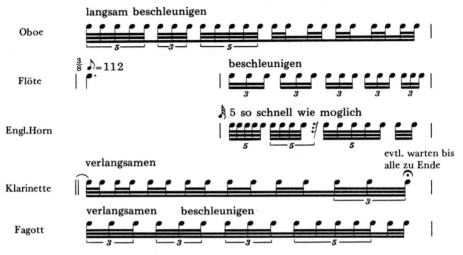

2.30 Proportional notation or space notation. In contrast to traditional notation where duration is indicated primarily by the type of note value used and only incidentally or not at all by the relative position of the notes, this type of notation depends on the spacing of notes to convey the full information on duration.

**EXAMPLE 3-53.** Cage: *Music of Changes*, beginning. Copyright © 1961 by Henmar Press Inc., New York. Reprint permission granted by publisher.

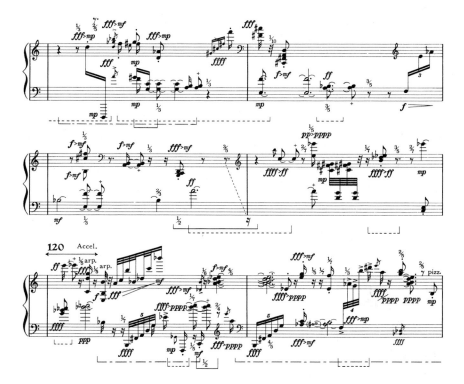

Cage has written the following instructions for this work:

The rhythmic structure, 3·5·6 3/4·5·3 1/8, is expressed in changing tempi (indicated by large numbers) (beats per minute). A number repeated at the succeeding structural point indicates a maintained tempo. Accelerandos and ritards are to be associated with the rhythmic structure, rather than with the sounds that happen in it.

The notation of durations is in space. $2\frac{1}{2}$ CM. = ♩ A sound begins at the point in time corresponding to the point in space of the stem of the note (not the notehead). In the case of a single whole note this stem-point is imagined before the note (as ♭ ), in the case of adjacent-in-pitch whole notes, between them (as ♪ ), in the case of a glissando, in the center of the duration indicated. A staccato mark indicates a short duration of no specific length. A cross (+) above an ♪ or at the end of a pedal notation indicates the point of stopping sound and does not have any duration value. Fractions are of a ♩ or of $2\frac{1}{2}$ CM. . . .

It will be found in many places that the notation is irrational; in such instances the performer is to employ his own discretion.

3.00   Completely new bases

   3.10   *Klavarscribo* and *Equiton*. These are among new notational systems whose principal purpose is to provide a clear-cut reference to the twelve-note tempered pitch system rather than to the traditional seven-note diatonic system. In *Klavarscribo* pitch is represented according to position on the piano keyboard and time is represented from top to bottom rather than left to right. In *Equiton* time is represented on the traditional horizontal axis, and pitches are represented according to placement between two lines representing the interval of the octave. In both systems note color (black or white) is used to represent aspects of pitches, making it necessary to devise new methods of representing durations. This is accomplished by using lines, dotted lines or dots to represent all pulses of the metric structure and placing the notes in relation to these. Thus in these systems the metric structure is always clearly notated; in traditional notation, on the other hand, the only clear indication of metric structure is the barline, while all other pulses of the metric structure must be implied from the written durations. Though it is beyond the scope of this chapter to give a complete explanation of those systems, the reader can gain some idea of their nature by comparing the following passages written in traditional notation with their transcriptions in *Klavarscribo* and *Equiton.*

**EXAMPLE 3-54.**

Traditional Notation

*Equiton*

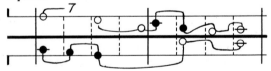

*Klavarscribo*

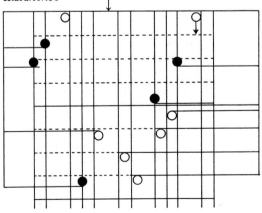

3.20 Verbal notation. Some composers of aleatoric music use verbal instructions wholly or partially in place of music notation. These may range from relatively precise formulations to vague hints to the performer. In Ex. 3-55, only dynamics and tempo modifications are given. Durations are given in the left margin, the first number indicating elapsed time and the second the time allotted for the event in seconds. Words in capital letters are read aloud by the performer, while the lowercase letters indicate actions to be performed.

**EXAMPLE 3-55.** Kagel: "FIN II/Invitation au jeu voice," in *Sonant* (1960/    ), double bass part. © 1960, Universal Edition. Used by permission of the publisher. Theodore Presser Company, sole representative United States, Canada and Mexico.

T/P
00″/10″    You may begin, the guitarist has given you the signal. Would you please play two pizzicati molto vibrato on the Vth string, at
    p    an interval of a minor ninth (LET'S JUST GET RID OF SOME MINOR OBJECTIONS TO BEGIN WITH); let ring.
10″/18″ mf    (IT IS PROGRAMME-MUSIC THAT YOU'RE PLAYING NOW; THE IDEA OF FIDELITY TO A TEXT MAY WELL BE AN ILLUSION.) Another pizzicato. Withdraw the finger of the left hand slowly from the string after the attack so as to produce a buzz, and drum on the soundbox with your right
    pp    hand (near the bridge). Apply the mute. ("IN BEETHOVEN, YOU MIGHT SAY THAT THE EFFECTS ARE DISTRIBUTED IN ADVANCE.")
28″/11″ f    Play six or seven times doublestops COL LEGNO BATTUTO

JETE   [music notation]   . At the same time move your hand between

the 2nd and the 5th position, change strongly the speed of the bow attack and the dynamic (go abruptly from PIANO TO
    mp    FORTE).
39″/24″ mf rall.    (In the 'Heures Seculaires,' Satie writes: "TO WHOM IT MAY
    f   ·    CONCERN, I ABSOLUTELY FORBID THE READING
     ·    OUT LOUD OF A TEXT DURING A MUSICAL PER-
     ·    FORMANCE. ANY INFRINGEMENT OF THIS RULE
    p   ·    WILL BRING DOWN MY JUST INDIGNATION UPON
     ·    THE WRONGDOER. . . ."

3.30 Graphic notation. This interesting trend lies on the border between visual and aural art. Some graphs or designs suggest pitch and durational aspects by the placement of design elements on vertical and horizontal axes. Others, like Logothetis' *Cycloide*, seem to have no reference at all to traditional concepts of pitch and rhythm notation, but rather are meant to inspire a certain sense of shape, movement, mood, or emotion in visual terms, which the performer then seeks to recreate in aural terms.

We might also mention that several methods of "notating" electronic music have been devised, including adaptations of traditional notation, schematic or graphic representation, verbal instructions, and instructions written in computer language.

For additional examples of notational innovations, the reader is referred to the bibliography at the end of this chapter (see esp. Karkoschka, Potter, and Read).

## CONCLUSION

We have attempted in this chapter not only to outline some of the innovations of twentieth-century rhythm, but also to show how they relate to traditional practice. To do so has meant a reexamination of aspects of common practice rhythm and an attempt to formulate concepts and terms which would be general enough to allow comparison of rhythmic characteristics over a wide spectrum of periods and styles. We have emphasized the importance of describing the aural effect of rhythmic events rather than the written symbols employed to represent them, but we have also considered how choice of notation may affect the character and meaning of a rhythmic event.

The importance of rhythm in twentieth-century music is evidenced not only by the efforts composers have made to seek out new possibilities, but also by the prominence given to rhythm in many works of this century. The most obvious examples of this would be the numerous works for percussion instruments alone like Varèse's *Ionisation* or Stockhausen's *Zyklus*, in which pitch and harmony are virtually eliminated as significant aspects, leaving primarily rhythm and to a lesser extent texture and timbre as bearers of the musical import of the work. In other works aspects of pitch and harmony may be dominated to a great extent by rhythm; this is frequently the case with Stravinsky, who has also stressed the importance of the temporal element in a statement in his *Autobiography* that can make a fitting conclusion to this chapter:

> The phenomenon of music is given to us with the sole purpose of establishing an order in things, including, and particularly, the co-ordination between *man* and *time*.[10]

## BIBLIOGRAPHY

Boulez, Pierre, "Sonate, que me veux-tu?" *Perspectives of New Music*, Vol. I, No. 2 (1963), 32–34.

---

[10]Igor Stravinsky, *Autobiography* (New York: W. W. Norton & Co., Inc., 1962), p. 54.

Cooper, Grosvenor W., and Leonard B. Meyer, *The Rhythmic Structure of Music*. Chicago: University of Chicago Press, 1960.

Creston, Paul, *Principles of Rhythm*. New York: Franco Columbo, 1964.

Haenselmann, Carl Ferdinand, *Harmonic Rhythm in Selected Works of the Latter Half of the Nineteenth Century*. Unpublished doctoral dissertation, Indiana University, 1966.

Karkoschka, Erhard, *Das Schriftbild der neuen Musik*. Celle, Moeck, 1966.

Potter, Gary M., *The Role of Chance in Contemporary Music*. Unpublished doctoral dissertation, Indiana University, 1971.

Read, Gardner, *Music Notation*. Boston: Allyn and Bacon, 1964.

Smither, Howard, *Theories of Rhythm in the Nineteenth and Twentieth Centuries*. Unpublished doctoral dissertation, Cornell University, 1960.

Westergaard, Peter, "Some Problems in Rhythmic Theory and Analysis" in Boretz, Benjamin and Edward T. Cone, eds., *Perspectives on Contemporary Music Theory*, New York, W.W. Norton, 1972, pp. 226–237.

## SUGGESTIONS FOR FURTHER STUDY

*In addition to works suggested in the chapter*

Elliott Carter, String Quartet No. 2.

Earle Brown, *Music for Cello and Piano*.

Igor Stravinsky, *Movements for Piano and Orchestra*.

Anton Webern, *Six Pieces for Orchestra*, Op. 6.

Béla Bartók, String Quartet No. 4.

Krzysztof Penderecki, *Threnody: To the Victims of Hiroshima*.

Witold Lutoslawski, *Trois Poemes d'Henri Michaux*.

chapter four

# Melody: Linear Aspects of Twentieth-Century Music

VERNON L. KLIEWER

For many musicians the study of melody in the twentieth century is problematical. Since many of us have been trained in the traditions of nineteenth-century musical thought, our conception of melody may exclude musical lines and contours that do not readily conform to ideals of such masters of melody as Schubert, Schumann, Brahms, Wagner and Wolf (to list only nineteenth-century melodists). Even if these masters of melody are taken as models, no unanimous agreement exists as to what constitutes *melody*. This is not to say that no attempts have been made to define melody,[1] but many extant explanations confine us to specific stylistic models, and they are too exclusive in their definitions.

There is general agreement that what is viewed as the *melodic* in music involves events occurring linearly. Occurrence of events in time is the property of many aspects of our experiential life. A mere succession of events (in music this might be successive articulations of the same sound) does not necessarily produce something melodic; the events occurring in time must

---

[1] The attempts at definition are too numerous to recount in this study. The interested reader will find a capsule definition of melody in Willi Apel's *Harvard Dictionary of Music,* 2nd ed., pp. 517–519. A catalog of sample definitions may be found in Arthur C. Edwards' *The Art of Melody,* xix–xxx. An attempt to formulate a theory of melody may be found in J. Smits van Waesberghe, *A Textbook of Melody.*

involve change of some kind to be understood as related or unrelated. Traditionally, the "events" making up a melody have been considered to be patterns of changing pitch levels and different durations, and this tradition continues to provide an important impetus for much twentieth-century music making. However, some musicians are expanding the limits, so that melody may be said to result where there are interacting patterns of changing events occurring in time. Such a generalized definition is all-inclusive, and it permits us to examine the linear aspect of twentieth-century music with a minimum of stylistic preconceptions.

## THE ELEMENTS OF MELODY

The essential elements of any melody are duration, pitch, and quality. In the past the interactions of duration (rhythm patterns) and pitch (changing pitch levels) have been considered primary melodic elements, while the qualitative dimension (patterns of changing colors, texture, or loudness) has been considered a secondary aspect of melody. Today, however, interacting patterns of changing qualities occurring in time may constitute the crucial linear thrust of a composition. Even though dimensional interaction is musically necessary, our survey first discusses each of the dimensions as an individual phenomenon.

### The Duration Dimension

It is a commonplace to state that music unfolds in time; yet without different patterns of durations melodies could not exist. In most music written before the twentieth century, the durational patterns are recurring events, often periodic, at all structural levels. Recurrence of durations and patterns of durations continue to play a vital melodic role; Ex. 4-1 illustrates simple periodic recurrence and patterning of time at various structural levels. Immediately apparent are the foreground rhythmic groupings: (1) the triplet anacrusis group in mm. 1–2 and the prolonging by repetition of the triplet anacrusis pattern from the last beat of the third measure to m. 5; (2) the contrasting duple-quadruple grouping of mm. 5–6; and (3) the dotted-quarter and eighth figure heard in mm. 7–10.

These easily apprehended groupings do not constitute a radical break with the past, even though such a rapid succession of different durations and patterns is not forecast by the opening gesture. Of greater durational significance is the ebb and flow resulting from event recurrence versus non-recurrence. A case in point is the periodic character established by the thrice-stated ♩. (m. 1–3) with two of its occurrences preceded by a triplet anacrusis figure. The third sounding of the triplet figure does not precede a longer duration. This change signals a new recurrent grouping projected

**EXAMPLE 4-1.** Hindemith: Organ Sonata in E-flat, I, mm. 1–11. Copyright 1937 by B. Schott's Soehne. Copyright renewed 1965. Used by permission. All rights reserved.

through time by an established duration unit (division by threes) and the
shifted longer duration ( 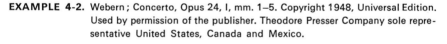 ) which is an outgrowth of the $\downarrow$. of
mm. 1–3. The entire projection becomes an extended upbeat to m. 5. Compared to the anacrusis pattern of mm. 1–2, this extended upbeat occupies four
beats, whereas the actual upbeat filled only one beat. It is apparent, then,
that rhythmic figures in this example are treated as recurrent events giving
the clear impression of periodicity, and that the phrase rhythm resulting
from upbeat-downbeat combinations is variable. The $\downarrow$. $\downarrow$ foreground
pattern in mm. 7–10 accumulates to produce an effect remarkably similar to
the extended anacrusis preceding m. 5. If perceived in this manner, the
upbeat occupies ten beats, and the rhythmic ebb and flow is the interaction
of recurrence at the level of beat and of non-recurrence in terms of lengths
of upbeats.

A progressive lengthening or shortening of the durational components of
a phrase may be a vital shaping force. From among the endless possibilities,
Ex. 4-2 shows one manner in which changing durations, together with changing colors, are an integral linear factor.

**EXAMPLE 4-2.** Webern; Concerto, Opus 24, I, mm. 1–5. Copyright 1948, Universal Edition. Used by permission of the publisher. Theodore Presser Company sole representative United States, Canada and Mexico.

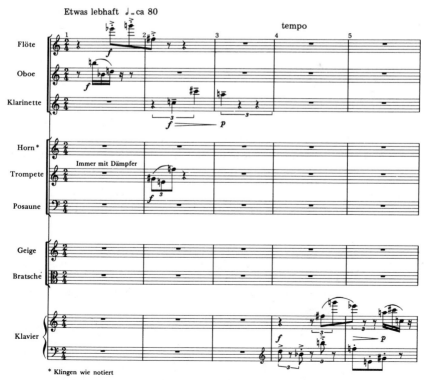

Each of the three-note motives of this opening melody has a different set of note values, from shortest duration to longest. In addition, the longest duration—quarter-note triplet—is performed with a ritardando. The overall rhythmic effect is one of expansion, which reinforces the expository character of these four measures.

The second phrase is a durational retrograde (as well as a pitch retrograde, $RI_1$) of the first; the *ritardando*, however, is now associated with the shortest note values. Even so, the two phrases form a strong periodic relation because of the clear-cut durational ordering: ♪♪ ♪ ♩ ♩ ♪ ♪ ♪ [2] Random ordering of durational events may seem to be operating in the structuring of some melodies. Example 4-3 illustrates such apparent randomness of rhythmic patterning. In this instance the random effect clearly results from the pervading non-recurrence of rhythmic figures and motives in a systematic order. Only five different durational values occur throughout; the longest unit is the ♪ (which is also the beat unit). Shown in a scalar manner, the durations occurring are:

Such scaling in itself implies the possibility of rhythmic subtleties; as the durations are arranged into rhythmic figures in Ex. 4-3 it is the order of presentation that produces the random quality we perceive.

In general, the passage is characterized by an alternation of patterns comprised of the four divisions and subdivisions of the eighth note (A pattern such as ♩. ♪ may be considered a variant of ♫♫ ). It is evident that the rapid succession of durational values and the number of articulations actu-

---

[2]The crescendo-decrescendo plan indicated in the illustration is analogous to the lengthening and shortening of durations; the actual loudness plan for both phrases is *f*━*p* .

[3]In this composition, this value usually occurs within a grouping such as

**EXAMPLE 4-3.** Maderno: *Honeyrêves* for flute and piano (flute only), mm. 10–25. By permission of the Edizioni Suvini Zerboni, Milano.

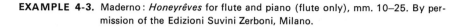

ally sounded per beat is important for the durational organization of this passage. The principle at work is durational variability.

Freedom of rhythmic expression may be the product of interpretation on the part of the performer. If the performer is given liberty to realize the durational relations, simple notational values provide a rhythmic effect not unlike that produced in highly organized or ordered rhythm, except that in any one instance the randomness is the product of a particular performance whereas in such instances as Ex. 4-3, the random quality is composed.

A simple notational scheme characterizes Ex. 4-4; the realization of the rhythm patterns is left to the performer. According to the performance instructions given by the composer:

The first flute part should be interpreted freely; the time divisions indicated by vertical lines need only be observed approximately. Rests in brackets ( ) are for the sake of orientation only. Rests without brackets, however, should be very accurately observed, the basic value being quarter note with a duration of one second.

The remaining instruments . . . accompany the soloist by playing in a way similar to that in which he plays; all that they need to observe is the sign of the conductor for the beginning of each section between as a guide, the duration of the individual sections . . . should never be exceeded.[4]

[4]Lutoslawski, *Jeux Venitiens,* p. 16.

**EXAMPLE 4-4.** Lutoslawski: *Jeux Venitiens*, III, A–C. © 1962 by Moeck Verlag, Celle/FRG. Used by permission of Moeck Verlag and Belwin Mills Publishing Corporation.

Permitting complete freedom to the performer makes the rhythmic organization wholly dependent upon the moment of performance. At any given performance the result may be heard as rhythmically structured or unstructured, depending upon the interpretation given. In Ex. 4-5 the improvisation is cadential, with the trumpet, horn, and trombone each providing a melodic

**EXAMPLE 4-5.** Schuller: Music for Brass Quintet, III, mm. 34–37. Reprinted by permission of Associated Music Publishers, Inc.

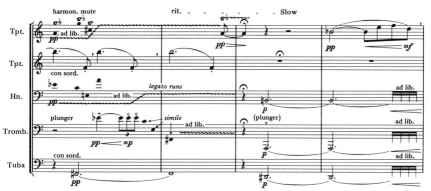

1. Tpt., horn & tromb improvise on the designated pitches in the manner indicated (pitch order and rhythmic duration free).

line of its own. Since the durations as well as pitch order are freely chosen, there is no way to predict beforehand what patterns and relations will be heard.

This brief survey of duration as a melodic element indicates only some of the potential of this important musical dimension.[5] Although the discussion has proceeded as if the duration dimension exists independently, it is apparent from each of the examples cited that other factors, such as pitch (or sound), must be present before musical time can be articulated.

### The Pitch Dimension

Equal in musical importance to the duration dimension is that of pitch. In music before the twentieth century, it is sufficient to speak of the pitch dimension as applying only to those aspects of sound having fixed and easily discernible frequency patterns (as, for example, A = 440 Hz). For the purposes of this discussion, *pitch* will refer to those aspects of sound that are classed as having highness or lowness, including non-fixed as well as fixed frequencies so that a wide array of melodic structures can be encompassed. Other aspects of musical tones, such as "loud," "dark," or "flute-like," are qualitative dimensions and are discussed in the next section.

Twentieth-century composers utilize a greater variety of pitch resources than has been the custom in any other historical period of Western music. As a consequence, it is extremely difficult to catalog the myriad possibilities of organizing pitch. This section of the essay briefly surveys some of the

---

[5]The reader should read the essay on Rhythm (Chapter Three), for a comprehensive discussion.

available pitch resources; later in the essay other examples also will be discussed.

Some compositions of the twentieth century continue to manifest the unique melodic possibilities of diatonic pitch materials. Such an instance is illustrated by Ex. 4-6. Here the pitch materials are clearly related to a simple diatonic scale. As an expression of key, however, the excerpt may appear ambiguous, especially if compared to compositions in major and minor keys of the eighteenth and nineteenth centuries; this ambiguity results from both the melodic and the harmonic ordering. As a musical gesture it is far from being vague; it is a tonal statement based on a certain limited set of diatonic pitch materials and generally reminiscent of an earlier melodic style.

**EXAMPLE 4-6.** Prokofiev: Piano Concerto No. 3, I, no. 28 to 3 mm. after no. 29. Copyright by Edition Gutheil. Copyright assigned to Boosey & Hawkes, Inc. Reprinted by permission.

During the twentieth century the twelve-note scale as a pitch resource is widely employed. In some instances these pitch materials continue to occur in musical contexts in which some of the pitches perform embellishing or decorative roles (i.e., they are chromatic embellishments of diatonic notes); in other instances the twelve-note scale (or a portion thereof) is used to establish contexts in which little or no pitch hierarchy is apparent. Generally, when the latter case prevails, factors other than pitch per se begin to ascend in melodic importance. In Ex. 4-7 the pitch material is derived from the twelve notes making up the total chromatic scale. In terms of pitch organization, no individual member of the melodic line appears to have greater significance than any other, even though our attention may be drawn to the highest and lowest pitches and to those notes with longer durations.

**EXAMPLE 4-7.** Webern: Variations for Orchestra, Opus 30, theme, mm. 1–4. © 1956, Universal Edition. Used by permission of the publisher. Theodore Presser Company sole representative United States, Canada and Mexico.

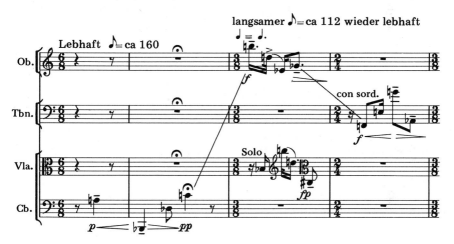

If hierarchical pitch ordering of the twelve notes is not an aspect of melodic organization, other factors of organization will predominate. Two such interrelated aspects in Ex. 4-7 are the contour and interval content of the four-note motives.

Similarly, all twelve pitch classes form the pitch resource in Ex. 4-8. As in the preceding example, each of the melodic strands (enclosed in the boxes) is a serialized statement. Each of the melodic statements presents the twelve-note series once, followed by a partial statement (either 10 or 11 of the pitch classes). Each of the melodic components is to be performed first as indicated; then each performer is to continue improvisationally corresponding to the scheme assigned. The pitch order assigned to a particular part is invariant. But melodicism in the general sense is not the most important aspect of the total musical effect; most important is the stacking of melodic lines into a dense contrapuntal texture. Thus, although pitch class succession is determined, the melodic effect is indeterminate.

EXAMPLE 4-8. Penderecki; *De Natura Sonoris,* no. 15–16. Copyright 1967 by Moeck Verlag. Used by permission.

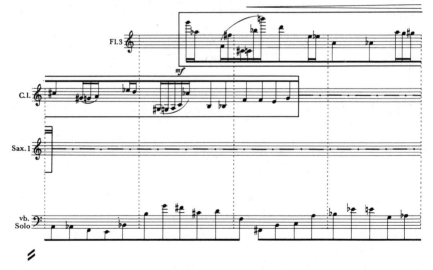

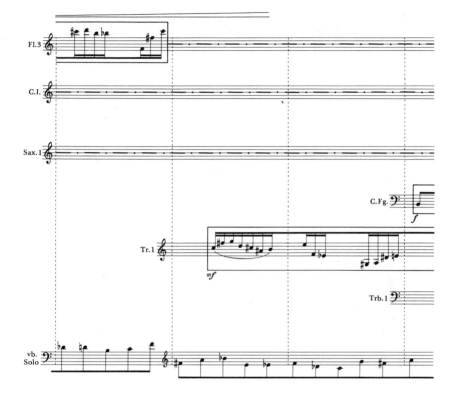

Mere highness and lowness of pitch (without fixed pitch characteristics) and gradual motion from one level to another may serve as the pitch basis of a melodic line. Example 4-9 is a case in point. Here the percussionist creates a melodic line by fluctuations in pitch produced by the tautness or slackness of a stretched skin. In the context of the composition, the percussion melody freely imitates the pitch structure of the cello parts, each of which begins at a fixed point in the pitch scale and glissandos to higher or lower approximate pitches. The counterpointed melodies differ from the previous examples in that changes of pitch are heard as moving from one frequency to another gradually rather than directly.[6]

---

[6]Such a portamento style has precedents in Eastern music and is also an aspect of melodic organization in compositions such as Davidovsky, *Electronic Study No. 2*; Stockhausen, *Gesang der Jünglinge*; Xenakis, *ST 4-1, 080262.*

**EXAMPLE 4-9.** Kagel: *Match,* ∃ — ♩. © 1967, Universal Edition. Used by permission of the publisher. Theodore Presser Company sole representative United States, Canada and Mexico.

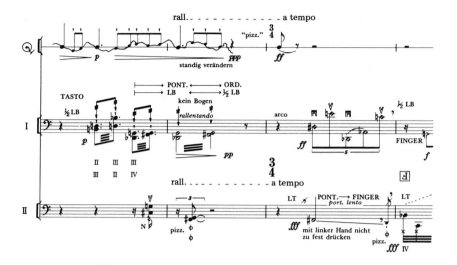

## The Qualitative Dimensions

One of the most striking features of linear organization that has evolved during the twentieth century is the increasing reliance upon the qualitative dimensions—color (timbre), texture, loudness, for example. It goes without saying that the qualitative aspects have always been present; but for the most part, earlier style periods place the qualitative dimensions in a secondary relation to pitch and rhythm. In such a role loudness, or any of the other qualitative dimensions, is not an element of linear ordering, but reinforces and highlights the more predominant pitch and rhythmic aspects. In some of today's compositions the qualitative aspects are linear elements taking on roles that in pre-twentieth-century music were almost exclusively reserved for pitch and rhythm.

Interestingly, emphasis on sound quality as a musical element reveals a growing awareness of novel ways of ordering pitches, as well as a use of pitch resources associated with earlier musical styles or with exotic musical cultures. For example, in nineteenth-century music, melody and harmony are complementary aspects, and may be called the two essential components of a musical context. And although harmony delineates structure, this delineation arises primarily not from the coloristic aspects of the different harmonic types, but rather from a system of contextual relations. However, harmony can become a coloristic-linear feature. In such instances melody and harmony are not separable components; they are one and the same. Such an occurrence is illustrated in Ex. 4-10. Here the melody *is* a chord stream (a result of parallel harmonies).[7] As such, this melody is a texture (note-against-note parallelism), a color (made up of major and minor harmonies), and a linear pattern (made of changing, parallel pitch levels). Considered as separable, each of the components of this melody does not represent a radical departure, but collectively, as an indivisible entity, they result in a "new" type of melody.

**EXAMPLE 4-10.** Debussy: *Preludes,* Book II, *Canope,* mm. 1–5. Copyright 1913, Durand et Cie. Used by permission of the publisher. Elkan-Vogel, Inc., sole representative United States, Canada and Mexico.

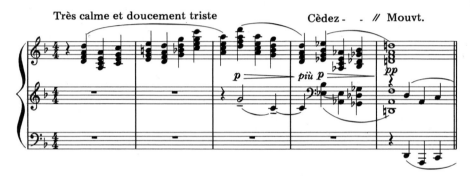

The coloristic aspect is even more striking when more than one instrumental color becomes a structural component of a single melodic statement. In Ex. 4-11 the first complete melodic idea involves three instrumental colors: flute, trumpet, and horn, in the color-order of flute (four notes), trumpet (single note), flute (three notes), and horn (one note). Changing pitch levels also are an important part of this melodic line, but its melodic uniqueness results as much from the integral changing of instrumental colors as it does from the changing pitch levels. This melodic statement is dependent for its structural existence upon the qualitative dimension of color (timbre), and not just pitch and rhythm. Melodies such as Ex. 4-11 are often classified as *Klangfarbenmelodie* (tone-color melody) to designate that color is a structural melodic element.

It is conceivable that a *Klangfarbenmelodie* could be created that consists of alternating colors, as in the *mélodie de timbres* in Ex. 4-12. A tone-color melody generally involves more than changing instrumental timbres; for example, the differences of attack and decay that are characteristic to the instruments

---

[7]Parallel harmony, in and of itself, is not a new compositional technique, but its structural significance is (it is a melodic, linear expression, not a melody and accompaniment).

**EXAMPLE 4-11.** Webern: Six Pieces for Orchestra, Opus 6, I, mm. 1–4. © 1956, Universal Edition. Used by permission of the publisher. Theodore Presser Company sole representative United States, Canada and Mexico.

being employed, and differences in loudness, contribute to the color dimension.

In Ex. 4-12 the horns and clarinets are to attack and decay in the manner of bells; the lowest note ($a^1$) is to be performed *fff* so as to continue the *mélodie de timbres*. It is the changing colors that are the predominant feature of this melody; the changing pitches take a secondary stance.

A melodic line can be entirely made up of changing patterns of sounds, without recourse to fixed pitches. One procedure is to use speech sounds as the "pitch" material. In Ex. 4-13 each of the voice parts is an independent line, and in each case the melodic line emerges from the patterned changes of phonetic sounds.

**EXAMPLE 4-12.** Messiaen: *Couleurs de la cité céleste,* no. 61 to no. 62. Copyright (1966) by Alphonse Leduc & Cie, 175 rue Saint-Honoré, Paris Ier, Owners and Publishers. Reprinted by permission.

\* Les cors et les clarinettes attaqueront *sfz* ⸻, dans l'esprit des cloches. Le piano marquera *fff* sa note grave, qui continue la "mélodie de timbres".

**EXAMPLE 4-13.** Ligeti: *Aventures,* mm. 20–22. Copyright © 1964 by Henry Litolff's Verlag. Reprint permission granted by C.F. Peters Corporation, New York.

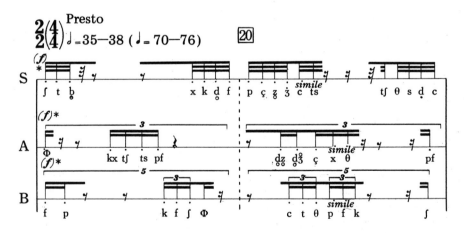

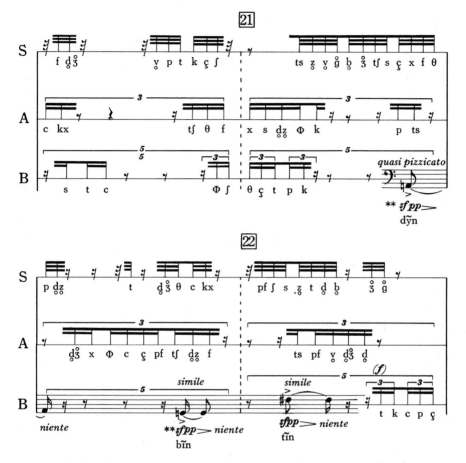

*Very intense whisper directed towards the audience ("stage whisper"). The unvoiced sounds should be articulated with exaggerated clarity. NB. Do not breathe out in the rests.

**If the baritone cannot be sure of hitting the A dead on, the 'cellist can play the note as well, as a very soft pizzicato.

The use of phonetic sounds can bring into play the structural principle of recurrence as easily as if pitches are the primary sound material. Even in the short excerpt given, this principle can be seen in operation. It is apparent that the melodic material is made up of the formative quality of the phonetic sounds, rather than the formative quality of words or changes in pitch level. In the last measure of this excerpt a pitch motive appears as a contrasting figure. The melodic line is structured by this contrast between phonetic sounds and pitched sounds.

Change in intensity (loudness) is generally considered to be a secondary musical quality, reinforcing the melodic shaping produced by other sound materials such as pitch or color. It is possible, however, to create a melodic line by simply changing from one loudness level to another. In Ex. 4-14 pitch

**EXAMPLE 4-14.** Carter: Eight Etudes and a Fantasy for Woodwind Quartet, Etude No. 7, mm. 1–7. Reprinted by permission of Associated Music Publishers, Inc.

is an unchanging quality whereas change of intensity and variability of points of attack are the elements that change to create the perceived linear motion. The staggering of the attacks establishes varied rhythmic patterns; these attacks also add to the illusion of increasing intensity.

The preceding discussion has referred predominantly to examples using conventional instruments as sound sources. Melodicism is just as unique to compositions based on *concrète* sound materials or sounds entirely electronically generated. No matter what constitutes the sound material, when changing patterns are conjoined, linear melodic properties tend to emerge.[8]

One graph of a melody occurring in an electronic composition is shown in Ex. 4-15. (As is generally known, a score is not essential for the production of

[8]Such a statement assumes that the illusion of motion through time is part of the musical image. For those who espouse a "spatial" aesthetic, the linear qualities must recede in significance, so that the sound presents the illusion of a "block" rather than a "line."

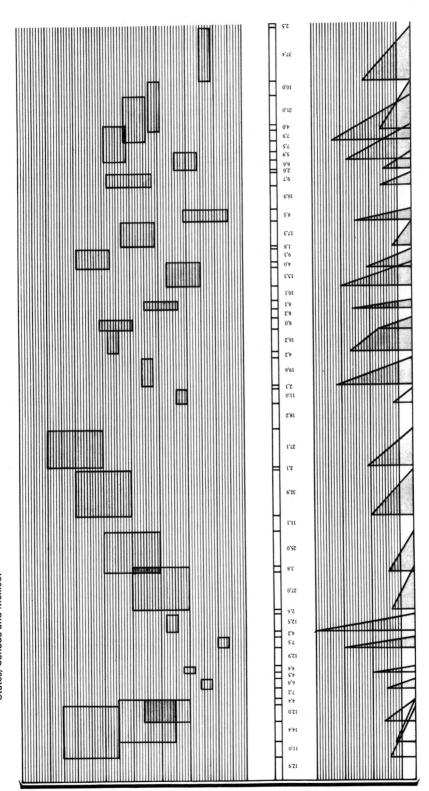

**EXAMPLE 4-15.** Stockhausen: *Studie II*, p. 14. © 1956 Universal Edition. Used by permission of the publisher. Theodore Presser Company sole representative United States, Canada and Mexico.

a totally electronic composition; in this case the composer provided the score *a posteriori*.) The segment shown is clearly concerned with points of color in time. Each of these colors is a mixture of five different sinusoidal tones which are pre-recorded and then used as musical elements to create the composition.

The upper portion of the musical graph shows the mixtures used to create this pointillistic melody. In each of the geometric shapes, the bottom line of the shape designates the lowest frequency of that mixture; similarly, the upper line of the geometric shape designates the highest frequency of that mixture. The width of the geometric shape (measured in centimeters) controls the duration of each note mixture. The bottom portion of the graph designates the intensity (loudness) of the attack and the release of the note. As can be seen, the characteristic attack is at a relatively high decibel level, and in many instances a rapid decay is used, creating the illusion of a sudden release. The melodic line that results appears pointillistic. As a matter of fact a strong contextual linear motion is perceived.

## MELODIC ORGANIZATION AND STRUCTURE

Our preceding discussion has presented some of the linear elements of twentieth-century music. In this section the emphasis will be on some of the aesthetic and structural aspects of line. As a point of departure, the notion of *relaxation and tension* is explored. This analogy to our experiential life serves a useful if generalized means for describing certain musical effects. The relaxation-tension notion has been employed at least since the time of Aristotle. Throughout the ensuing discussion it is important to keep in mind that analogy is being employed in the descriptive process.

### Tension and Release

The illusion of an increase in musical tension can be produced by the combination of various factors. Two important means are reiteration (tension created by the desire for a change) and gradual motion to a higher pitch. Both of these factors are illustrated in Ex. 4-16. The repetitions heard in mm. 79–80 are based on the figure presented in m. 78. An increase in tension is created by the note repetitions and partial presentation of the interval content of m. 78, spread through mm. 79–81. By repeating the tritone (m. 79), obliquely "expanding" to the major seventh (m. 80) and then to a minor tenth (m. 81), a classic pitch-climax (tension) is produced. The release effect is created by the rapid descent in pitch, in this case returning to the lowest note of the pattern.

**EXAMPLE 4-16.** From *Time Cycle, Four Songs for Soprano, Clarinet, Cello, Percussion, and Piano-Celeste* by Lukas Foss; III. "Sechzehnter Januar." Copyright © MCMLX, MCMLXII by Carl Fischer, Inc., New York. Copyright © MCML-XIV by Carl Fischer, Inc., New York. International Copyright Secured. All rights reserved. Music reprinted by permission of Carl Fischer, Inc. New York.

Melodic tension can occur as the direct result of shortened note durations in combination with other motion factors. Such is the case in Ex. 4-17; here two eighth notes stand at the exact midpoint of the melody. The durations prior to m. 5 and following m. 7 are repeated quarter notes, while mm. 5 and 7 consist of dotted quarters preceded or followed by eighth rests. The rhythmic patterning beginning with the third eighth note in m. 6 through m. 11 is a retrograde of the durations heard in mm. 1–6. A major portion of the tensional change is the result of altering the length of time a particular pitch is being heard. The tension is released by retrograding the durations and returning to pianissimo. The increase in tension in Ex. 4-17 is a subtle matter, but this subtlety becomes an important structural factor in the variations made on this theme.

The ways in which tension and release patterns may be evoked and in which this analogy influences our interpretations are as numerous as are melodic contexts. It is also obvious that for the analogy to be useful it must

**EXAMPLE 4-17.** Webern: Symphony Opus 21, II, mm. 1–11. Copyright 1929, Universal Edition. Used by permission of the publisher. Theodore Presser Company sole representative United States, Canada and Mexico.

apply to the total context and not just the linear aspect as has been done in this section.

### Continuity and Coherence

Continuity and coherence are vital musical forces and important aesthetic and structural principles for melody. The discussion of these two principles can give only an indication of the ways in which they occur in twentieth-century music. Since they are complementary principles, continuity and coherence are presented simultaneously.

The impression of continuity and coherence is often the result of rhythm and pitch patterning. The anacrusis-thesis rhythmic relation (or its variant) is structurally important in the first movement of Bartók's Second String Quartet (mm. 118–123 are given in Ex. 4-18). Recurrences of this basic rhythmic idea provide continuity and simultaneously create a coherent melody. A subsidiary rhythmic event ( ♩ ♪ ) is heard in m. 119, which while providing contrast to the initiating rhythmic pattern, completes the statement by its rhythmic symmetry ( ∪ — ∪ — ∪ — ). The continua-

**EXAMPLE 4-18.** Bartók: String Quartet No. 2, I, mm. 118–123. Copyright 1920 by Universal Edition; Renewed 1956. Copyright assigned to Boosey & Hawkes, Inc., for the U.S.A. Reprinted by permission. Permission granted by Universal Edition A.G., Vienna, for all countries of the world except USA.

tion of the ⏑ — pattern in mm. 120–121 is evident, even though the rhythmic pattern contributes to an increase in melodic tension because of the increased frequency of contextual accents.

As important a factor as rhythm is in contributing to the continuity and coherence of Ex. 4-18, pitch patterning is just as crucial. The melodic excerpt given in Ex. 4-18 has as its basic pitch material a symmetric four-note set, $d^2$ $c^2\sharp$ $g^1\sharp$ $g^1$. After the sixteenth-note upbeat figure in m. 118, this four-note set is repeated several times. By its recurrence, pitch continuity becomes a structural fact, producing melodic coherence. As is evident, recurrence is an essential aspect of both continuity and coherence.

In some compositions the strongest coherence factor is produced by structural step progressions. In Ex. 4-19 two progressions descending by half steps are clearly audible. As shown in the graph, the upper progression begins in the first measure, coincidental with the statement of an important descending melodic motive; the beginning of the lower progression coincides with the last note of the motive, $g^1\flat$.

**EXAMPLE 4-19.** Berg: Four Songs, Opus 2, No. 2, mm. 9–17 (with graph). Copyright 1928, Universal Edition. Used by permission of the publisher. Theodore Presser Company sole representative United States, Canada and Mexico.

Both step progressions appear to have the same note as their pitch goal. The lower progression does not move directly to its apparent goal, A, stopping short by two half steps in m. 6. At this point a new melodic shape interrupts the straightforward descent, recalling the opening of the descending step progression.[9] In this case, the coherent structure is the direct result of interacting descending step progressions.

Recurrence of a melodic contour or pitch motion pattern may be crucial for melodic continuity. Example 4-20 illustrates such a procedure. From m. 10 to the beginning of m. 13, the contour of each melodic figure is a simple arch, with its ending at a lower pitch than its beginning. During m. 13 another shape is introduced, basically one with descending pitch motion. This shape also is stated three times, with the third statement occupying less

---

[9]In actuality the motion initiated in the lower step progression has as its goal E♭, which is realized in the accompaniment. The entire context should be studied, since the two step progressions discussed interact with other descending progressions in the accompaniment.

**EXAMPLE 4-20.** Dallapiccola: *Cinque frammenti di Saffo,* I, mm. 10–16. By permission of the Edizioni Suvini Zerboni, Milano.

time than the first and second (also the case with the third statement of the first shape). The interval of the minor third is of considerable significance for both continuity and coherence; even though there is no exact restatement of the melodic pattern, inclusion of the minor third in structurally important positions creates a continuity based on elemental recurrence and makes the apparently dissimilar figures cohere.

Contour and the number of events in a melodic motive are other means by which apparently disparate statements can be formed into highly coherent structures. Each of the four-note motives in Ex. 4-21 is a subset[10] of the prime

**EXAMPLE 4-21.** Webern: Variations for Orchestra, Opus 30, mm. 1–3. © 1956, Universal Edition. Used by permission of the publisher. Theodore Presser Company sole representative United States, Canada and Mexico.

---

[10]For an explanation of set types, see Chapter Six, Section 2.3.

form of the twelve-tone row used in this composition. Although each of the motives is performed by a different instrument (*Klangfarbenmelodie*) and has a different rhythmic pattern, the separate statements cohere because of the contoural similarities between the motives and because each contains four different pitches. The trombone motive is a contoural inversion of the contrabass motive, and the clarinet motive is a contoural variant of the contrabass. (In context the oboe statement is imitated by inversion by the viola.) Continuity is also felt as a direct result of the groupings by fours.

### Cadence

Continuity and coherence are organizational principles that operate at various levels, from the smallest formal unit to the entire composition. To be artistically effective, these principles cannot be limited to simple repetition but must exist in contexts where musical events are differentiated by one means or another. The introduction of contrasting events, interruptive devices, and cadential punctuations are important means for differentiating, highlighting, and separating musical events in time (while continuity and coherence exert control between events). Although cadences are the product of the total context, this discussion focuses on aspects of melodic cadence.

In tonal compositions hierarchical pitch relations are perceived because of their structural functions. Cadence is one such structural function, and is not just a property of pitch, but of rhythm as well. Example 4-22 is an excerpt from a tonal composition that functions as a connection between two fugues in different tonalities. Both of the phrases shown (phrases one and two of this Interludium) exhibit the quality of moving from one tonal emphasis to another. Considering only the melodic aspect for the moment, it is clear

**EXAMPLE 4-22.** Hindemith: *Ludus Tonalis,* Interludium in F, mm. 1–8. Copyright 1942 by B. Schott's Soehne. Copyright renewed 1970. Used with permission. All rights reserved.

that the pitch motion is from F to E♭ in the first phrase. When the E♭ is interpreted in its linear context it does not represent the root of a tonality. Nevertheless, in terms of melodic activity, the motion is from $f^1$ to $f^2$ to $e^1♭$. The cadence pitch $e^1♭$, is reached by step motion from an octave above. The descending pitch motion and the under-third embellishment are decisive cadential factors; the rhythmic patterning is less so, since the similar pattern continues as the cadence pitch is reached.

In both phrases the contrapuntal relations ultimately are more important structurally than the independent linear patterns. But in each line pitch direction is clearly established. For example, the line beginning with C (left hand part) moves by step in contrary motion to the upper line. As in the principal melodic line, the bass cadence pitch, A♭, is approached by an embellishing skip. The cadential activity at the end of the second phrase is similar, except that the pitch motion is by step.

The effect of cadence often is as much a result of halting an activity abruptly as it is of gradually moving to a close. One such abrupt halt is shown in Ex. 4-23, an excerpt from the beginning of the recapitulation. The motive

**EXAMPLE 4-23.** Bartók, String Quartet No. 4, I, mm. 93–95, first violin. Copyright 1929 by Universal Edition; Renewed 1948. Copyright assigned to Boosey & Hawkes, Inc., for the U.S.A. Reprinted by permission of Boosey & Hawkes, Inc., and Universal Edition.

heard at the end of the excerpt is basic to the structure of the movement, and its position at the end of this phrase serves to connect it with what has gone before. But because of specific identity it functions to close this phrase in an abrupt fashion.[11] As such, the motive is now a cadential pattern. In retrospect, the silence following the statement of the motive is also part of the cadential property associated with the statement of the motive. An "abrupt" cadence tends not to produce as strong a feeling of closure as one in which the motion patterns reveal a gradual progression.

A change in tempo or duration is often associated with cadences. This is particularly true in those instances in which pitch direction and hierarchy are not primary organizational factors. Changes in tempo and duration often produce subtleties of articulation. Since change in tempo automatically changes the duration relation, the "strength" of a cadence is proportionate

---

[11]The term "abrupt" should not be interpreted as denoting a negative quality; rather, it is an important means for delineating form.

to how much of a tempo change takes place. A change in duration might well be sudden, as by the introduction of a longer note value or a subtle device such as a fermata. Both gradual change (tempo change) and abrupt change (longer duration) are shown in Ex. 4-24. Particularly noteworthy is the role of tempo change in the sectional cadencing activity of mm. 7–9. The designation *wieder langsamer* (slower again) followed by *rit.* reveals that an abrupt change in tempo and *ritardando* are being used to create the impression of a close.[12] The next tempo designation is *lebhaft* ( ♪ = ca. 160), which retrospectively aids in providing tempo perspective.

A cadencing effect may result from the gradual discontinuance of a particular event. This is particularly true in those contrapuntal textures in which closes of lines do not always coincide. A unique example is shown in Ex. 4-25. Here the seven violas create a one-note *Klangfarbenmelodie* which is premised on individual attacks, on tone decay in the form of either an ascending or descending glissando, and on a diminuendo from *mf* to *pp*.[13] In a sense all of the conventional properties of a cadence are present: a change in pitch, even though the highest or lowest pitch is not specified; a change in dynamics; and the effect of slowing down because the attacks are not equidistantly spaced. When the total "decay" of the violas is accomplished, a very strong cadential effect is produced.

The methods for producing cadence effects are too numerous to catalog. It is true that the twentieth century is witnessing a multiplicity of cadence types. This discussion has stressed primarily the punctuating, concluding properties of musical cadences without attempting to make a catalog of cadence types.

As an element of musical organization cadence serves to define the ends of formal units. The formal units themselves often are projections of basic shapes, motives, or themes. It should be stressed that these elements of musical organization are continuations of past techniques, even though unique ways of presentation are always being brought forward. This portion of our discussion will isolate some examples.

---

[12]Register also plays a part in this sectional close.

[13]It may be shocking to conceive of this texture as a melody, but because of the successive attacks the viola color takes on the characteristics of a melodic event, i.e., a pattern of changes.

**EXAMPLE 4-24.** Webern: Variations for Orchestra, Opus 30, mm. 1–9. © 1956, Universal Edition. Used by permission of the publisher. Theodore Presser Company sole representative United States, Canada and Mexico.

**EXAMPLE 4-24** continued.

**EXAMPLE 4-25.** Penderecki: *Anaklasis,* p. 6, top system. Copyright 1960 by Hermann Moeck Verlag. Used by permission.

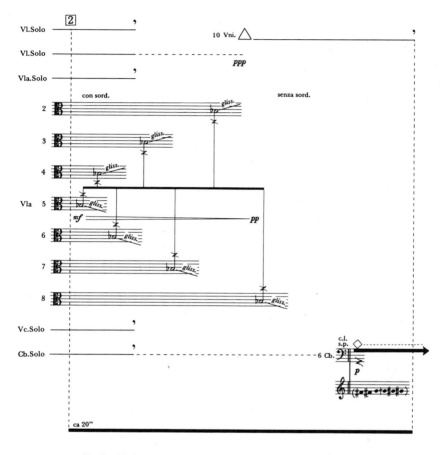

### Basic Shape

Frequently a line evolves from a germinal figure or a basic shape. Three excerpts will illustrate the potential of such elemental structures. The first excerpt (Ex. 4-26) shows a melodic fragment and the germinal figure on which it is based. As can be seen, the melodic theme derives its essential material from the germinal figure. The use of the melodic germ is simple: it consists primarily of repetitions of the figure and rudimentary rhythmic and pitch additions (such as the skip of a sixth ($e^2 - c^3$) and the filling in of the perfect fourth, m. 2).

A basic shape is melodically important in Ex. 4-27. The first three melodic notes are the presentation of the shape; the next three notes (not including the repetition of $f^1$) are a continuation of that shape. In its initial presentation the shape is defined as a descending pattern bounded by a major third;

**EXAMPLE 4-26.** Stravinsky: Symphony in C, mm. 1–2 and no. 5 to 4 after no. 5. Copyright 1948 by B. Schott's Soehne. Used with permission. All rights reserved.

**EXAMPLE 4-27.** Schoenberg: Opus 11, 1, mm. 1–3. Copyright 1910 by Universal Edition. Renewed 1938 by Arnold Schoenberg. Used by permission of Belmont Music Publishers, Los Angeles, California 90049.

in its second presentation it is a descending melodic pattern bounded by a perfect fourth.

Another type of basic shape is shown in Ex. 4-2. The shape as presented by the oboe consists of three notes and a large and a small interval. Four statements of this shape are shown: the flute performs the shape in retrograde inversion, the trumpet in retrograde, and the clarinet in inversion. Each of the statements of this shape (which actually performs the function of a motive) is presented in a different rhythmic guise. The composite result is a *Klangfarbenmelodie*.

## MELODIC PROCESSES IN TWENTIETH-CENTURY MUSIC

The preceding survey of melodic elements and elements of organization and structure exposes some of the ingredients and materials of twentieth-century melody. Now these factors will be viewed as they interact as melodic processes[14] in artistic, musical expressions.

### Expansive Linear Processes

It is held by many that the "long line" melodic idea that developed to such a high form in the nineteenth century has lost its fascination for twentieth-century composers. While this may be largely true, twentieth-century music still has many melodies in which the expansive quality that is associated with the "long line" is very much present.

Expansiveness is an integral characteristic of the melodic line shown in Ex. 4-28. After an initial three-note gesture, the phrase reaches its structural apex (m. 10) rapidly. The motion toward the close of the phrase gives the impression of occupying more time, partly because of the lengthened durations. The overall contour and rhythmic structure of this melody are little different from earlier models. Pitch organization, however, differs markedly: (1) the smallest melodic interval is the major second, which means pitch hierarchy cannot be established by conventional means; (2) reliance upon the major second as the smallest melodic component reduces the pitch and interval resources (a symmetric hexachordal basis, expressed in abstraction as a whole-tone scale); (3) the structural pitches A♭ and D are a tritone apart, creating the impression of non-differentiation of pitch materials (directly related to the symmetric arrangement of the pitch materials). The primary differentiating dimension is duration; increasing duration defines the phrase apex (the climax m. 10) and the melodic cadence.

---

[14]Although the presentation will contain some chronological ordering, it is not to be construed that this is a "History of Twentieth-Century Melody."

**EXAMPLE 4-28.** Debussy: *Preludes,* Book I, *Voiles,* mm. 7–14. Copyright 1910, Durand et Cie. Used by permission of the publisher. Elkan-Vogel, Inc. sole representative United States, Canada and Mexico.

Implications of traditional structural organization are often clearly present. Such is the case of the melody in Ex. 4-29, both in and out of the total context. The tonal relations are unique and interesting. Characteristic of the tonal plan is the inclusion of f♮ and c♮ at important structural

**EXAMPLE 4-29.** Shostakovich: Symphony No. 10, IV, no. 145 to 1 m. before no. 146. © Copyright 1955 by MCA Music, A Division of MCA, Inc., 445 Park Avenue, New York, N.Y. 10022. All Rights Reserved. Used by Permission of MCA Music; Musikverlag Hans Sikorski, Hamburg, copyright owner for the German Federal Republic, Scandinavia, Spain, Portugal, Greece, Turkey and Israel; Anglo-Soviet Music Press Ltd. for the United Kingdom of Great Britain and Northern Ireland, the British Commonwealth & Dominions (excluding Canada), all British Colonies, Protectorates and Mandated Territories, and South Africa; and G. Ricordi & Co.

positions, as in the third measure. These pitches are more than chromatic embellishments; they are integral members of the tonality. The implication of such inclusions is that the pitch resources are greater than those that make up the traditional seven-note diatonic scales. Chromaticism is not the sole factor because the composer has created the line by joining together motivic cells. Each of these cells has its own identity as well as operating in the total context. For example, the first phrase consists of three motivic ideas; the second, mm. 2–3, encloses as much time as the figures framing it. Because of its length and pitch content, this second motivic statement of the first phrase is the peak of the melodic arch, both in contour and in the tension created. The second phrase rises to a higher melodic peak, namely $e^3\flat$, the tension of which is resolved by the descending sequential patterns returning to the cadence pitch, $d^2$. In both of these phrases, recurrence of motivic cells is an important organizational feature; but only in the sequential pattern is repetition the rule. Overall continuity results from the characteristic weak-beat endings of the motives; it is this feature which creates the impression of much repetition.

Melodies with "classic" long-line characteristics have been favored by some twentieth-century composers. The excerpt shown in Ex. 4-30 illustrates

**EXAMPLE 4-30.** Hindemith: Piano Sonata No. 2, I, mm. 1–10. Copyright 1936 by B. Schott's Soehne. Copyright renewed 1964. Used with permission. All rights reserved.

Ruhig bewegt ( ♩. etwa 64)

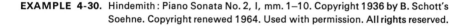

the "classic" concept well. Intervallically, the melody is constructed along tertian chord outlines. As in the previous example, motivic sequence is an important organizational feature, giving an illusion of increasing length while simultaneously creating a forward drive to the restatement of the initial melodic idea in m. 10. The sequences expand the tonal relations because repetition provides organizational relationships. Described in such terms this melody is not very much different from its historical prototypes. However, its relation to the total context marks it as a more recent melodic expression.

The continuation of conventional melodic processes is most evident in those compositions in which tonality still is an important structural feature. The examples cited so far serve primarily as reminders of the potentials that still exist for creating important tonal musical expressions. Continuation of conventional processes can also be observed in compositions in which tonality does not play a structural role.

Melodies and melodic patterns can be easily derived from tone rows, which predetermine the pitch order a composer selects to use in a particular instance. By using recurring rhythmic figures and motives certain aspects of convention can be conserved, as in Ex. 4-31.

In Ex. 4-31 the theme of the movement and the row forms coincide (not only in the portion cited, but throughout the movement), but it is the rhythmic patterns that initially help us to hear a melodic line. As with many tonal predecessors, this melody contains repeated note groups of eighths moving to a longer duration. Tonal hierarchy is not an aim (although in isolation the melody may suggest hierarchical ordering), and such a scheme is negated by the pitch ordering selected for this line. The notes with longer

**EXAMPLE 4-31.** Schoenberg: String Quartet No. 4, Opus 37, I, mm. 1–6. Copyright 1939 by G. Schirmer, Inc. Used by permission.

durations may seem structurally important from an organizational point of view: they provide the points of the melodic contour. It is the motion from one point to another that provides the qualitative motion we perceive.

Motive and figure may be incorporated into melodic lines more subtly than in Ex. 4-31, but even in subtle usage there is no doubt that the processes involved are continuations of past techniques. Such is the case in the vocal melody shown in Ex. 4-32. The pitch materials are derived from different forms of a twelve-tone row. In this instance overlapping is used ($F\sharp$ in m. 3 is the last note of $I_0$ and the first note of $R_0$). More important is the interval content of the series and the ways in which these appear in the melody. For instance, four subsets of adjacent notes contain similar interval content, either (0 1 4) or (0 3 4). Structurally, these occur at important points in the

**EXAMPLE 4-32.** Webern: Cantata No. 2, Opus 31, I, mm. 8–22. Copyright 1951, Universal Edition. Used by permission of the publisher. Theodore Presser Company sole representative United States, Canada and Mexico.

melody. The first line of text begins with $I_0$ and as a consequence "Schweigt auch die" is melodicized by an (0 1 4) subset. The first phrase ends with the words "sie immer," melodicized by an (0 3 4) subset. This latter subset does not occur because it is the last three notes of the set [the last three-note subset is (0 1 2)]. Similarly, "Sonne scheint," corresponding to the end of a stanza, is melodicized by an (0 1 4) subset. Thus, three structural points—the beginning, middle, and end of a stanza—have similar pitch motives. Such is the case for the beginning and end of the next stanza also. This particular twelve-tone series was selected partly because it contains these subsets. Musically, the pitch motives are identifiable because of their similarities and because the composer has placed them in structurally important positions.

On first hearing melodic lines may appear to consist of unrelated melodic figures. Such apparent unrelatedness may arise from the fact that no duplicates of surface patterns occur, either in rhythm or pitch. In Ex. 4-33 the phrases unfold through an accumulation of short, figural statements, which together create an illusion of a longer line. In part, the complementary phrases derive their long-line characteristics from contour and loudness; in addition, the second phrase (mm. 39–42), with its fewer rests, appears to be continuous.

While the melodic elements may appear unrelated at first, particularly if recurrence of motives and figures is expected, upon closer examination factors of structural coherence other than contour and loudness become apparent. Most notable is the submotivic organization (in some respects similar to Ex. 4-32, but not derived from serialization of pitches). This is observable in the use of linear materials, basically the minor third and the perfect fifth. Each of the figures is made up of successions of minor thirds. The perfect fifth appears in the manner of an interpolation: as an interruptive feature (the chord in m. 35), as a connective interval (m. 36), as a prefix (m. 38), and as a cadential interval (mm. 40–41).

Although recurrence of motives and figures does not take place, the reliance upon a limited number of melodic intervals provides coherence and continuity at the submotivic level. The submotivic recurrence makes motivic recurrence (or, for that matter, the recurrence of any larger pattern) an unessential organizational aspect. With recurrence as a substructural factor, the actual melodic line exhibits a random, improvisational quality that is ever-changing on the surface, but highly limited below the surface.[15]

Perpetual change as an organizational concept is characteristic of the twentieth century. This concept appears to resemble the traditional technique of variation, which has led some writers to describe much music of

---

[15]It is the submotivic treatment that bears a resemblance to serial technique.

**EXAMPLE 4-33.** Carter: String Quartet No. 2, I, mm. 35–42. Reprinted by permission of Associated Music Publishers, Inc.

our time as "perpetual variation." In a manner of speaking this is true; in serialized compositions the pitch order may be invariant while the rhythmic patterning is highly variable. In Ex. 4-33 the melodic intervals are basically invariant, but the melodic presentation is highly variable, both in its pitch and its rhythmic content.

### Non-Expansive Linear Processes

Although the expansive quality of the long line is important, there are some processes in which the extended line per se is not a melodic ideal. Both Ex. 4-32 and Ex. 4-33 are dependent for their long-line effect upon successions of melodic fragments. An alternative to the long-line quality is to create melodic events that are nonexpansive; rather than being temporal, linear, and goal-oriented, melodic events appear as linear strata and tend to take on a spatial, objectified characteristic. In general, melodic stratification begins to appear when the linear aspects consist principally of segmental groupings; as a consequence, the long line recedes in structural significance, and characteristics of objects existing in space tend to become prominent.[16]

Stratification of musical events has gained considerable significance in the twentieth century. Example 4-34 illustrates the emergence of such procedures. A twice-stated three-note motive is the principal melodic statement; this three-note motive is accompanied by a harmonic-linear idea that is repeated in octave transpositions, first in patterned groups of threes, then in groups of twos.[17] Since the motive and its accompaniment are repeated, and since the double pedal creates a static harmonic field, mm. 1–8 take on the aura of a unified object existing as much in space as in time, and forming the first linear stratum of this composition. Within the stratum there is linear activity, but it is a localized quality, characteristic of this particular event. The unified-object concept is reinforced because a substantial change (mm. 9–11) coincides with a new event rather than being integral to the projection through a single event, the stratum created by mm. 1–8.[18]

Interrelations between successive strata may be discernible, as in Ex. 4-34, or they may be remote. If the latter situation prevails, the segments

---

[16]Music, by its very nature, exists in time; nevertheless, that is not the same as creating the illusion of the passage of time. It is this image of the passage of time that is referred to as the temporal quality of music. To create an image of non-passage or suspension of time is to create a stratified, spatial image.

[17]The harmonic-linear idea of measures 3 and 4 is obviously derived from measures 1 and 2.

[18]At the submotivic level the second stratum, beginning in measure 9, is a temporal compression of intervallic content of both the principal and the subsidiary accompanimental motives.

**EXAMPLE 4-34.** Debussy: *Reflets dans l'eau,* mm. 1–11. Copyright 1905, Elkan-Vogel, Inc. Used by permission.

will probably appear to consist of new material. Such may be the initial interpretation of Ex. 4-35.[19] The principal linear ideas are stated by a choir of woodwinds and solo trumpet. These ideas are separated from one another

---

[19]A study of individual woodwind lines will reveal similarities of linear organization.

**EXAMPLE 4-35.** Ives: *The Unanswered Question,* p. 5. Copyright 1953 by Southern Music Publishing Company, Inc. Used by permission.

in real time and by color, as well as consisting of individualized pitch patterns. The total effect is that of stratified linear events occurring above an unvarying continuum (in this instance a choir of barely audible strings playing *ppp con sordini*). Creation of linear strata is a means of projecting the program of Ex. 4-35: the trumpet raises "The Question"[20] and a few seconds later an "Answer" is proposed by the woodwind choir. This alternation of "Question" and proposed "Answer" characterizes the composition as a whole. Since no definitive "Answer" is forthcoming, no musical synthesis occurs.

Imitative contrapuntal textures with alternating instrumental choirs lend themselves to linear stratification; the texture unifies each block of activity. In Ex. 4-36 the procedures are not unlike those found in some compositions from the Renaissance. The segmental grouping is characterized by blocks of color; within each block there is considerable activity consisting of imitative statements of a five-pitch serialized "Theme." Two aspects of linear organization are demonstrated by Ex. 4-36: (1) each stratum consists essentially of imitative statements of a melodic subject; and (2) the alternating blocks of color set up a linear pattern which governs the form of the movement, whereas the imitative texture governs each linear stratum.

**EXAMPLE 4-36.** Stravinsky: *In Memoriam Dylan Thomas*, mm. 1–8. Copyright 1954 by Boosey & Hawkes, Inc. Reprinted by permission.

---

[20]The first statement of the "Question" is not given in the excerpt.

**EXAMPLE 4-36** continued.

Attack density[21] may be influential in the stratification of linear events. The duration of the third phrase, mm. 5–9 of Ex. 4-37 is equivalent to 28 ♪'s. In this span of time (the tempo being determined by the smallest note-value) there are 42 attacks, or an average of approximately $1\frac{1}{2}$ attacks per eighth note, with the greatest number of attacks occurring in m. 6. By comparison, the duration of the first phrase, mm. 1–3, is 16 eighth notes; during this time there are 15 attacks, most of which occur in m. 1. From these observations it may be concluded that attack density is a linear as well as a

**EXAMPLE 4-37.** Stockhausen: *Klavierstücke,* Number 2, I, mm. 1–9. © 1954, Universal Edition. Used by permission of the publisher. Theodore Presser Company sole representative United States, Canada and Mexico.

---

[21]The number of attacks in a given amount of time.

**EXAMPLE 4-37** continued.

structural factor. Attack density shapes the phrases and gives each one of them an identity. The sudden increase in the attack density of the third phrase coincides with an abrupt increase in loudness, and as such is also important for the stratification process. Although the composition is for a monochromatic instrument, the use of registral extremes and the sudden changes in loudness between adjacent attacks produces an overall effect not unlike *Klangfarbenmelodie*.

Less conventional sound sources and unspecified pitches may be combined in segmental groups to create linear statements; Ex. 4-38 is an illustration. Measures 1–5 constitute the first unified block; each of the voice parts has its own rhythmic patterning so that few simultaneous attacks occur. The sound material is an unmodulated *h*; an attack density increase occurs in both the alto and bass parts. In m. 6 the bass is assigned an active role, with the performers choosing the amount of time each of the segments is to occupy; this total block is to occupy from 23 to 28 seconds. Although the material is specified, the precise temporal occurrence is indeterminate and dependent upon the performers. Measures 7 and 8 have determined durations and are to be performed with fixed pitches.

One important linear process in Ex. 4-38 is the alternation of specified tempo with *senza tempo*. Another is the change from one vocable to numerous groups of pitched and unpitched sounds in m. 6 of the bass part, and the return to one vocable in mm. 7–8 in the soprano and alto.

Complete or partial freedom on the part of the performer to elect the

**EXAMPLE 4-38.** Ligeti: *Aventures,* mm. 1–9. Copyright © 1964 by Henry Litolff's Verlag. Reprint permission granted by C. F. Peters Corporation, New York.

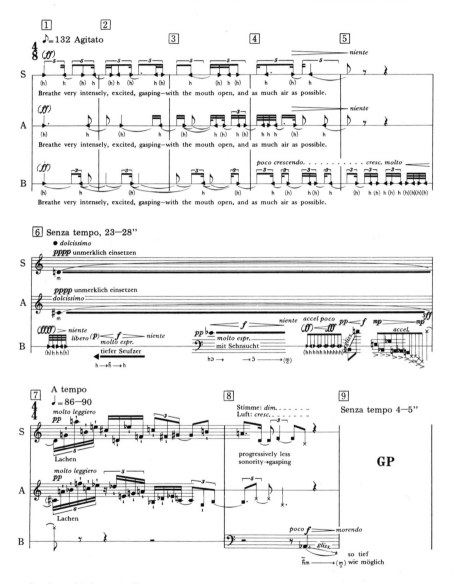

order in which melodic segments are to occur opens up infinite possibilities. In simplistic terms this means that melodic processes are the result of a performance rather than being made available by a performance. Example 4-39 shows a small portion of a partially indeterminate composition. Each of the instruments has an independent line, and each of these lines consists of numerous melodic segments designated by interrupted "barlines" with a

**EXAMPLE 4-39.** Lutoslawski, *Jeux Venitiens,* I. Copyright 1962 by Hermann Moeck Verlag, Celle.

caesura above. The length of a caesura is optional with the performer. In performance each of the instrumental lines loses its individuality in the density of sound, and this density of sound depends in part upon the length of the caesura. Thus, although there are seven lines of linear activity, what emerges is a stratified mass of sound.

The composition consists of eight sections, designated A B C D E F G H. The beginning and end of each section is given by the conductor. Section A, played by the woodwind and percussion group (not given above), is to have a duration of twelve seconds. When the conductor gives the downbeat, the players begin performing the segments in the order notated. At the sign for the end of Section A the players automatically begin Section B (also not shown). Section C (beginning immediately as the conductor signals the end of B) is played by the woodwinds, timpani, and percussion (the parts for the latter two groups are not shown). For Section C, E, and G, the individual parts need not be played from the beginning, but may begin with a phrase that appears between two caesuras. Since the order of the melodic segments in Sections C, E, and G is indeterminate, recurrence of material does not tend to become a structural feature; rather (as a hearing of the work will bear out), the form of the work becomes apparent because of relative activity and textural density. The linear element here is thus structurally important as it contributes to activity and density, not because of its melodicism.

Improvisation of lines may be based on specific notational events or it may be based on graphic or verbal instructions. A hypothetical graphic linear event might be notated as follows:

If no other instructions are given, the performer is free to realize the graphic score in a manner he deems suitable. The resultant linear event cannot be determined by the listener in advance. In this respect the line is indeterminate, and ideally will remain so because each performance of the event will probably be different from its predecessors.

## CONCLUSION

Melody as a musical phenomenon has undergone enormous changes during the twentieth century. In many instances melody continues to fulfill the same structural roles that it did in the past; in some instances melody is best thought of as a series of linear events either occurring successively or simultaneously.

The musical effects that are produced by melodic-linear statements in twentieth-century music are undoubtedly more varied than in any other period of music, because the resources being drawn upon are much greater and therefore less predictable. In some circles indeterminate linear activity is the objective, while in other circles the opposite is just as viable. In either case, the linear structure may be similar to a long-line aesthetic; or the linear structure may take on the characteristic of a spatial object, which is a highly unified structure, but appears to exist in space rather than time.

In conclusion, our use of the term "melody" has been inclusive rather than exclusive. Such a procedure permits the inclusion of many types of linear activity that ordinarily would not enter into a discussion of melody. The open-endedness of this essay suggests that, whether a linear event reminds us of the past or whether a linear event appears to be so novel that it seems a completely new procedure, the study of melody must be a continuing process.

## SUGGESTIONS OF COMPOSITIONS FOR FURTHER STUDY

Babbitt, *Composition for Four Instruments*.
Barber, Piano Sonata.
Bartók, Concerto for Orchestra.
Berg, Violin Concerto.
Berio, *Circles*.
Boulez, *Improvisation sur mallarmé; Le marteau sans maître*.
Brown, *Available Forms I*.
Cage, *Music of Changes*.
Carter, Piano Sonata 1945/46.
Copland, Piano Variations; Symphony No. 3.
Dallapiccola, *Quaderno Musicale di Annalibera*.
Davidovsky, *Synchronisms*.
Erb, Sonata for Harpsichord and String Quartet.
Foss, *Echoi*.
Gaburo, *Antiphony III; Antiphony IV*.
Griffes, Piano Sonata.
Hindemith, Sonata for Flute and Piano.
Messiaen, *Mode de valeurs et d'intensités*.
Penderecki, *Threnody: To the Victims of Hiroshima*.
Powell, *Events for Tape Recorder*.
Prokofiev, Symphony No. 7.
Schoenberg, Five Pieces for Orchestra, Op. 16.
Schuman, Symphony No. 3.
Stravinsky, Movements for Piano and Orchestra; Octet.
Webern, Cantata, Op. 29; Five Movements for String Quartet, Op. 5; Songs, Op. 3.

# chapter five

# The Vertical Dimension in Twentieth-Century Music

HORACE REISBERG

## INTRODUCTION[1]

What is twentieth-century harmony? It is essential to understand that twentieth-century music is a diversity of practices rather than a period of time and that all the harmonic materials of the past are available to the composer. What makes harmonic materials of the past part of our time is their being used in new ways. In this chapter twentieth-century harmony will be considered from two points of view: (1) the materials of harmony and (2) some of the uses of harmony. Considered as materials there are essentially two categories: (1) tertian and (2) non-tertian approaches to building chords and sonorities. The latter may be systematic, i.e., superposing the same interval (fourths, fifths, etc.) or combinations of two or more interval types or sounds, i.e., non-systematic.

The evolving of the major-minor tertian system shows increasing use of

---

[1]It will be recognized that the following discussion does not develop an encompassing theory of vertical organization in twentieth-century music. In fact, any essay dealing with the vertical dimension that hopes to present the main developments in this century must be selective rather than all-inclusive. For the most part, the harmonic materials are isolated from their larger contexts, thus decreasing the deeper understanding that accrues when they are related to earlier and later events in a composition.

the higher "dissonant" partials of the overtone series in addition to the eight that were the basis of music in the common practice period of the eighteenth and nineteenth centuries. This led to the use of the diatonic ninths, elevenths and thirteenths, as well as the more striking, decorative dissonances—the major seventh and the minor ninth—of the earlier tonal period. These harmonic structures ultimately became stylistically common in tonal music and became the consonances of the early part of our century.

What then makes harmony in twentieth-century music different from the past? Apparently, the differences have much to do with the gradual weakening and breakdown of the major-minor tonal system, principally caused by the increased chromaticism that developed in the nineteenth century. When the resultant chromatic harmonic structures were given structural significance, they replaced the more basic structural diatonic pitches and chords of the typical classical approach, and the clear functional meaning of the chords in a tonality was thereby markedly decreased. The expansion of tonality in which the more traditional syntax was loosely applied, and the growth of contrapuntal, chromatic contexts, created situations in which the conventional contrasts between tension and stability became obscured. Harmonies became products of linear motions and the freer use of all twelve pitch classes of the tempered octave. Since each voice in a texture may be functionally logical in itself, this became an important aspect in the breakdown of tonality. The combinations of the lines (chords) obscured tonality because of almost continual chromatic activity and modulation. As a result, functional harmony ceased to be the only viable determinant of tonal organization.

The traditions of musical syntax (the creation and strengthening of pitch focus) that developed over a period of centuries have gone through radical change in much twentieth-century music. Even in compositions that are totally tertian in their materials, the dictum that any chord (and pitch) may follow any other becomes the prevailing rule!

As chords gradually lost their structural functions in a constant chromatic atmosphere they became functionally unclassifiable. They became aggregates of sounds or pitches chosen for their individual characteristics of tension or relaxation (based on their interval structure) and were syntactically placed in relation to the prevailing compositional context. For pre-twentieth-century composers the various functions of a harmony within a tonality dictated a limited group of choices; as they gradually enlarged the scope of choices, the relatively predictable syntax of the past was changed.

## TRIADS AND HIGHER TERTIAN CHORDS

Major and minor triads are rarely used in twentieth-century music as the sole chordal materials of a composition. They most often occur in context with other chords (tertian or non-tertian) or in shorter passages of free root relations. In the following, non-functional passage of root-position major triads, there is no clearly defined tonality, nor predictable pattern of chordal changes. A high degree of tension is created by the unusual voice leading, parallel motion, and the predominance of root relations other than the perfect fifth.

**EXAMPLE 5-1.** Schuman: Symphony No. 4, II. Copyright 1944 by G. Schirmer, Inc. Used by permission.

Tenderly, simply ♩ = ca 66

*Ode to Napoleon*, by Schoenberg (Ex. 5-2), contains many unusual passages using tertian melodic figures and chords. These materials are derived from the twelve-tone series on which this composition is based. In the measures cited, the piano part juxtaposes major and minor triads (mainly inversions) in hocket-like procedure. In m. 220 the simultaneous presentation of the triads creates polychords; the string parts above the piano combine to form more complex tertian sonorities.

Examples 5-1 and 5-2 may suggest that when tertian chords are used, non-tertian sonorities are excluded. On the contrary, it is more common to find tertian harmonies combined with other types of chord structures. The complex layered texture illustrated in Ex. 5-3 contains the four types of triads in the piano part (e.g., m. 30, augmented; m. 33, major, diminished, and minor) as well as several non-tertian chords. The counterpoint lines of the piano and of the three other instruments produce vertical combinations that obscure the "conventional" origin of some of the melodic and harmonic resources.

**EXAMPLE 5-2.** Schoenberg: *Ode to Napoleon Buonaparte,* mm. 217–221. Used by permission of Belmont Music Publishers, Los Angeles, California 90049.

**EXAMPLE 5-2** continued.

**EXAMPLE 5-3.** Schoenberg: *Pierrot Lunaire,* Op. 21, "Mondestrunken." Copyright 1914 by Wien Universal. Renewed 1941 by Arnold Schoenberg. Used by permission of Belmont Music Publishers, Los Angeles, California 90049.

**EXAMPLE 5-3** continued.

### Sevenths, Ninths, Elevenths, and Thirteenths

The chords produced by the addition of thirds to triads are used as freely as the simpler chords in common practice period music. These higher order tertian structures have become separated from the previous functional harmonic meanings, and are often heard as colorful sound structures in which the so-called dissonances tend to become less tense, even stable, by consistent usage. The use of a chord as color or as sound for its own sake became the hallmark of some composers, particularly Debussy and Ravel. Debussy's music shows the first radical abandonment of Romantic chromaticism and of most functional traditions. The trends which freed sound from being subsidiary to the key system, however, are apparent throughout the nineteenth century.

Parallel seventh chords above a dyadic pedal produce a coloristic effect in Ex. 5-4. As such, conventional voice-leading principles are irrelevant. It is obvious, however, that the parallel chords are linear features as much as they are harmonic. It is linearization that makes the sonorous character of the passage more important than the individual chords.

**EXAMPLE 5-4.** Creston: Symphony No. 2, I. Copyright 1954 by G. Schirmer, Inc. Used by permission.

Example 5-5 illustrates a more conservative usage of seventh chords. The association with pre-twentieth-century chord syntax and voice leading results from the motion of the root position bass line and the resolutions of dissonance (as m. 8, resolution of $MM_7$ and mm. 10–12, resolution of suspension).

**EXAMPLE 5-5.** Bartók: Concerto for Orchestra, II. Copyright 1946 by Hawkes & Son (London) Ltd.; Renewed 1973. Reprinted by permission of Boosey & Hawkes, Inc.

Ninth chords as well as other tertian chords are characteristic sonorities in Ex. 5-6. Some of the arpeggiated figures outline elevenths and thirteenths. Parallel and similar voice leading and close position of the chords are also characteristic of this excerpt.

For a final example illustrating higher tertian chords, we return to impressionism. It was mentioned above that Debussy and Ravel were fond of the coloristic effect produced by chords, whether in chord streams or in more traditional relations. The short excerpt shown in Ex. 5-7 contains several incomplete thirteenth chords in varied chord-to-chord relations.

### Added-note Chords

So-called added-note chords are first found in the music of Debussy. They are considered to be additions to tertian chord structures in that nonchord tones become chordal members. One of the most popular early additions to the triad was the sixth above the root, particularly at a cadence; this harmonic device was adopted in many jazz compositions in the twentieth century. Other common additions were seconds and perfect fourths.

Originally these added tones provided new color to the triad. The sixth added to the tonic triad at the end of Ex. 5-8 provides a pungency to the cadence. The added D♯ is anticipated in the prominent major seconds in m. 2. The F♯ root is added to the major seconds in m. 3.

**EXAMPLE 5-8.** Debussy: *Preludes,* Book I, No. 7. Copyright 1910, Durand et Cie. Used by permission of the publisher. Elkan-Vogel, Inc., sole representative United States, Canada and Mexico.

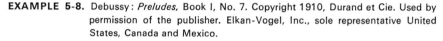

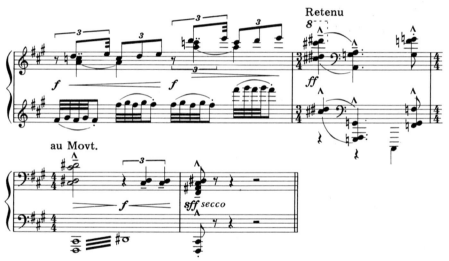

However, when heard consistently or found with frequency in a composition, it is reasonable to consider all the notes in any chord as equal, not as additions. The harp ostinato in Ex. 5-9 could be interpreted as an A♭ minor triad with added sixth, or as a mm₇ with F as root. But the latter interpretation conflicts with the recurring A♭ minor chord in the three trumpets as well as the strength of the recurring perfect fifth in the bass and the continued A♭ ostinato when the chord above changes to a B♭ major triad. The listener, therefore, recognizes the triad as the foundation with the F as an addition.

Other twentieth-century composers also used added notes for color and to make new vertical sonorities. Sometimes they are found in parallel motion.

Within its narrow confines Ex. 5-10 can be perceived as consisting of seventh chords with added ninths. However, since the passage continues for several more measures in similar fashion, the added notes are easily heard as integrated chord members. The conclusion to be drawn from Exx. 5-9 and 5-10 is that added-note sonorities tend to be ambiguous if the same kinds of chords are not previously emphasized without the added notes.

**EXAMPLE 5-9.** Debussy: *Nocturnes,* "Fêtes." Copyright 1914, Durand et Cie. Used by permission of the publisher. Elkan-Vogel, Inc. sole representative United States, Canada and Mexico.

**EXAMPLE 5-10.** Stravinsky: *Petrushka,* "Russian Dance." Copyright by Edition Russe de Musique. Copyright assigned to Boosey & Hawkes, Inc. Copyright 1947; Revised version Copyright 1948; Renewed 1974. Reprinted by permission.

### Harmonic Parallelism[2]

Parallel voice leading[3] seems to proclaim a conception of sound divorced from functional relations, and is thus a denial of the principles of organization that governed the traditional tonal system. This symbolic declaration that sound structures have their own individual integrity is one of the most important changes from pre-twentieth-century practice. Parallel harmony

---

[2]Harmonic parallelism is also known by the more recent terms *planing* or *harmonic planing.*

[3]Also see Exx. 5-4 and 5-6.

becomes the movement of vertical blocks of sound moving in thick bands like a heavy brush on a canvas; it contributes to making sound (chord) a color (timbre); it suggests sound (chord) as an indivisible texture rather than a combination of linear entities in which each line has its own identity as well as being a complementary part of the total texture; it is "anti-harmonic" because it consists essentially of coloristic couplings of a melodic line. It may also be said that divorcing chord from the varied multi-linear dimension eliminates harmony as a viable mode of musical organization and structure. Although a great deal of music in our century continues to have a controlled vertical parameter, the history of twentieth-century music shows a decrease in the importance of harmony as a compositional determinant.

Many composers in the earlier decades of this century incorporated parallelism in their music. Major-minor seventh chords (in third inversion) played by strings *divisi* add the dimension of instrumental color to coloristic harmonies in the next example. Since the harmonic stream functions as a melody, there is little structural significance attached to the chords in this brief excerpt.

**EXAMPLE 5-11.** Ravel: *Daphnis and Chloë,* Suite No. 2. Copyright 1913, Durand et Cie. Used by permission of the publisher. Elkan-Vogel, Inc. sole representative United States, Canada and Mexico.

This new technique also occurs as intervallic parallelism, as Ex. 5-12 illustrates. Here the harmonic basis is tritones moving in contrary motion as well as in all voices descending. When the parallel motion begins, the combined tritone-lines produce a stream of chords containing tritones, major thirds, and major seconds (traditionally, French augmented sixth chords; in jazz, a seventh chord with flatted fifth).

**EXAMPLE 5-12.** Strauss: *Elektra.*

In the next illustration planing occurs as an ostinato on two levels in contrary motion to one another. The upper level, piano, has incomplete seventh chords; the lower, flute and clarinet, has perfect fourths. The contrary motion of the two layers and their separation by range suggests another development in this century's harmonic practice: the use of bichordal structures.

**EXAMPLE 5-13.** Schoenberg: *Pierrot Lunaire,* "Columbine." Copyright 1914 by Wien Universal. Renewed 1941 by Arnold Schoenberg. Used by permission of Belmont Music Publishers, Los Angeles, California 90049.

The expressive possibilities of two chords in parallel motion are exploited in Ex. 5-14. Here major triads in root position and in second inversion are combined to produce a bichordal effect. The planing is within each chord type, and in a context of contrary motion.

**EXAMPLE 5-14.** Schuman: *Three Score Set for Piano.* Copyright 1944 by G. Schirmer, Inc. Used by permission.

### Polychords (Bichords)

Combining tertian sonorities to make polychords is another means to create fresh-sounding harmonic materials and new modes of pitch organization. It is, of course, clear that complete ninth, eleventh, and thirteenth chords contain more than one triad, especially when the units are spaced separately (Ex. 5-15).

**EXAMPLE 5-15.**

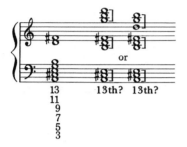

It is highly improbable that the second chord will be interpreted as a thirteenth chord. Since each of the three bracketed chords has its own identity, even though they are heard simultaneously, a polychordal group of levels or strata is a result. An outgrowth of polychordal procedure, when carried through a passage or section, is a "counterpoint of chords." Such contrapuntal levels become clearer when rhythmic and pitch class differentiation exists between levels. In contrapuntal extremes, each chord stratum has a life of its own without much pretense of close relationship or cooperation between the levels.

One of the more famous early bichordal examples is in Stravinsky's *Petrushka* (Ex. 5-16). In this bichordal combination two triads a tritone apart are harmonically joined. The conflict between C major and F♯ major is an important structural element in the work. The tritone relation makes the chord separation obvious as does the horizontalization of the C major chord in the trumpets and cornets.

A great deal of the music in *Rite of Spring* is related to a structural bichord. At the beginning of the *Dance of the Adolescents* (Ex. 5-17), we hear this chord in an ostinato for eight measures, then the bottom triad is arpeggiated while three of the four pitches of the upper chord appear in the English horn. The bassoons add a third group, consisting of arpeggiated C major and E minor triads.

**EXAMPLE 5-16.** Stravinsky: *Petrushka,* p. 15. Copyright by Edition Russe de Musique. Copyright assigned to Boosey & Hawkes, Inc. Copyright 1947; Revised version Copyright 1948; Renewed 1974. Reprinted by permission.

**EXAMPLE 5-17.** Stravinsky: *Rite of Spring,* "Dance of the Adolescents." Copyright 1921 by Edition Russe de Musique. Copyright assigned 1947 to Boosey & Hawkes for all countries of the world. Reprinted by permission.

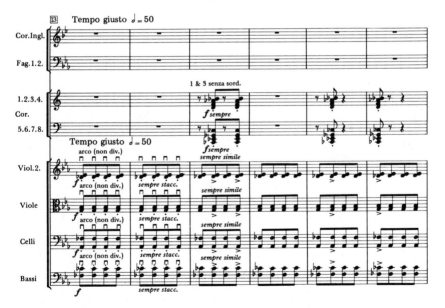

**EXAMPLE 5-17** continued.

A logical continuation of polychordal technique is polytonality, the simultaneous presentation, on different strata, of two or more keys or tonalities. It is possible to have a tonality without the functional hierarchy that produces a major or minor key. As in bichordal music, separations of register are necessary to effect polytonality. Composers also often contrast the texture and rhythm between the tonal levels.

**EXAMPLE 5-18.** Honegger : Symphony for Strings, III. Used by permission of Editions Salabert, Paris.

The next two examples are strongly contrasted in texture and vertical structure. The violin duet is an imitative contrapuntal juxtaposition in which the tonics are a tritone apart and the two lines are differentiated by rhythmic and contrapuntal means as well as tonal.

**EXAMPLE 5-19.** Bartók : 44 Violin Duets, "Song of the Harvest." Copyright 1933 by Universal Edition, Ltd. ; Renewed 1960. Copyright and Renewal assigned to Boosey & Hawkes, Inc. Reprinted by permission of Boosey & Hawkes, Inc., and Universal Edition.

**EXAMPLE 5-19** continued.

The second passage is much more complicated, having three tonal centers and a much thicker texture. One of the tonal centers is heard only because of the rearticulated B♭ pedal. The left hand part revolves around E as tonic, while the right hand is in C♯. The separation of levels is enhanced by the thirds on the bottom against the perfect fifths on top and by the contrary motion of the two hands.

**EXAMPLE 5-20.** Bartók: Sonata for Piano, I. Copyright 1927 by Universal Edition; Renewed 1954. Copyright and renewal assigned to Boosey & Hawkes, Inc. Reprinted by permission.

### Serialized Harmony[4]

Although serial organization of the pitch parameter in music is most often associated with atonal compositions in which non-tertian sonorities are the

---

[4]For a full discussion of serial techniques see Chapter 6.

norm, the compositional method does not necessarily preclude either tonal suggestion or tertian harmonic materials.

There are some compositions in the twelve-tone genre which have structurally significant tertian chords. One of the best-known of such works is Berg's Violin Concerto. The first two measures of Ex. 5-21 are obviously in G minor. However, hierarchic functional relations of the past are not present. Many writers believe that because the triad was the precompositional criterion in diatonic and (usually) chromatic tonality, most twentieth-century music based on tertian structures is inherently tonal, although it may be conceived within an expanded conception of tonality.

**EXAMPLE 5-21.** Berg: Violin Concerto. Copyright 1936, Universal Edition. Used by permission of the publisher. Theodore Presser Company sole representative United States, Canada and Mexico.

Dallapiccola often has triadic trichords (three-note segments) in his twelve-tone sets. In Ex. 5-22 the fourth trichord (m. 5) of the series is used structurally at significant places in the form, especially in the opening and closing phrases of the movement.

**EXAMPLE 5-22.** Dallapiccola: *Quaderno Musicale,* "Simbolo." By permission of the Edizioni Suvini Zerboni, Milano.

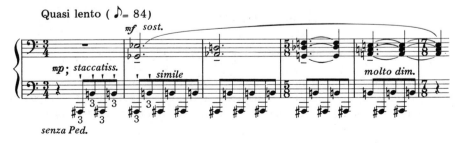

As mentioned above, Schoenberg used triads as primary material in the twelve-tone work, *Ode to Napoleon.* The bracketed notes in the set below show the triads derived from the series.

**EXAMPLE 5-23.** Basic Set from Schoenberg's *Ode to Napoleon.*

In this composition the piano part usually has passages consisting largely of triads, while the string quartet and reciter have contrasting figurations.

**EXAMPLE 5-24.** Schoenberg : *Ode to Napoleon Buonaparte.* Used by permission of Belmont Music Publishers, Los Angeles, California 90049.

## NON-TERTIAN HARMONY

### Intervallic Consistency

With the freeing of music from its obligation to a key system that was absolute in its tertian-based harmony and tonal organization, composers began introducing chords that were generated by other intervals or combinations of intervals. There are, generally, two approaches to new sonorities. The first involves a consistent systematic superposing of like intervals, such as perfect fourths, perfect fifths, seconds, and sevenths.

**EXAMPLE 5-25.** Non-tertian chords with consistent intervals.

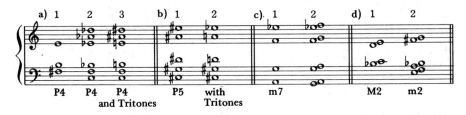

The second kind of non-tertian sonority contains a variety of interval types, resulting in mixed-interval chords. In a strict sense some of the chords in the example above are heard as mixed-interval chords even though one interval type is predominant. Scriabin's "mystic" chord, for example, is spelled in fourths, but it contains an enharmonic major third as well as two augmented fourths.

**EXAMPLE 5-26.** Scriabin: Mystic chord.

All of these chord types began to occur sporadically in late nineteenth-century impressionistic music. They became more prominent in the twentieth century, but it is rare to hear a complete composition based on any one type; it was soon found that when used consistently they all had a severely restricted potential and allowed little flexibility of style.

### Quartal Chords

Among the first of the new sonorities to be widely used was the quartal chord, which implies superposed perfect fourths. Debussy used perfect-fourth dyads and trichords with octave doublings, and in parallel motion, to imitate organum in his piano prelude "The Sunken Cathedral." They are found at the beginning and the end of the work, and provide a decided contrast to the tertian harmony in other portions of the composition.

**EXAMPLE 5-27(a).** Debussy: *Preludes,* Book I, "The Sunken Cathedral." Copyright 1910, Durand et Cie. Used by permission of the publisher. Elkan-Vogel, Inc. sole representative United States, Canada and Mexico.

**EXAMPLE 5-27(b).** Debussy: "The Sunken Cathedral," ending. Copyright 1910, Durand et Cie. Used by permission of the publisher. Elkan-Vogel, Inc. sole representative United States, Canada and Mexico.

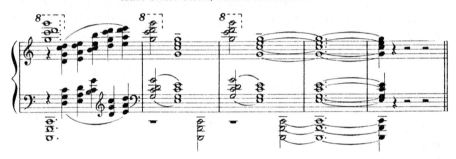

Quartal harmony is of structural significance in Schoenberg's First *Chamber* Symphony (Ex. 5-28), in which the perfect fourth is the foundation of the primary harmonic and melodic materials. Even though there are evidences of a tonal center (E) in the excerpt, tonality does not depend on hierarchic functions.

Charles Ives also wrote chords built in perfect fourths, before such techniques became generally known in the United States. The short song, "The Cage" (Ex. 5-29) written in 1906, is constructed entirely with quartal harmonies; the vocal part has a conjunct melody whose notes may or may not coincide with the pitches of the chords.

The perfect fourth is also a staple in Berg's opera *Wozzeck,* with much of the linear and vertical pitch organization determined by this interval. It is worthwhile quoting Berg, from a lecture he gave in 1929, to explain his choice of pitch materials.

The other result of my current investigations is the way I have met the need to provide folk-like tuneful elements, and thus the need to establish a relation within my opera between art-music and folk-music, something that in tonal music is quite

**EXAMPLE 5-28.** Schoenberg: *Chamber* Symphony No. 1, Op. 9. Copyright 1924 by Wien Universal Edition. Used by permission of Belmont Music Publishers, Los Angeles, California 90049.

**EXAMPLE 5-29.** Ives: 114 Songs, "The Cage," Copyright 1955 by Peer International Corporation. Used by permission.

Note: All notes not marked with sharp or flat are natural.

taken for granted. It was not easy to distinguish these levels so clearly in this so-called atonal harmony. I believe I succeeded by filling out everything that extends musically into the folk-like sphere with an easily recognizable primitive quality that is adaptable even within atonal harmony. For example: preference for symmetrical construction of the periods and sentences, incorporation of harmonies in (parallel) thirds and especially in fourths, and indeed of melodies dominated by the whole-tone scale and the perfect fourth, whereas otherwise in the atonal music of the Viennese School diminished and augmented intervals prevail. Another such means of harmonically primitive music-making is so-called "polytonality." We find such a folk-like infusion in the military march (with its "wrong-note bases") and in Marie's lullaby (with its fourth chords).[5]

The first of the following two piano reductions from Act I of *Wozzeck* is from the beginning of the aria known as Marie's lullaby. Each chord has a third in the middle which joins the top and bottom. One may quibble about calling these quartal chords but it is clear that vertical (and horizontal) fourths are predominant intervals.

**EXAMPLE 5-30.** Berg: *Wozzeck*, Act I, Scene 3. Copyright 1931, Universal Edition. Used by permission of the publisher. Theodore Presser Company sole representative United States, Canada and Mexico.

The second excerpt (Ex. 5-31) is completely dominated by the perfect fourth. Two, three, four, six, and seven notes of superposed intervals intensify the crescendo in the music. Also note the parallelism and the descending whole-tone melodic fragments.

It is important to remember that quartal chords are rarely the basis of a complete composition but are used as the foundation of a section or, more characteristically, incorporated in passages where other types of sonority are also present. They can provide a dramatic contrast to the surrounding harmony.

---

[5]Hans F. Redlich, *Alban Berg* (Vienna, 1957), p. 328.

**EXAMPLE 5-31.** Berg: *Wozzeck,* Act I. Copyright 1931, Universal Edition. Used by permission of the publisher. Theodore Presser Company sole representative United States, Canada and Mexico.

### Quartal Chord With Tritones and Other Intervals

When successive sonorities are restricted to superpositions of any one interval—in other words, symmetric structuring—they tend to become static and lacking in forward propulsion. Composers soon realized the limitations of quartal chords as a primary constructive element for a composition and began to use them as one of a variety of chord types.

A variant of quartal harmony combines perfect fourths with tritones and other intervals. The following chords are all six-voice quartal chords, but each one has a tritone between notes 4 and 5, counting from the lowest note. It is a passage of planed sonorities which negates pitch focus and is harmonically static.

**EXAMPLE 5-32.** Satie: *Le Fils des Étoiles.* Used by permission of Editions Salabert, Paris.

The trichord containing a perfect fourth and a tritone became very popular with Schoenberg, Berg, and Webern. (Of course, it was used by many other composers, and still is.) Many works by these three Viennese composers use this chord for important harmonic ideas. Sometimes called a tritone-fourth chord or "Viennese fourth," three of the sonority's intervals were dissonances in music of the common practice period. The emphasis on the strong outside interval, the major seventh, removes it from the mild dissonance of stacked perfect fourths.

**EXAMPLE 5-33.** "Viennese fourth chord."

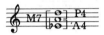

The quartal chord with tritone is often used in Webern's Variations for Piano. The final eleven measures of the third movement demonstrate its importance by the frequency with which such a sonority appears.

**EXAMPLE 5-34.** Webern: Variations for Piano, Op. 27, III. Copyright 1937, Universal Edition. Used by permission of the publisher. Theodore Presser Company sole representative United States, Canada and Mexico.

The earlier excerpt, Ex. 5-30, illustrated two perfect fourths separated by thirds. In the next example, perfect fourths are separated by seconds. The manner in which the chords are constructed makes it difficult to decide whether the perfect fourth or the perfect fifth is the predominant interval. The major second can also be understood as an added note.

**EXAMPLE 5-35.** Sessions: *From My Diary*, IV. © Copyright Edward B. Marks Music Corporation. Used by permission.

A four-note chord with two perfect fourths joined by a minor second is repeated hundreds of times in a piano work by Stockhausen (Ex. 5-36). The chord is never transposed throughout the composition, and is found only in the first two-thirds of the piano piece. Like the quartal chord with tritone ([0 5 6]), the quartal chord joined by minor second ([0 5 6 11]) occurs with great frequency in the twentieth century.

**EXAMPLE 5-36.** Stockhausen : *Klavierstück IX*, mm. 1–6. © 1967, Universal Edition. Used by permission of the publisher. Theodore Presser Company, sole representative United States, Canada and Mexico.

## Quintal Chords

   The perfect fifth is also used for chord generation by many composers in the twentieth century. Chords built on this interval have similar characteristics to quartal chords (the perfect fourth and fifth belong to the same interval class) and are used and varied with other intervals like the quartal chords. Two examples will illustrate its characteristics. The cello part in Ex. 5-37 clearly presents a reiterated quintal chord. It is heard with other chords above it that suggest perfect fourths with octave doublings.

   An extraordinary sound and timbre is created by Varèse in the final seventeen measures of the composition for percussion, *Ionisation,* when the pitched percussion instruments enter. Except for the massive tone cluster at the bottom of the piano keyboard, the main intervals in the passage are the perfect fifth and the diminished fifth. The right hand of the piano part is a quintal chord with tritone and is very similar to the chord built with a tritone and a perfect fourth. Only a portion of the total texture is quoted (Ex. 5-38).

**EXAMPLE 5-37.** Bartók: String Quartet No. 4, V. Copyright 1929 by Universal Edition; Renewed 1948. Copyright assigned to Boosey & Hawkes, Inc., for the U.S.A. Reprinted by permission of Boosey & Hawkes, Inc., and Universal Edition.

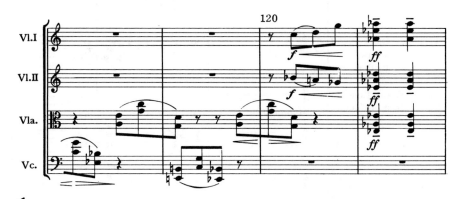

**EXAMPLE 5-38.** Varèse: *Ionisation,* at No. 13. Courtesy of Colfranc Music Publishing Corp, copyright owners.

10. . . . . . . . . . Cloches

*Sonna à doueble 8va*

11. . . . . . . Glockenspiel
à clavier
(with resonators)

12. . . . Grand Tam-tam
(tres profound)

attaque sèche (peroutèe) Laissez vibrer, durée indiquée

13. . . . . . . . . . .Piano

Pèdale
jusqu à la fin

*8va bassa* - - - - - - - - - - - - - - - - - - -

\*) Piano 3rd line Oppure ⸭ to the end as rhythmically indicated.

### Chords Based on Seconds

The use of major and minor seconds and their inversions as chordal material originates with harmony based on the whole-tone scale and from added-tone chords. In music employing whole-tone scale materials, many of the chords suggest that they are being built with major seconds. However, they rarely are grouped in clusters, but are spaced apart with intervening intervals of various sizes. Often seconds occur as sevenths and as ninths, which are compound seconds. They also appear as dyads as in the following example. All the notes in the passage fall within the whole-tone scale on C.

**EXAMPLE 5-39.** Debussy: *Preludes*, Book II, No. 12. Copyright 1913, Durand et Cie. Used by permission of the publisher. Elkan-Vogel, Inc. sole representative United States, Canada and Mexico.

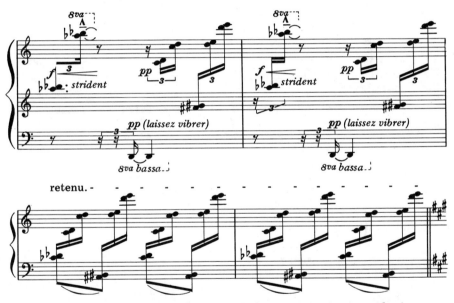

Example 5-40 has four-note chords built from two major seconds chosen from adjacent pitch classes in four-note segments of two forms of the twelve-tone set that is the basis of the composition. The harp part also derives its melodic materials from the series.

Bartók frequently uses seconds horizontally and vertically as important compositional material. In No. 107 of *Mikrokosmos* the main harmonic structures are built with seconds separated by minor thirds. In Ex. 5-41, from No. 144, he is concerned with the relations of seconds to sevenths. Minor seconds expand outward in both voices to major seconds, clusters, and other chords. The major sevenths are interpreted as minor seconds which are inverted: D-E♭ becomes E♭-D.

**EXAMPLE 5-40.** Webern: Symphony, Op. 21, II. Copyright 1929, Universal Edition. Used by permission of the publisher. Theodore Presser Company sole representative United States, Canada and Mexico.

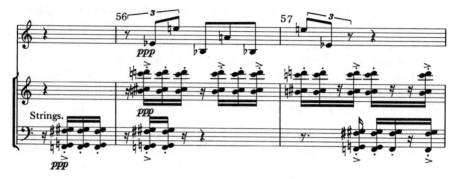

**EXAMPLE 5-41.** Bartók: *Mikrokosmos,* No. 144 ("Minor Seconds, Major Sevenths"). Copyright 1940 by Hawkes & Son (London) Ltd.; Renewed 1967. Reprinted by permission of Boosey & Hawkes, Inc.

## TONE CLUSTERS

Henry Cowell, the first composer to explore and discuss tone clusters theoretically,[6] was also one of the first to apply them consistently in his music (Ives preceded Cowell in using tone clusters in his Concord Sonata of 1909–1910). Cowell first performed a work with these new sounds in 1912. He believed that chords based on adjacent seconds were inevitable, since they are built from those partials that come after the thirds in the overtone series. He pointed out that "the natural spacing of so-called dissonances is as seconds, as in the overtone series, rather than sevenths and ninths. . . . Groups spaced in seconds may be made to sound euphonious, particularly if played in conjunction with fundamental chord notes taken from lower in the same overtone series. This blends them together and explains them to the ear."[7]

The publication *Piano Music by Henry Cowell* contains a variety of compositions with many unusual pianistic techniques. Most of them, like the tone cluster, provide new timbres and modes of expression. These techniques are often used in combination with more traditional elements, including a clearly diatonic tonal conception with key signature. One of the most unusual is *Tiger Rag*, composed in 1928. It abounds in tone clusters, large and small, performed in various manners to create different colors and articulations. The final ten measures give a good indication of this variety (Ex. 5-42). In the top system, the enormous tone clusters are played with the forearms. The small cluster chords in the middle system with the + sign are to be played with a slightly clenched fist, while in the last four measures fingers are used. The effect of the large clusters is more in the sphere of color, even noise, than pitch. Unlike most tonal and non-tonal linear dissonances, tone clusters are essentially static. The individual pitches are of secondary importance; it is the *sound mass* that is foremost.

Tone clusters are of vital structural significance in Bartók's Fourth String Quartet. A four-note major-second cluster and a four-note minor-second

---

[6]Henry Cowell, *New Musical Resources* (New York: Something Else Press, 1969), pp. 111–139.

[7]*Ibid.,* p. 115.

**EXAMPLE 5-42.** Cowell: *Tiger Rag.* Reprinted by permission of Associated Music Publishers, Inc.

cluster dominate a great deal of the harmonic material in the first movement. The cluster notes are also spread out texturally to sound as ninths, seconds, and sevenths.

The whole-tone cluster first occurs in a brief imitative passage near the beginning of the movement as an expansion of tetrachordal minor-second clusters. The cadence chord in m. 13 with its seven pitch classes is a combination of the minor-second and major-second clusters.

**EXAMPLE 5-43.** Bartók: String Quartet No. 4, I. Copyright 1929 by Universal Edition; Renewed 1948. Copyright assigned to Boosey & Hawkes, Inc., for the U.S.A. Reprinted by permission of Boosey & Hawkes, Inc., and Universal Edition.

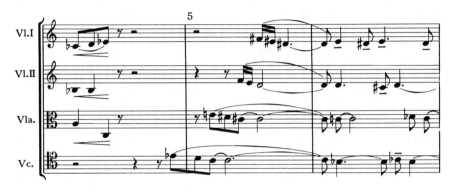

**EXAMPLE 5-43** continued.

One of the largest clusterings of individual pitches that has been written is the intensely emotional ending of *Threnody* by Penderecki. The large band of sound consists of fifty-two stringed instruments playing in quarter tones. This massive approach to sound seems to be the final development of sound for its own sake; in sound as mass, the total vertical (and horizontal) sound negates the identity of the single pitch and chord. The composer has notated the pitches because he desires the particular timbre of the register in which the sound band is heard. Except for the simultaneous sounding of many pitches, harmony no longer exists in this example.

**EXAMPLE 5-44.** Penderecki: *Threnody: To the Victims of Hiroshima.* Copyright 1969 by Polskie Wydawn Muzyczne. Used by permission of Polskie Wydawn Muzyczne and Belwin Mills Publishing Corp.

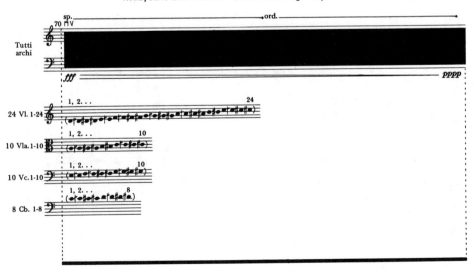

## PITCH CLASS DENSITY

An important change in twentieth-century chord structure has to do with chord density of pitch classes, i.e., the number of pitch classes present in any one chord. In the eighteenth and nineteenth centuries composers usually avoided overlaying their works with chords of more than four pitch classes; ninth chords, and even 11ths and 13ths, are often represented by a chord of four pitches, rarely occurring as complete sonorities. Most composers in our century do not restrict themselves in this manner. However, the sonorities are not usually heard as a complex of discrete, functional pitches, but as a sound aggregate with its own distinct color and expressive properties. The following is an extraordinary early example of a dense chord, expectedly used for expressive and dramatic, rather than harmonic functional purposes.

**EXAMPLE 5-45.** Beethoven: Symphony No. 9, IV, mm. 208–209.

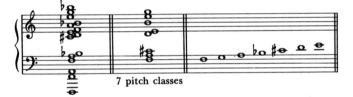

7 pitch classes

Many compositions in our century also utilize thick and complex harmonic textures; it is quite common to find chords with six or more pitch classes. Where a Romantic composer would often double (triple, etc.) three to five pitches to make a rich orchestral timbre, the chords could still be reduced to their simple structure of triads or higher tertian sonorities. But doublings are a secondary consideration when a chord (particularly a mixed-interval chord) contains eight or ten pitch classes. A doubled note in such a sonority would hardly bring a much greater emphasis to it when one considers the already apparent complexities in such a dense vertical structure. See Exx. 5-46(a) and 5-46(b).

Examples exist of harmonic structures using all twelve pitches of the chromatic scale. The Penderecki tone cluster in Ex. 5-44, of course, has many more pitch classes because of the divisions into quarter-tones. With electronic synthesizers it is possible to create simultaneities using even smaller divisions, thus greatly enlarging the spectrum of pitch classes.

**EXAMPLE 5-46(a).** Berg: *Wozzeck,* Act III. Copyright 1931, Universal Edition. Used by permission of the publisher. Theodore Presser Company sole representative United States, Canada and Mexico.

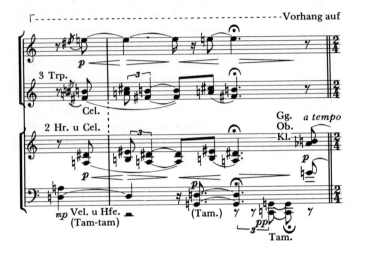

**EXAMPLE 5-46(b).** Varèse: *Intègrales*. Courtesy of Colfranc Music Publishing Corporation, copyright owners.

## MIXED-INTERVAL CHORDS

We have seen that non-tertian chords based on particular intervals are freely mingled with tertian sonorities and vice versa. Equal-interval chords are often altered to make them "impure" as in the case of quartal and quintal chords with tritones, or chords based on seconds with varying intervals between the seconds. Nevertheless, all of these sonorities have one characteristic generic interval.

An important procedure in twentieth-century chord construction that has not been discussed is the building of sonorities that are not characterized by one consistent interval. We shall refer to such sonorities as mixed-interval chords. They tend to lend themselves particularly to atonal music since they are usually "dissonant" structures.

Chords with mixed intervals can best be described by their intervallic content. In chords having only one interval type, root determination is usually irrelevant.[8] Generally, the abandonment of tonality signals the end of the necessity for a concept of root progression. The content of mixed-interval sonorities is limited only by the imagination of the composer. These chords adhere to no functional traditions and are interesting because of their activities within atonal contexts, their beauty as sound, and their relative degrees of tension or stability. Several excerpts of mixed-interval chords follow with little discussion.

In Ex. 5-47 tertian segments are present in mm. 128 and 129, but except for the MMM$_9$ on the second beat of m. 128, none of the chords, as totalities, have relations to past forms. The complete chords are highly dissonant, with each chord containing at least one major seventh or minor ninth.

Measures 1–10 of Ex. 5-48 seem tertian in their chord structuring, particularly because thirds are the predominant interval type (there are several minor triads in the first seven measures). Nevertheless, the intervals separating the two staves most often suggest mixed-interval simultaneities. The perfect fourth and perfect fifth, which are associated with thirds in the upper parts in mm. 1–10 become more obviously structural intervals in mm. 11–20, ultimately resolving the tension through linear contrary motion in mm. 18–20.

---

[8]In *The Craft of Musical Composition* Hindemith develops a theory of root determination for all chord structures, whether tertian or not. However, when complex chord structures are heard, especially mixed-interval ones, too often his root designations are based on an *a priori* theory rather than on aural perception. His theory is based on the root of the strongest, or most stable, interval in the chord. A hierarchy of intervals is determined by theoretical concepts. There is, of course, no doubt that certain intervals and pitches *may be* prominent in *any* chord due to doublings, spacing, instrumentation, rhythm, or dynamics, etc.

**EXAMPLE 5-47.** Schoenberg : *Erwartung*, Op. 17, Scene IV. Copyright 1922 by Wien Universal Edition. Renewed. 1950 by Edward Stevermann. Used by permission of Belmont Music Publishers, Los Angeles, California 90049.

**EXAMPLE 5-48.** Copland: Sonata for Piano. Copyright 1942 by Aaron Copland; Renewed 1969. Reprinted by permission of Aaron Copland, Copyright Owner, and Boosey & Hawkes, Inc., Sole Publishers and Licensees.

**EXAMPLE 5-48** continued.

In Ex. 5-49, every chord has a different interval content (and all except one have a strong dissonance); yet the tension of each chord changes by the pitch and textual rhythm, the voice leading, and the essentially outward movement of the soprano and bass parts. Also, the intervallic content is continually changing, although some chords have similarities. The cello obbligato duplicates very few of the pitches found in the immediate vocal sonorities.

The multiple-stop chords from Elliott Carter's String Quartet No. 1 (Ex. 5-50) provide a rich variety of mixed-interval structures. Every one of the sonorities (including the viola) has one or more sharp dissonances. It is interesting that most of the chords do not have doubled octaves, although there is no rigid attempt to exclude doublings as is often the case in twelve-tone music. The expansion of chordal range and increased chord density contributes to the climax in mm. 294–296.

Varèse's music is characterized by its sonority color, harmonic stasis, and a high degree of chord tension. The excerpt in Ex. 5-51 is one of many that could be cited from his *Intègrales*.

**EXAMPLE 5-49.** Horace Reisberg: *Do Not Go Gentle Into That Good Night.*

**EXAMPLE 5-49** continued.

**EXAMPLE 5-50.** Elliott Carter: String Quartet No. 1. Reprinted by permission of Associated Music Publishers, Inc.

**EXAMPLE 5-51.** Varèse: *Intégrales*. Courtesy of Colfranc Music Publishing Corporation, copyright owners.

**EXAMPLE 5-51** continued.

Since mixed-interval chords are most commonly found in music that is customarily described as atonal, we can expect them to be fundamental to vertical structure and organization in twelve-tone and other serial music. As quoted in *Harmonielehre*, Schoenberg speaks of his earlier atonal music and notes the "tendency to produce in the second chord tones that were lacking in the first. . . . Then, too, I have noticed that doublings of a tone, octaves, seldom occur . . . the doubled tone would acquire a preponderance over the others and thus become a sort of root, which it hardly ought to be. . . ."[9] The polyphonic, linearly produced harmony became more and more dissonant and achieved what he called "emancipation of the dissonance." The "emancipation" refers to his belief that the "dissonant" higher partials are really consonances that are simply located farther up in the overtone series. Theoretically, all twelve tones of the chromatic scale were resources equally available to the composer. The precompositional harmonic reference of seven-tone diatonic tonality—the consonant triad—no longer had primacy, and no *a priori* harmonic reference took its place except the *avoidance* of major and minor triads.

In the endeavors to deny tonality, non-tertian mixed-interval chords became the norm. Complex polyphonic textures with strongly dissonant simultaneities are the hallmark of the style. This was the ultimate result of

---

[9]William W. Austin, *Music in the 20th Century* (New York: W. W. Norton & Co., 1966), p. 204.

constant chromaticism, in which dissonance, as the result of contrapuntal movement of lines, became incorporated into vertical, nontertian sonorities.

One example from Schoenberg's pre-twelve-tone period will suffice to illustrate the completely free chromatic polyphony in which the twelve tones of the chromatic scale have attained equality. The past diatonic and consonant norms are gone. All twelve pitch classes have been presented before the clarinet's A♭. In these nine short measures there is an incredible variety of mixed-interval chords.

**EXAMPLE 5-52.** Schoenberg: *Pierrot Lunaire,* "Gebet an Pierrot." Copyright 1914 by Wien Universal. Renewed 1941 by Arnold Schoenberg. Used by permission of Belmont Music Publishers, Los Angeles, California 90049.

**EXAMPLE 5-52** continued.

The chords at the beginning of Op. 33a (Ex. 5-53), by Schoenberg, are four-note segments of a twelve-tone set. The vertical arrangement of the pitches is not determined by the serial adjacencies. In this instance Schoenberg chose certain constants: Class 1 intervals forming a second in the first and sixth chords; Class 1 intervals forming a seventh in the first, third, fourth, and sixth chords; and Class 5 and Class 6 intervals in the first, second, fourth, and fifth chords; the second and fifth chords have characteristics of more traditional chordal types.

The highly disjunct lines in Ex. 5-54 combine to form an almost chordal texture. The composer asks for three absolutely equal parts. The vertical-

**EXAMPLE 5-53.** Schoenberg: *Klavierstück*, Op. 33a. Copyright © 1929 Wien Universal Edition. Renewed 1956 by Gertrude Schoenberg. Used by permission of Belmont Music Publishers, Los Angeles, California 90049.

**EXAMPLE 5-54.** Boulez: Second Piano Sonata, p. 3. Copyright 1950, Heugel et Cie. Used by permission of the publisher. Theodore Presser Company, sole representative United States, Canada and Mexico.

les 3 parties absolument égales

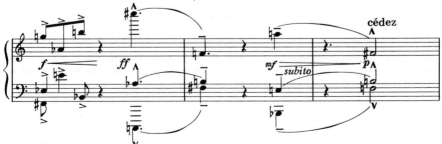

horizontal texture contains a variety of mixed-interval chords with changes in degree of consonance and dissonance.

Mixed-interval chords are commonly produced through the serial technique termed combinatoriality. (See Chapter Six for a full explanation of the term.) Since the purpose of combinatoriality is non-repetition of pitch classes, the resulting twelve-pitch aggregates will have a variety of non-tertian mixed-interval chords. The following prime and inversion forms of a set and an example from the composition in which they are used illustrate the technique. The dyads and trichords contain a variety of intervals.

**EXAMPLE 5-55(a).** Combinatorial Set Transpositions. Schoenberg: *Klavierstück*, Op. 33b.

**EXAMPLE 5-55(b).** Schoenberg: *Klavierstück*, Op. 33b. Copyright 1932 by Arnold Schoenberg. Renewed 1959 by Gertrude Schoenberg. Used by permission of Belmont Music Publishers, Los Angeles, California 90049.

## NEGATION OF HARMONY

Many of the viewpoints expressed in this chapter, together with a large number of the music illustrations strongly suggest that harmony, when viewed as the controlling aspect of the vertical dimension, has been declining since the dissolution of the major-minor tonal system. This implication is especially true in free atonal and serial compositions which are, to a great extent, contrapuntally motivated. We have seen that even music which is tonally oriented, in the sense of pitch focus, usually does not depend upon the referential laws of the functional system.

The simultaneities formed by the various parts in dissonant linear textures often do not seem to refer to a pre-conceived controlling norm; they also appear peripheral or secondary. A term that is often used to describe the forming of these simultaneities is *linear harmony*.

Linear harmony is an appropriate term for the vertical dimension in the first movement of Bartók's Music for Strings, Percussion and Celesta. The movement does have an ultimate tonal reference to A♮, but the main organizational procedures are melodic and contrapuntal. A typical example is the piling up of four of the five fugal entries at the beginning of the movement. No systematic chord generation is perceivable except the general principle of dissonances being present in every three- and four-note simultaneity.

**EXAMPLE 5-56.** Bartók: Music for Strings, Percussion, and Celesta, I. Copyright 1937 by Universal Edition; Renewed 1964. Copyright & Renewal assigned to Boosey & Hawkes, Inc., for the U.S.A. Reprinted by permission of Boosey & Hawkes, Inc., and Universal Edition.

**EXAMPLE 5-56** continued.

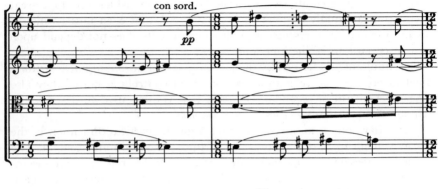

Because all voices in Ex. 5-56 have similar melodic and rhythmic materials, the total effect is homogeneity of sound from measure to measure. The excerpt in Ex. 5-57 is radically different. Each line has its own unique character, and pitch repetitions and doublings between lines are avoided. The total effect is a kind of highly chromatic polyphony. Except for chords in the piano part in mm. 7 and 10, chordal organization is not a relevant factor. Another aspect that removes the vertical from importance is the layering technique of the texture. The two upper instruments are one layer, the piano is another, and the reciter is a third layer.

More recent music shows the same negation of the harmonic principle as a controlled element in contemporary music. The complex texture in Ex. 5-58 is characterized by extremely disjunct lines and rapid changes of register within the lines. Counterpoint is the primary textural activity, and one may ask whether the vertical element exists at all. The only guide is consistency of vertical dissonance which, in the context, is stable and therefore consonant. It is a matter of changing degrees of tension. This kind of music makes even clearer what Schoenberg meant by the phrase "emancipation of the dissonance."

**EXAMPLE 5-57.** Schoenberg: *Pierrot Lunaire*, Op. 21, "Mondestrunken." Copyright 1914 by Wien Universal. Renewed 1941 by Arnold Schoenberg. Used by permission of Belmont Music Publishers, Los Angeles, California 90049.

**EXAMPLE 5-57** continued.

**EXAMPLE 5-58.** Boulez: Second Piano Sonata. Copyright 1950, Heugel et Cie. Used by permission of the publisher. Theodore Presser Company, sole representative United States, Canada and Mexico.

Each instrument in the Carter String Quartet No. 2 is assigned its own characteristic intervals. This alone would suggest a separation of the lines, but the character of each instrument's music is also quite different. In addition, the composer directs the players to be more widely spaced than usual in performance.

**EXAMPLE 5-59.** Carter: String Quartet No. 2. Reprinted by permission of Associated Music Publishers, Inc.

Another linear texture in which simultaneous combinations are apparently unrelated to the musical activity is cited in Ex. 5-60. The tempo, being very fast, makes it even more unlikely that the vertical is to be considered an important factor.

The tendency to remove the vertical dimension as an important structural force in music is found most often in music dating from about 1945–1950. The emphasis on rhythm, timbre, and texture, and an increasingly complex counterpoint suggests new organizations of sound which seem to be unrelated to past tradition. The conception of sound existing for its unique sonorous value is not new, of course; what is new is the use of vertical structures as masses and blocks of sound.

There is a view of sound that considers all pitches aggregated within a prescribed space and time as a single macrocosm of sound, whether or not the pitches are in motion. Within prescribed limits, these pitches are meant to operate more or less freely, depending upon the degree of control imposed by the composer. Xenakis describes his particular kinds of aggregates as "clouds" of sounds. There are numerous moving pitches, including glissandi, within the macroscopic space of the clouds. Their individual identities are not important. The timbre, rhythm, and registral disposition of the sounds in the total aggregate are more crucial than the perception of precise pitches. The vertical is there, but is heard as a texture and/or timbre.

**EXAMPLE 5-60.** Boulez: *Le Marteau sans maître,* I, mm. 1–11. © 1954, Universal Edition. Used by permission of the publisher. Theodore Presser Company, sole representative United States, Canada and Mexico.

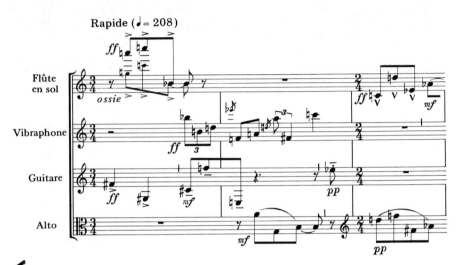

Example 5-61 is an example of the aggregation of pitches into what the composer calls a "sound." The music figures in the boxes are to be played without interruption in a varying and indeterminate order until the conductor gives the signal to go on to the next box (page 2 in the score). The unit of sound—horizontally and vertically—is the aggregate of the material in the boxes. It is as if each group of pitch conglomerations is a solitary event taking place in an allotted time span.

**EXAMPLE 5-61.** Joel Chadabe: *Monomusic*, p. 1. Used by permission.

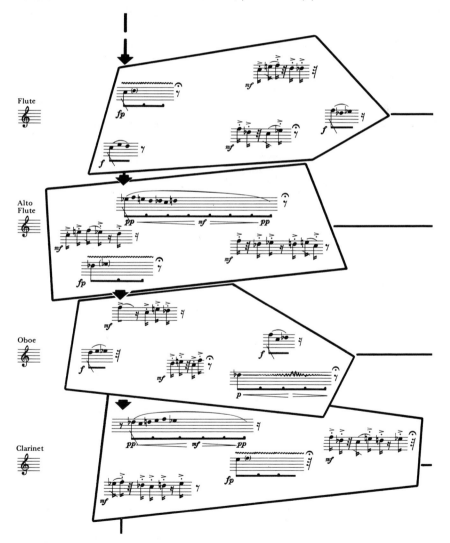

The groups of notes in boxes are similarly played in Berio's *Circles* (Ex. 5-62). The group of very small notes in the upper part of the score is heard as an intricate moment of sound, like a long grace note, which functions as an upbeat to the material in the following box.

Varèse anticipated many of the stylistic developments in music since World War II. *Intègrales* (1926; see Ex. 5-63) and *Ionisation* (1931) are based on sound masses in which rhythm, timbre, and dynamic intensity are the focal points. *Desèrts*, from 1954, exhibits similar characteristics. Harmony and melody have no traditional meaning here; in fact, pitch and sound repetition is so characteristic that a certain static effect within the sound masses is evident. The subtle changes in color and rhythm provide dynamic variety.

The irrelevance of "harmony" in the more recent developments in instrumental and vocal music is echoed in electronic compositions. The acoustical possibilities of electronic modes of sound production allow the composer to create sounds that are not accessible with traditional instruments. Electronic equipment can produce all frequencies perceivable by the ear, and allows a fantastic control over time relations and timbres that is impossible to achieve with human performers and the traditional means of sound generation.

Although it is possible to analyze the make-up of any sound with modern equipment, the individual components of an electronic sound are not important. The timbre, density, attack, amplitude, duration, etc., of a sound are the musical material, not the elements that make the sound.

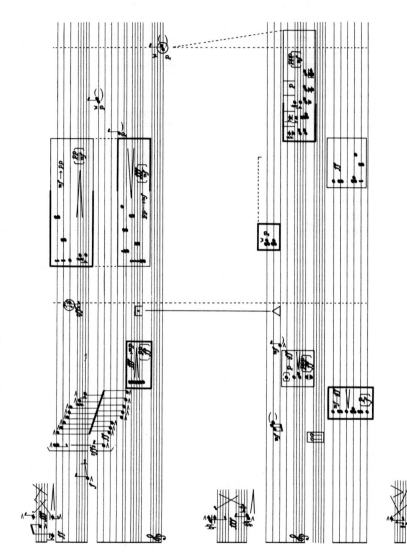

EXAMPLE 5-62. Berio: *Circles*. Reprinted by permission of Associated Music Publishers, Inc.

**EXAMPLE 5-63.** Varèse : *Intègrales,* p. 24. Courtesy of Colfranc Music Publishing Corporation. copyright owners.

This mode of thinking tends to preclude a conception of a texture of several lines, or parts, as in the past. The tendency away from a linear approach to music, in favor of sound as the determinative material, has been mentioned often in this chapter. One can go back as far as the rudimentary examples of Debussy, or the more advanced and subtle approach of Schoenberg in *Summer Morning By a Lake*, the third piece of Op. 16 (Ex. 5-64). His subtitle (*Colors*) shows his intention. Notice the very subtle pitch and color changes between instruments within a basically static texture.

A recent work (1967) by Kenneth Gaburo (Ex. 5-65) uses live instruments and vocal sound, as well as electronic sound generation. The geometric shapes in the score give a graphic suggestion of phrase shapes, sound durations, and sound intensity. The voice part is composed of recorded sounds and their transformations. This is represented by phonetic symbols.

**EXAMPLE 5-64.** Schoenberg: Five Pieces for Orchestra, III. Copyright © 1952 by Henmar Press Inc., New York.

The change of chords in this piece has to be executed with the greatest subtlety, avoiding accentuations of entering instruments, so that only the difference of color becomes noticeable.

The conductor need not try to polish sounds which seem unbalanced but watch that every instrumentalist plays accurately the prescribed dynamic, according to the nature of the instrument. There are no motives in the piece which have to be brought to the fore.

**EXAMPLE 5-65.** Gaburo: *Antiphony IV*. Used by permission.

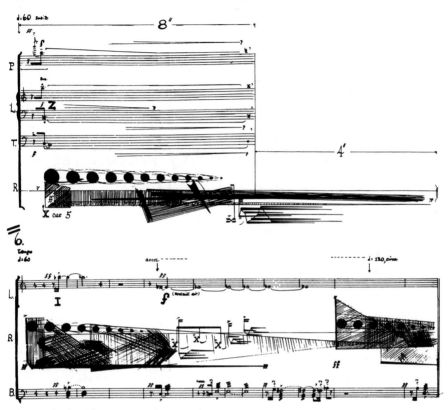

A great many compositions could be cited from our modern period (since about 1950), in which the vertical dimension has ceased to be a prime element of musical construction. Vertical structures still exist, but their function within the organization of sound has little or no resemblance to the central position that harmony held in pre-twentieth-century music. Although this essay has not been chronologically organized, the discussion shows that the history of "harmony" in our century points to a gradual decline of controlled vertical organization. It may be that since major-minor tonality and its attendant functional harmony no longer meets the needs of composers, it was inevitable that vertical organization would go through a process of dissolution.

chapter six

# Sets and Ordering Procedures in Twentieth-Century Music

GARY E. WITTLICH

During the early twentieth century it became clear to many composers that the triadic tonal system was no longer a viable one for the creation of new musical art works. Merely to decorate traditional tonal schema with elaborate chromaticism was not in the final analysis a satisfactory solution to the question of how to create something new and aesthetically satisfying in music. What was necessary was a radical revision of musical thought which could result in the establishment of a new musical dialectic, something that neither the short-lived impressionist school nor the magnificent early and revolutionary contributions of Stravinsky really provided, though obviously these works helped to make the break with traditional music.

Much experimentation in musical composition took place in the early twentieth century. Among the numerous ideas that came to the fore, one has proved to be systematic enough conceptually and sufficiently viable compositionally to have made a significant impact on the course of musical thought. This is the twelve-note (also called twelve-tone or dodecaphonic) method invented by Arnold Schoenberg.

Schoenberg believed that in music ". . . there is no form without logic, no logic without unity."[1] To provide both logic to guide the compositional process and a means of guaranteeing unity within a musical work, he devised his method of pitch organization, the basis of which is an ordered set or series (hence the term *serial*) of the twelve pitch classes[2] provided by the equal-tempered tuning system. In this method, the relationship of the notes to one another is guaranteed primarily by the interval succession defined by the note ordering of the basic set. Essentially, twelve-note music restores intervallic relations to the prominent position this aspect of the pitch dimension occupied in music prior to the establishment of the major-minor tonal system.

The primary purpose of this chapter is to present the basic elements of the twelve-note method as employed by composers during the second quarter of this century. To the extent that factors such as rhythm, texture, form, and the like may be related to or determined by the twelve-note structure of a work, these will also be discussed. Generally, however, the reader should refer to the other chapters of this book for explication of these details. Following the discussion of twelve-note music is a brief examination of extensions of the twelve-note concept to the serial control of dimensions other than pitch to create examples of so-called multi-serialized music. The final portion of the chapter is devoted to a brief look at some pre-serial atonal music, in particular works by Schoenberg and Webern that preceded and gave rise to the invention of the twelve-note method. This body of music is placed last in the chapter since its details may be more easily understood—and appreciated—in relation to the more systematically organized twelve-note works. All technical terms used in the chapter are defined at the end.

As a point of departure, we provide the following set of general principles underlying the twelve-note method as conceived by Schoenberg and adopted in spirit by his followers:

1. A twelve-note set is an ordered arrangement of the twelve pitch classes.
2. Four forms of the set are possible: prime (or original), retrograde (the prime in reverse order), inversion (the prime with inverted intervals), and retrograde inversion. Each form may begin on any one of the twelve pitch classes, thus providing a matrix of 48 different ordered versions of any one twelve-note set. (Limitations on the number of versions available will be noted later.)

---

[1] Arnold Schoenberg, "Composition With Twelve Tones," in *Style and Idea* tr. Dika Newlin (New York: Philosophical Library, 1950), p. 143. The reader is referred to this essay for an understanding of Schoenberg's reasons for and certain aspects of his method.

[2] The term *pitch class* is preferred to *pitch* since it is more general; that is, *pitch class* refers to a note and any and all of its octave duplications, while *pitch* implies a specific frequency. A list of terms and their definitions appears at the end of this chapter.

3. The order of notes within a form is fixed and only immediate repetitions of a note are allowed before all other notes of the form appear. As an exception, trills of adjacent notes are allowed.
4. Any note of the set may appear in any octave.
5. A twelve-note work consists of successive statements of forms of the set (and their transpositions) selected and disposed according to the composer's desires.

## 1.0 THE TWELVE-NOTE SET

Example 6-1 shows the four forms of the basic set from Schoenberg's Fourth String Quartet. The four forms, prime (P), retrograde (R), inversion (I), and retrograde inversion (RI) are read in the direction of the arrows.

**EXAMPLE 6-1.** Schoenberg: String Quartet No. 4, Op. 37, I. Copyright 1937 by G. Schirmer, Inc. Used by permission.

P →                           ← R      I →                           ← RI

For purposes of discussion, the set is represented in an abstract version with all notes appearing within one octave. A note not preceded by an accidental is presumed to be natural. These notational practices will be followed in general throughout the chapter.

The interval structure of the set serves as a limitation on the permutational variety made possible by the transposed forms. Transposition does not affect the interval structure of a set of notes, and thus a twelve-note set generates only four rather than forty-eight different interval sequences: P, R, I, and RI. And this number may be cut in half by constructing the set as a self-contained mirror pattern in which the interval succession is the same in prime and retrograde ordering (examples of this type of set will be dealt with shortly). Thus, perception of the structure of a set or of a set segment depends primarily on one's ability to perceive and to remember interval patterns. However, in contrast to traditional music, in which a melodic element is generally characterized by the preservation of its contour, twelve-note music is characterized by a rather great variety of melodic shapes, in part because the notes of the set forms employed may appear in any octave, which may cause intervals to be compounded and/or inverted. Thus the interval structure of the set can be and generally is considerably varied during the course of a composition.

Variety can also be created by other factors, such as the vertical alignment of parts (each of which might have a different set form), by reorderings, and by changing patterns of rhythm, dynamics, articulation, and timbre. In general, the twelve-note set serves as an unobtrusive unifying agent whose organizing role is more felt than directly perceived, notwithstanding the continuous reiteration of the set and its associated forms throughout a composition.

## 1.1 Numbering

To facilitate discussion of twelve-note works, it is common practice to number the notes of a set as shown below. The set is that of Ex. 6-1 above. The numbers below the letters are *pitch class numbers* determined by semitone distances measured *above* some more or less arbitrarily selected starting note numbered 0. Thus, in pitch class numbers, 0–11 is a major seventh, 0–7 a perfect fifth, and so forth.

| Order nos. | 0 | 1 | 2 | 3 | 4 | 5 | 6 | 7 | 8 | 9 | 10 | 11 |
|---|---|---|---|---|---|---|---|---|---|---|---|---|
| Pitch | D | C♯ | A | B♭ | F | E♭ | E | C | A♭ | G | F♯ | B |
| Class nos. | 0 | 11 | 7 | 8 | 3 | 1 | 2 | 10 | 6 | 5 | 4 | 9 |

Here D is 0 because the linear ordering first given in the composition begins on D. It makes no difference which note is chosen as 0 so long as all other notes are numbered in semitones above 0 and all other forms are related to the prime form beginning on 0. The zero element may change for different movements of a multi-movement composition, as for example in the third movement of Schoenberg's Fourth Quartet, which begins with a unison statement of the prime form of the set transposed to begin on C (see Ex. 6-24).

The numbers above the letters are *order numbers*, that is, the numbers associated with the ordinal positions of the notes in the set. The numbers 0–11 are used (rather than 1–12) so that both the order and pitch-class numbering schemes correspond. Numbers appearing in musical examples throughout this chapter will be order numbers.

## 1.2 Transposition and Inversion of Numerical Sets

When using the set of numbers 0–11 to denote pitch classes, we adopt the following principles:

1. Transposition (T) amounts to adding a constant number (from 0–11) to each member of given pitch class set. For example, given the set (1 4 7), transposition a perfect fifth higher amounts to adding the number 7 (seven semitones) to each pitch class of the set:

$$
\begin{array}{lrrr}
\text{given:} & 1 & 4 & 7 \\
\text{add:} & 7 & 7 & 7 \\
\hline
 & 8 & 11 & 14
\end{array}
$$

From any number(s) exceeding 11, subtract 12 until the result falls within the range of 0–11. In this case, 14 becomes 2. The resultant set is (8 11 2). Transposition is always assumed in a upward direction.

2. Inversion (I) amounts to complementing pitch classes, that is, subtracting each given pitch class from 12. For example, the inversion of a perfect fifth is a perfect fourth. This is found by subtracting 7 from 12 to get 5. Under simple inversion, 0 remains 0 since $12 - 0 = 12$, and (because 12 exceeds 11) $12 - 12 = 0$.

3. Tranposed Inversion (TI) amounts to the operation of inversion followed by transposition. For example, given the pitch class set (1 5 6), the inversion transposed a perfect fourth higher is determined as follows:

$$
\begin{array}{rccc}
\text{given:} & 1 & 5 & 6 \\
\text{I:} & 11 & 7 & 6 \\
\text{add:} & 5 & 5 & 5 \\
\hline
\text{result:} & 16 & 12 & 11 \\
\text{subtract:} & 12 & 12 & \\
\hline
\text{T}_5\text{I:} & 4 & 0 & 11
\end{array}
$$

Thus the inversion transposed five semitones higher of (1 5 6) is (4 0 11).

Another and shorter way to obtain the same results is to add to each member of the given set that number necessary to produce a constant sum representing the interval of transposition:

$$
\begin{array}{rccc}
\text{given:} & 1 & 5 & 6 \\
\text{add:} & ? & ? & ? \\
\hline
\text{sum:} & 5 & 5 & 5
\end{array}
$$

The missing numbers are 4, 0, and 11 (the last sum being $6 + 11 - 12$).

4. To determine the absolute interval succession of a string of pitch classes, always subtract the left number from the right, adding 12 where necessary to the right. For example, given the string of pitch classes 4 7 3 11 2, the succession of intervals is 3 8 8 3.

The reader familiar with modulus (base 12, or "clock-face") arithmetic will recognize the above principles as deriving from this system. The number 12 is the modulus of the system (that is, the number of numbers in the system). It is common practice to speak of the "set of pitch classes (mod 12)."

### 1.3 The Matrix of Set Forms

When examining a twelve-note composition for its set structure, it is helpful to list the possible set forms for reference. A convenient method of listing the forms is the matrix (sometimes called a "magic square") shown on page 393. Both letter-name and numerical pitch class matrices are given for the set of Ex. 6-1. In the matrix, all rows read from left to right are prime forms, and all columns read from top to bottom are inversions. Reading in the opposite directions gives the retrograde forms.

```
P→                              ←R    P→                              ←R
I↓ D  C♯ A  B♭ F  E♭ E  C  A♭ G  F♯ B   I↓0 11  7  8  3  1  2 10  6  5  4  9
   E♭ D  B♭ B  F♯ E  F  C♯ A  G♯ G  C      1  0  8  9  4  2  3 11  7  6  5 10
   G  F♯ D  E♭ B♭ A♭ A  F  C♯ C  B  E      5  4  0  1  8  6  7  3 11 10  9  2
   F♯ F  C♯ D  A  G  A♭ E  C  B  B♭ E♭     4  3 11  0  7  5  6  2 10  9  8  1
   B  B♭ F♯ G  D  C  C♯ A  F  E  E♭ A♭     9  8  4  5  0 10 11  7  3  2  1  6
   C♯ C  A♭ A  E  D  E♭ B  G  F♯ F  B♭    11 10  6  7  2  0  1  9  5  4  3  8
   C  B  G  A♭ E♭ C♯ D  B♭ F♯ F  E  A     10  9  5  6  1 11  0  8  4  3  2  7
   E  E♭ B  C  G  F  F♯ D  B♭ A  A♭ C♯     2  1  9 10  5  3  4  0  8  7  6 11
   A♭ G  E♭ E  B  A  B♭ F♯ D  C♯ C  F      6  5  1  2  9  7  8  4  0 11 10  3
   A  A♭ E  F  C  B♭ B  G  E♭ D  C♯ F♯     7  6  2  3 10  8  9  5  1  0 11  4
   B♭ A  F  F♯ C♯ B  C  A♭ E  E♭ D  G      8  7  3  4 11  9 10  6  2  1  0  5
   F  E  C  C♯ A♭ F♯ G  E♭ B  B♭ A  D      3  2 10 11  6  4  5  1  9  8  7  0
                              RI↑                                     RI↑
```

To construct a matrix, list the original prime form as the top row and the inversion of this form as the leftmost column. All subsequent rows will be prime forms beginning on successive notes of the inversion. All subsequent columns will be inversions starting on successive notes of the original prime form. The principal diagonal (upper left to lower right) will always be the zero element, in this case the note D.

### 1.4 Index Numbers

An index number associated with the symbols P and I refers to the pitch-class number on which these forms *begin*. For example, $P_0$ is the prime form beginning on 0, $P_1$ the prime a semitone higher, and so forth, through $P_{11}$. Similarly, $I_0$ is the inversion beginning on 0, $I_1$ the inversion a semitone higher, etc. For retrograde forms, the index refers to the *last* note. For example, $R_0$ is the retrograde of $P_0$, $R_1$ the retrograde of $P_1$, etc., and $RI_0$ is the retrograde of $I_0$, $RI_1$ the retrograde of $I_1$, etc. This convention ties together the P and R and the I and RI forms, e.g., $P_0$ and $R_0$ refer to prime and retrograde versions of the same ordered collection.[3]

### 2.0 TYPES OF TWELVE-NOTE SETS

For the purpose of the following discussion twelve-note sets are grouped into two separate but by no means mutually exclusive categories: sets with tonal implications and sets with no apparent tonal implications. In general the sets of the former category are deployed compositionally so as to suggest

---

[3]This procedure of numbering R forms dates from about 1960. In sources appearing prior to that time, and in some cases still, R forms are often indexed according to their first notes.

changing or momentary tonal centers, while those of the latter category are stated so as to avoid tonal implications. However, either type may be manipulated to imply tonal or atonal contexts, and even the compositions utilizing "tonal" sets tend ultimately to resolve activity in favor of atonal or ambiguous tonal contexts.

### 2.1 Sets With Tonal Implications

Perhaps the most famous set of this type is found in Alban Berg's last completed work, the Violin Concerto. The set and an excerpt from the work appear in Ex. 6-2.

**EXAMPLE 6-2(a).** Berg: Violin Concerto (1935). Copyright 1936, Universal Edition. Used by permission of the publisher. Theodore Presser Company sole representative United States, Canada and Mexico.

**EXAMPLE 6-2(b).** Berg: Ibid., mm. 11–14. Copyright 1936, Universal Edition. Used by permission of the publisher. Theodore Presser Company sole representative United States, Canada and Mexico.

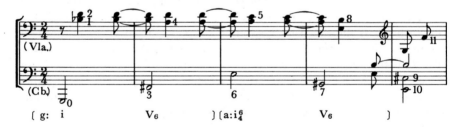

The tonal possibilities of the set are indicated in Ex. 6-2(a). The particular spatial version given is played by the solo violin in mm. 15–18. The tonal implications of the set are made clear in the compositional presentation shown in Ex. 6-2(b). The final four notes of the set are also used in a tonal context in the concluding portion of the concerto as the initial notes of the chorale tune *Es ist genug!* ("It is enough") which is made the subject for a set of variations. (For another set with similar tonal implications, see Ex. 6-31.)

Another twelve-note work with tonal implications is Hans Werner Henze's *Apollo and Hyacinth*, for alto voice, piano, and eight instruments. The set and an excerpt from the work appear in Ex. 6-3. Unlike the clear suggestion of tonal centers found in Berg's Concerto, Henze juxtaposes the triads of his set in this excerpt to suggest a polytonal texture. The notes E and B sounding

**EXAMPLE 6-3.** Henze: *Apollo and Hyacinth* (1957). Copyright 1967 by B. Schott's Soehne, Used with permission. All rights reserved.

as the lowest part in the excerpt are not adjacent notes in the set but are selected to suggest another traditional rooted sonority along with the three above it. This type of purposeful juggling of the linear order of a set (see also the previous example) is common in twelve-note compositions and will be taken up separately later in this chapter.

A third example of a tonal type of set is that used by Luigi Dallapiccola in his group of piano pieces *Quaderno musicale di Annalibera*. Each of the two hexachords (six-note groups) of the set can be related to a particular tonal center, though Dallapiccola does not stress particular tonal regions but rather vaguely suggests tonal patterns. Notice in the excerpt that the upper notes of the right hand trace the famous motive on Bach's name (B♭ A C B), in this case transposed to begin on E♭. Reference to Bach is also suggested by the title of the work, *Musical Notebook of Annalibera,* which recalls Bach's composition similarly named for Anna Magdalena Bach. This and other similarly derived motives can also be found in other twelve-note works, e.g., Schoenberg's Variations for Orchestra, Op. 31, Webern's String Quartet, Op. 28, and Berg's *Chamber* Concerto.

**EXAMPLE 6-4.** Dallapiccola: *Quaderno musicale di Annalibera* (1952), No. 1, "Simbolo," mm. 1–5. By permission of the Edizioni Suvini Zerboni, Milano.

Before looking at other sets, we note another characteristic of the set employed by Dallapiccola in the *Quaderno*. In the excerpt below from the sixth piece, each of the eleven intervals from the minor second through the major seventh is present. Sets with this characteristic are appropriately called *all-interval* sets. Such sets provide the utmost in built-in interval variety and have been used by numerous composers.

**EXAMPLE 6-5.** Dallapiccola: *Quaderno,* No. 6, "Fregi," mm. 1–4. By permission of the Edizioni Suvini Zerboni, Milano.

## 2.2 Sets With No Apparent Tonal Implications

The majority of twelve-note sets do not imply nor are they normally deployed to create or suggest tonal contexts, although even within these "atonal" sets it is common to find small note groups, or cells, that in some contexts might be perceived as tonal in nature.

One set cited frequently in writings about twelve-note music is that of Webern's Concerto for Nine Instruments, Op. 24, shown in Ex. 6-6. Each three-note cell of this set contains the same intervals: 1, 3, and 4. Further, each of the trichords *b*, *c* and *d* is derived from *a*: *b* is an RI form of *a*, *c* is an R form, and *d* is an I form. Sets built in this manner are called *derived* sets.[4] As one might expect with a set so carefully constructed, Webern exploits the trichordal structure in the Concerto (e.g., see Ex. 6-12).

**EXAMPLE 6-6.** Basic set from Webern: Concerto, Op. 24 (1934).

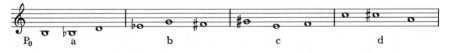

Another set with derived segments is that of Webern's String Quartet, Op. 28, in which the second tetrachord is a transposed retrograde form and the third a simple transposed form of the first tetrachord.[5] Notice that the outer

---

[4]The term originates with Milton Babbitt; see his article "Some Aspects of Twelve-Tone Composition," *The Score and I. M. A. Magazine,* 12 (June, 1955), p. 59.

[5]The symbol T denotes transposition.

tetrachords are BACH collections, although, as the excerpt below from the opening of the first movement demonstrates, the nature of the writing obscures the motive.

**EXAMPLE 6-7.** Webern: String Quartet, Op. 28 (1937–38) 1, mm. 1–6. Copyright 1939, Universal Edition. Used by permission of the publisher. Theodore Presser Company sole representative United States, Canada and Mexico.

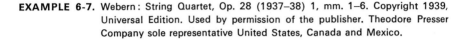

### 2.3 Set Type

Before looking at other atonal sets, we introduce another analytical aid, the *set type*. The term set type is used in this discussion to denote a generic interval collection. For example, in the set of Webern's Concerto (Ex. 6-6), each trichord consists of the same set of intervals, though each is uniquely ordered. For convenience, we may represent each of these trichords by the symbol (0 1 4), that is, a type of pitch class set that includes the three intervals (0 1), (0 4), and (1 4) or, simply, the intervals 1, 3, and 4 as measured in semitones. In the twelve-note set of the String Quartet (Ex. 6-7), each tetrachord is an (0 1 2 3) set type, that is, a collection containing six intervals: three interval 1, two interval 2, and one interval 3.

To determine a set type, consider a set of pitch classes in its *normal form*, that is, in the particular ascending order with the smallest interval between the first and last notes.[6] For example, the normal form of the first trichord of

Ex. 6-6 is . To derive the set type, associate 0 with the

first note and number upward in semitones, giving (0 1 4). Similarly, the

normal form of the first tetrachord of Ex. 6-7 is , and
the set type is (0 1 2 3).

Some sets can be reduced to a normal form in which the smaller intervals

are at the top (to the right) of the collection, e.g.,    To

determine the set type of this and all similarly arranged sets, associate 0 with the top note and read from right to left (downward) in semitones. If the numbers are rearranged in ascending order, the set type is (0 1 5) in this case.[7]

The set type is a convenient abstraction for reducing the multiplicity of interval collections to basic types. It is analogous to the familiar notion of the triad which normally suggests a collection of intervals arranged in root position and which is representative of any and all transpositions and inversions i.e., $\frac{6}{3}$ and $\frac{6}{4}$). At the same time, however, the set type concept extends beyond the notion of chord quality to one of complete generality of interval structure. For example, the set type (0 1 5) refers to both of the collections (EFA) and (EG♯A), which are transposed retrograde inversions of each other,[8] while triads are generally regarded exclusively in terms of quality, even though major and minor triads contain exactly the same inter-

---

[6]Babbitt, Milton, "Set Structure as a Compositional Determinant," *Journal of Music Theory* V/1 (April, 1967), p. 77.

[7]When read from left to right, (E G♯ A) is (0 4 5), but (0 4 5) is RI₅ of
(0 1 5):     (0 4 5)    The two sets are identical in terms of interval content,
             I₅(5 1 0)    and this is true of any sets related by inversion.
             RI₅(0 1 5)

[8]The notion of set type derives from Allen Forte's "A Theory of Set-Complexes for Music," *Journal of Music Theory* VIII 12 (Winter, 1964), pp. 136–83. In the article, Forte lists all possible set types with their interval class contents.

vals. In the music with which we will be concerned in this chapter, the root concept is no longer valid. Furthermore, except for linear set statements, ordering is often not a perceivable aspect of the pitch materials; this is particularly true of pre-serial atonal music and of some freer twelve-note compositions.

### 2.4 Symmetry

Returning to the set from Webern's Quartet (Ex. 6-7), the diagram below demonstrates another feature of its interval structure, namely *symmetry*. This kind of mirror symmetry (found also in the sets of Webern's Symphony, Op.

|   | G | F♯ | A | A♭ | C | C♯ | A♯ | B | E♭ | D | F | E |
|---|---|---|---|---|---|---|---|---|---|---|---|---|
| intervals | 1 | | 3 | | 1 | | 4 | | 1 | | 3 | 1 |

21, Cantata 1, Op. 29, and Variations for Orchestra, Op. 30) provides a limitation on the total potential of the set, for in such cases there are only twenty-four different forms possible rather than forty-eight; there will always be some retrograde inversion form identical with some prime, and, similarly, some retrograde form identical with some inversion. Thus, when dealing with a work based on a symmetrical set,[9] designations of set forms may be limited to P and R (or I) forms, the particular designations depending on the details of the work. The use of such sets is indicative of a trend in twentieth-century music toward symmetry of all kinds, particularly by serial composers and by other composers who have apparently thought along serial lines, e.g., Bartók, Scriabin, and Stravinsky in many of his pre-serial works. Later in the chapter examples of other kinds of symmetry will be noted.

Symmetry of a different kind is noted in the following twelve-note set from Luigi Nono's *Il canto sospeso*. When the set is arranged as shown below, each interval of the first half of the set is found in its complementary form in the second half with the complements appearing in retrograde order as shown by the brackets. Appropriately, such collections are called *symmetrical all-interval* sets.

Intervals: 1 2 3 4 5 6 7 8 9 10 11

---

[9]Symmetry here refers to the type characteristic of a set whose interval succession is the same read forwards or backwards. Such sets, whether of twelve or fewer notes, have the property that some retrograde inversion will reproduce the original set, e.g., the set (B C E F) under RI₆.

### 2.5 Embedded Subsets

The majority of sets have no particular symmetrical features, but in most there will be subsets of the same set type embedded within the set that aid in unifying the collection. Consider as an example the set given earlier from Schoenberg's Fourth String Quartet. Solid brackets mark (0 1 5) trichords, and slurs mark (0 1 2) types. The successive tetrachords marked by dotted brackets are (0 1 2 5) types, while the vertical line separates two (0 1 4 5 6 8) hexachords.

**EXAMPLE 6-8.** Embedded set types in the set from Schoenberg's String Quartet No. 4.

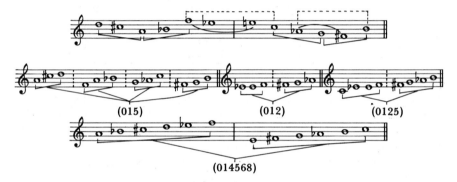

Each of the set types shown, especially the (0 1 5) trichord and the hexachord types, plays an important role in the organization of the work (see Section 5.0 of this chapter for a discussion of the set structure of a portion of the third movement of the Quartet.) In general, details of the sort described here can be found in most twelve-note sets. It is not always the case that the subsets revealed by analysis of the set play prominent roles in the composition from which it is taken, but careful examination of the set can usually lead one to discoveries about the pitch and interval structure of a composition by suggesting ways in which the set might logically be employed (more will be said about this in the following pages).

### 3.0 COMPOSITIONAL PRESENTATIONS OF SETS

The manner in which sets appear compositionally varies from work to work and, generally, within a work. Sometimes the set is exposed initially as a melody, while in other cases the notes of the set may appear initially as a series of chords. In most compositions the basic set is revealed clearly at some point by a linear ordering to which the various transposed forms can be related, although there are twelve-note works in which the basic set as a particular ordered collection can only be inferred by piecing together ordered segments appearing at various points within the composition. Moreover, in some twelve-note works specific ordering as such is secondary in importance to the preservation of the unordered content of set segments. The remaining portion of this discussion of twelve-note music is devoted to details of set presentation, beginning with linear statements.

### 3.1 Linear Set Presentation

Frequently the set is exposed as an unaccompanied melodic line, as for example in the excerpt from the opening measures of George Rochberg's Symphony No. 2, shown in Ex. 6-9. Here the set is articulated in three discrete note groups. Throughout the work the rhythmic patterns, the pitch and interval relations and the contours of this opening statement serve as prominent unifying elements.

Another and somewhat more common procedure of linear set presentation is shown in Ex. 6-10 from Dallapiccola's *Canti di liberazioni* for chorus and orchestra. The set is exposed in successive segments through several voices and is joined (aided by the common tone, C) to another set form ($R_7$, the last note of which does not appear in the example) to create a long and lyrical line. The joining of two set forms to comprise a thematic unit serves to underscore Ernst Křenek's pertinent observation that theme and set are not necessarily synonymous.[10] In fact, most twelve-note music is characterized more by motivic than by thematic unity; themes in this music are generally not twelve notes long.

---

[10]Ernst Křenek, *Studies in Counterpoint* (New York: G. Schirmer, Inc., 1940), p. 3.

**EXAMPLE 6-9.** George Rochberg: Symphony No. 2 (1955–56), I, mm. 1–4. © 1958, Theodore Presser Company. Used by permission.

**EXAMPLE 6-10.** Dallapiccola: *Canti di liberazioni* (1955), No. 2, mm. 1–6. By permission of the Edizioni Suvini Zerboni, Milano.

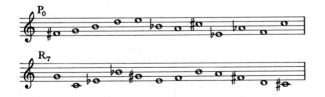

### 3.2 Segmentation

It is easily demonstrable that the human mind has definite limitations regarding the perception and memory of discrete stimuli.[11] Generally, one can distinguish among and remember about five to seven different items presented successively. Throughout history composers have recognized the limitation of memory and have organized their music accordingly. Most tonal themes, for example, do not contain more than six or seven different pitches (excluding repetitions) without including some sort of punctuation or melodic and/or rhythmic grouping. Similarly, most twelve-note sets are not presented compositionally as a series of twelve separate notes. Rather, they are usually deployed in smaller segments of varying lengths, with the upward limit commonly being six different notes. And as the manner of presentation more radically departs from tradition (say, Webern as compared with Schoenberg), it is often the case that segments become smaller and rests become more frequent in order to aid the listener in his perception of the materials.

Often the set is so structured as to suggest possibilities for statement in segments. For example, consider the opening of Webern's Concerto, Op. 24 (Ex. 6-11), which bases its pitch organization on the derived set shown earlier in Ex. 6-6. Here the four trichordal segments of the set are stated by different instruments, creating a type of linear presentation often described by the term *Klangfarbenmelodie*, that is, a melody of tone colors. Many composers have been influenced by this procedure, e.g., Dallapiccola, Stravinsky (especially in his late works), Boulez, Stockhausen, and Babbitt.

Example 6-12 from the first of Webern's Three Songs, Op. 25, demonstrates how a particular set type derived from the twelve-note collection upon which a work is based can be employed as a unifying agent by associating it with a particular rhythm. The opening measures of the song establish the mode of presentation used throughout. The set is unified by the (0 1 4) cells shown by the brackets. The triplet sixteenth-note rhythmic figure is associated only with this set type. Its frequent appearance in the song thus provides a strong cohesive element. Adding to the unity is that the piano plays only this triplet pattern, a few single notes, linear dyads, and four-note chords made up of dyad pairs. The dyads and tetrachords, however, are not tied to particular set types.

Common to many twelve-note compositions is the division of the set into two hexachords (e.g., Exx. 6-13, 6-20, 6-24). The reasons for hexachordal segmentation are numerous. For one, *complementary* hexachords (i.e., any pair of hexachords which together give all twelve pitch classes) will generally

---

[11]In this regard see George Miller's *The Psychology of Communication* (Baltimore: Penguin Books, 1967), especially Chapter 3.

**EXAMPLE 6-11.** Webern: Concerto, Op. 24, I, mm. 1–5. Copyright 1948, Universal Edition. Used by permission of the publisher. Theodore Presser Company sole representative United States, Canada and Mexico.

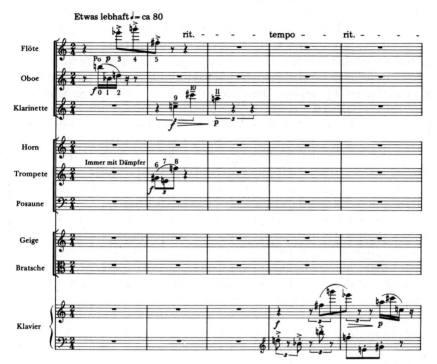

**EXAMPLE 6-12.** Webern: Three Songs, Op. 25, "Wie bin ich froh," mm. 1–3. ⓒ 1956, Universal Edition. Used by permission of the publisher. Theodore Presser Company sole representative United States, Canada and Mexico.

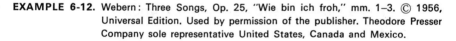

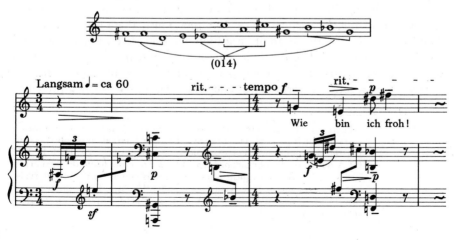

contain the same intervals (recall the single set type representative of both hexachords of the set from Schoenberg's Fourth Quartet); they will always have the same interval class content.[12] Thus there is a natural intervallic affinity of the two halves of a twelve-note set. Second, six different notes represent a perceivable unit and thus a logical division of the set. And third, the equal two-part partition of the set figures prominently in a particular method of simultaneously presenting sets or parts of sets (see Section 4.2).

In contrast to those works in which the set is rather consistently segmented into equal parts throughout, there are numerous compositions in which segments of various sizes appear. In the opening of George Rochberg's Symphony No. 2 (Ex. 6-9), the set is segmented into $4 + 3 + 5$ different notes with the cells in the presentation linked by common tones. In this work, as in many others, rhythmic groupings appear to be at least as important a unifying factor as the statement of particular ordered segments of the set.

In still other examples, the segmentation of the set is governed by other serial details, as for example by a set of durations (see Section 7.0). In general, it may be said that in twelve-note music foreground unity is carried by motives built of set segments of two to six notes in length. In some cases the set is partitioned into equal parts, while in others the size of the segment varies. Often the specific manner of segmentation employed depends upon the structural details of the set, though sometimes it appears that the segments are somewhat arbitrarily selected. In most works the type of segmentation varies throughout. Generally, later sections are freer in the nature of the segmentation than those sections in which the basic materials of the work are initially exposed.

### 4.0 SIMULTANEOUS SET PRESENTATION

One of the significant problems confronting the twelve-note composer is that of organizing the vertical space. In atonal music there is no predicated harmonic basis like the triad in traditional music. Likewise, there is no preexistent scheme, such as the major-minor tonal system, according to which successions of chords can be understood, no matter how the chords may be derived from a set. Furthermore, to infer ordering from a vertical presenta-

---

[12]There are fifty discrete hexachordal set types. Of these, there are fifteen cases in which pairs of set types have the same interval class contents, but not the same intervals. For example, given the set (C C♯ D D♯ F F♯ E G G♯ A A♯ B), the first hexachord is a (0 1 2 3 5 6) type, while the second is a (0 1 2 3 4 7) type. Obviously these collections contain different intervals, but they do contain exactly the same interval classes. For a discussion of this anomaly, see Allen Forte's "A Theory of Set-Complexes for Music," *op. cit.*, esp. pp. 143–48.

tion of pitches is difficult if not impossible. Primarily for these reasons, twelve-note music tends mainly to be contrapuntal rather than homophonic, though it is true that the textures found in traditional music also appear in twelve-note contexts. In the following discussion, some common procedures of organizing the vertical space in this music are examined.

### 4.1 Aggregates

One of Schoenberg's chief concerns in his development of the twelve-note method was the avoidance of octave doublings in multi-part textures. The doublings, he felt, could create the impression of a tonic, which could in turn give rise to the expectation of procedures associated with tonal music. In his words, "The use of a tonic is deceiving if it is not based on *all* the relationships of tonality."[13]

One solution to the problem of avoiding doublings is shown in Ex. 6-13 taken from the opening measures of Schoenberg's Wind Quintet, Op. 26. Here the flute presents in turn the two hexachords of the set while the accompanying parts provide the complementary hexachords. In this way twelve-note *aggregates* (i.e., essentially unordered collections of the twelve pitch classes) result without octave duplications. The aggregates are marked A in the example.

Later in the same work, Schoenberg applies another technique to create aggregates by stating trichordal segments from an R form in one voice (bassoon) while stating hexachordal groupings from the same form as accompaniment (Ex. 6-14).

A common procedure for deriving chords from a set of twelve notes is to select adjacent notes as chord members. In the opening measures of Schoenberg's Fourth Quartet (Ex. 6-15), this procedure is applied to provide chords to accompany the line played by the first violin. Here the set is segmented trichordally and the combinations of chords are set off against the line systematically so as to produce a succession of aggregates (the trichords are marked *a, b, c, d*). This scheme of melodic and accompanimental trichords continues through m. 16, at which point a new section begins. On the whole, systematic control of aggregate structures characterizes this work.

---

[13] Schoenberg, *op. cit.*, p. 108. Italics added.

**EXAMPLE 6-13.** Schoenberg: Wind Quintet, Op. 26 (1924), I, mm. 1–6. Copyright 1925 by Wien Universal Edition, New York. Renewed 1952 by Gertrude Schoenberg. Used by permission of Belmont Music Publishers, Los Angeles, California 90049.

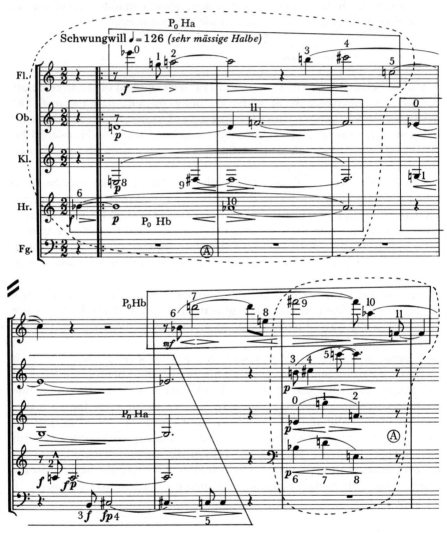

**EXAMPLE 6-14.** Schoenberg: Wind Quintet, IV, mm. 117–124. Copyright 1925 by Wien Universal Edition, New York. Renewed 1952 by Gertrude Schoenberg. Used by permission of Belmont Music Publishers, Los Angeles, California 90049.

**EXAMPLE 6-15.** Schoenberg: String Quartet No. 4, I, mm. 1–6. Copyright 1937 by G Schirmer, Inc. Used by permission.

## 4.2 Combinatoriality

An important aspect of the vertical combinations of Schoenberg's Fourth Quartet and one of his contributions to twelve-note composition in general is combinatoriality. Consider the simultaneous combination of the $P_0$ and the $I_5$ forms of the set from this work:

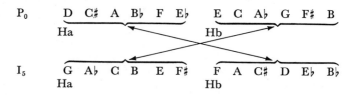

The pitch class contents, though not the ordering, of the two hexachords (labelled *Ha* and *Hb*) are duplicated in opposite positions in the two forms. This allows control of the vertical space to the extent that these two forms (and other similarly related P and I forms of this set, e.g., $P_1/I_6$) can be combined as shown without duplicating pitch classes. The vertical alignment thus produces two successive aggregates. Throughout the quartet combinatoriality of the type described is the primary basis for the association of set forms. An example from the second theme section of the first movement is given below in which four successive aggregates are shown. The two upper and the two lower instruments are paired to present the set forms.

**EXAMPLE 6-16.** Ibid., I, mm. 27–28. Copyright 1937 by G. Schirmer, Inc. Used by permission.

The type of combinatoriality found in this work is technically called *hexachordal inversional combinatoriality* and is common in Schoenberg's music beginning with his Variations for Orchestra, Op. 31 (1927–28). In addition to this type, there is also the type in which hexachords may be complemented under simple transposition. For example, given the hexachord (C D E F G A), transposition by tritone gives (F♯ G♯ A♯ B C♯ D♯). Further, this set is symmetrical and under $RI_9$ reproduces itself. When all three conditions (transposition, inversion with or without transposition, and inversional symmetry) are met by a single hexachord, *all-combinatoriality* results.[14]

There are six all-combinatorial hexachords, which along with their set types and the specific conditions under which they produce complementary hexachords are given in Table 1.

Each of the first three sets are called *first order all-combinatorial source sets*. These produce complements under one case of transposition and one case of

---

[14]The various types of combinatoriality and the conditions under which they arise are described by Milton Babbitt in his article "Set Structure as a Compositional Determinant," in the *Journal of Music Theory* V/1 (April, 1961), pp. 72–94. Combinatoriality resulting from transposition or inversion only is called *semi-combinatoriality*.

**TABLE 1**

| Set | Type | Complements Produced Under |
|---|---|---|
| 1.  C  C♯  D  D♯  E  F | (0  1  2  3  4  5) | $T_6$ and $I_{11}$ |
| 2.  C  D  D♯  E  F  G | (0  2  3  4  5  7) | $T_6$ and $I_1$ |
| 3.  C  D  E  F  G  A | (0  2  4  5  7  9) | $T_6$ and $I_3$ |
| 4.  C  C♯  D  F♯  G  G♯ | (0  1  2  6  7  8) | $T_{3,9}$ and $I_{5,11}$ |
| 5.  C  C♯  E  F  G♯  A | (0  1  4  5  8  9) | $T_{2,6,10}$ and $I_{3,7,11}$ |
| 6.  C  D  E  F♯  G♯  A♯ | (0  2  4  6  8  10) | $T_{1,3,5,7,9,11}$ and $I_{1,3,5,7,9,11}$ |

transposed inversion. The fourth set is a *second order* type and produces its complement under two cases of transposition and of transposed inversion, while the fifth set is complement producing under three instances of transposition and of transposed inversion and is a *third order* type. The last set, a whole-tone scale, is a *fourth order* source set and is complement-producing under six cases of transposition and transposed inversion. These set types have been used by numerous composers, though in many cases, for example in Schoenberg's and Webern's compositions, the combinatorial potential is not fully (and in some cases not at all) realized.[15]

The idea of combinatoriality can be extended to tetrachords, trichords, dyads and to single notes. For example, consider the remarkably complex combinatorial possibilities of the set from Milton Babbitt's Composition for Twelve Instruments (1948) shown at the top of page 413.[16] Aggregates are given by each column; by hexachords (e.g., $P_0$Ha and $R_8$Ha or $P_8$Ha and $R_4$Ha), by initial trichords (e.g., of $P_0$, $I_9$, $R_0$ and $RI_9$), by initial dyads (e.g., of $P_{0,4,8}$ and $RI_{1,5,9}$), as well as by other combinations.

Another method of controlling vertical combinations is found in the fifth movement of Webern's last completed work, the Cantata No. 2, Op. 31. In Ex. 6-17, which is characteristic of all choral portions of the movement, the voices are deployed in pairs with the interval between members of each pair and the interval class between the two pairs (i.e., between the alto and tenor) remaining constant. Each choral sonority is therefore the same set type throughout—(0 1 4 6) in this case. Variety is achieved by changing contours within the voice parts and by rhythm and dynamics.

---

[15]This is probably due at least in part to the fact that the twelve-note method was not fully investigated as to its systematic potential until about 1945, the point at which Milton Babbitt completed a doctoral dissertation dealing with this topic.

[16]Babbitt, *op. cit.*, p. 81.

| $P_0$ | 0, | 1, | 4, | 9, | 5, | 8, | 3, | 10, | 2, | 11, | 6, | 7. |
|---|---|---|---|---|---|---|---|---|---|---|---|---|
| $P_4$ | 4, | 5, | 8, | 1, | 9, | 0, | 7, | 2, | 6, | 3, | 10, | 11. |
| $P_8$ | 8, | 9, | 0, | 5, | 1, | 4, | 11, | 6, | 10, | 7, | 2, | 3. |
| $I_1$ | 1, | 0, | 9, | 4, | 8, | 5, | 10, | 3, | 11, | 2, | 7, | 6. |
| $I_5$ | 5, | 4, | 1, | 8, | 0, | 9, | 2, | 7, | 3, | 6, | 11, | 10. |
| $I_9$ | 9, | 8, | 5, | 0, | 4, | 1, | 6, | 11, | 7, | 10, | 3, | 2. |
| $R_0$ | 7, | 6, | 11, | 2, | 10, | 3, | 8, | 5, | 9, | 4, | 1, | 0. |
| $R_4$ | 11, | 10, | 3, | 6, | 2, | 7, | 0, | 9, | 1, | 8, | 5, | 4. |
| $R_8$ | 3, | 2, | 7, | 10, | 6, | 11, | 4, | 1, | 5, | 0, | 9, | 8. |
| $RI_1$ | 6, | 7, | 2, | 11, | 3, | 10, | 5, | 8, | 4, | 9, | 0, | 1. |
| $RI_5$ | 10, | 11, | 6, | 3, | 7, | 2, | 9, | 0, | 8,. | 1, | 4, | 5. |
| $RI_9$ | 2, | 3, | 10, | 7, | 11, | 6, | 1, | 4, | 0, | 5, | 8, | 9. |

**A**

**EXAMPLE 6-17.** Webern: Cantata No. 2, Op. 31 (1941–43), V, mm. 1–3. Copyright 1951, Universal Edition. Used by permission of the publisher. Theodore Presser Company sole representative United States, Canada and Mexico.

In Webern's Cantata No. I, Op. 29, a similar but more elaborate scheme characterizes the choral portions of the first movement. In this movement the succession of four-voice chords reflects the symmetrical nature of the set upon which it is based. Only three different set types are created by the combination of P and I forms, and these are presented in a scheme which is, like the interval structure of the set itself, a palindrome. The details of the set are shown in Ex. 6-18 along with a portion of the first choral entry. Note that the three tetrachordal set types also reflect the structure of the set in that they too are symmetrical.

In Exx. 6-17 and 6-18, neither combinatoriality nor the systematic presentation of aggregates plays a discernible role in the structure of the movements. Rather, the concern is with harmonic unity as achieved by schemata that may be viewed as logical atonal substitutes for tonal harmonic progressions.

**EXAMPLE 6-18.** Webern: Cantata No. I, Op. 29 (1938–39), I, mm. 14–19. © 1954, Universal Edition. Used by permission of the publisher. Theodore Presser sole representative United States, Canada and Mexico.

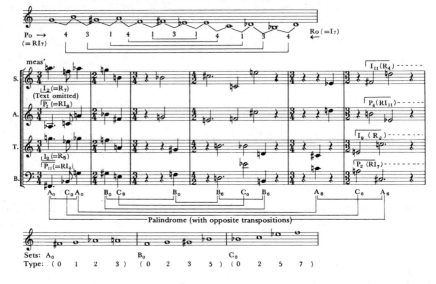

## 4.3 Polyphonic Details

In many works, particularly those by Webern and by composers influenced by his writing, the musical fabric is woven by elaborate and strict canons. In the example following, the two voices are in canon at the distance of an eighth note throughout. But here, as in most twelve-note works employing canons, the contrapuntal device itself is of secondary importance (from the standpoint of perception) to the unity created by the rhythmic and pitch details (these and other details of this movement are discussed in Sections 4.4 and 7.0 of this chapter).

**EXAMPLE 6-19.** Webern: Variations for Piano, Op. 27 (1936), II (complete). Copyright 1937, Universal Edition. Used by permission of the publisher. Theodore Presser Company sole representative United States, Canada and Mexico.

Another example of canonic treatment is found in the third piece from Dallapiccola's *Quaderno musicale*, entitled "Contrapunctus primus." This piece begins with a canon in quasi-diminution at the unison, using the $P_1$ form of the set (see Ex. 6-10 for the $P_0$ form).

**EXAMPLE 6-20.** Dallapiccola: *Quaderno musicale,* No. 3, "Contrapunctus primus" (complete). By permission of the Edizioni Suvini Zerboni, Milano.

**EXAMPLE 6-20** continued.

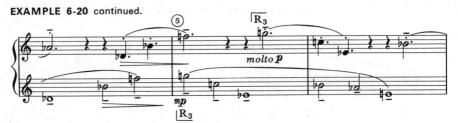

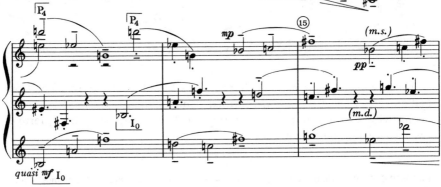

In the ninth measure a third voice joins the leader in simultaneous mirror inversion, and in m. 13 this voice is made the leader in a second canon structured like the first. Observe also that the intervals between the voices emphasized by the two-voice portion (thirds, fourths, and fifths) are likewise emphasized in the later portions, even though other intervals do appear. It is generally true in twelve-note music that the composer controls the vertical dimension so that particular interval and/or pitch class combinations arise, even in instances such as this one in which linear writing is clearly predominant. By carefully organizing both the linear and vertical elements, including the rhythmic, timbral, and dynamic aspects, the composer is able to provide for the unification of the total texture.

### 4.4 Invariance

One criterion often applied by the composer in selecting set forms to be employed in a work is *invariance*, that is, the preservation of one or more segments of a set (a single note may be considered a segment) under transposition or transposed inversion. The most common twelve-note invariant is the preservation of the interval structure of a set under transposition. Another invariant property is provided by combinatoriality, in which segmental pitch class content is preserved by the combinatorially related sets. The following examples will serve to introduce this important aspect of twelve-note composition as a factor in the simultaneous presentation of set forms. Additional references will be made to invariant properties, particularly those affecting set succession, in subsequent sections of the chapter.

A particularly interesting and systematic example of invariant structure is found in the second movement of Webern's Variations for Piano (see Ex. 6-19). The entire movement employs a succession of paired P and I forms, the particular transpositions of which preserve throughout the vertical pairs of pitch classes formed initially by the simultaneous presentation of $P_0$ and $I_2$. The dyads (or monads in the case of the notes A and E♭) are bracketed in the example below.

P₀:  G♯  A  F   G  E  F♯  C   C♯  D  B♭  B  E♭

I₂:  B♭  A  C♯  B  D  C   F♯  F   E  G♯  G  E♭

Other P/I pairs appearing in the movement are $P_7/I_7$, $P_2/I_0$ and $P_5/I_9$. In order to preserve the vertical pairs, all that is necessary is to associate a pair of P and I forms whose initial notes form one of the dyads in the example. Or looked at in another way, so long as the sum of the indices of the P/I pair is some constant number (or that number $+ 12$), the vertical pairs will be preserved. In this case the sum of the indices is 2 (or 14).

This same procedure is followed in the first movement of Webern's Symphony, Op. 21, in which two pairs of P and I forms participate in a double canon. In this case, the dyads created by the initial canonic voices are preserved throughout the first and third sections of the movement (the rough equivalent of a sonata form exposition and recapitulation, respectively), while a different collection of pitch-class pairs is preserved throughout the middle section.[17] In the first movement of Webern's Cantata No. I (see Ex. 6-18), this procedure is applied to pairs of P/I forms in order to create precisely ordered successions of tetrachordal set types in the choral portions. Especially in this latter work, the aural effect of the organization by means of invariant vertical elements is one of stability and cohesion.

In contrast to the clearly systematic invariant features evident in the Webern examples is Ex. 6-21 taken from the second movement of Stravinsky's Movements for Piano and Orchestra. Here the four combined set forms provide invariant dyads, trichords, and hexachords, but not so systematically as in Webern's works cited above. These invariant elements aid in unifying the final portion of the movement, which serves as a synthesis of the materials presented previously. Note in the example that the dyads ($B\flat A\flat$) and ($F\sharp G$) appear as adjacencies in all four of the set forms, and ($E\flat E$) and ($BC$) appear in three of the four forms. Trichordal invariants, both ordered and unordered, are found in $P_0$ and $I_0$, while unordered hexachordal content is preserved within these same forms. Further, the simultaneous presentation of $P_0$ and $R_0$ retains all adjacencies between the two sets but in reverse order.

Before going on to details of set succession, it is well to point out that although many sets reveal invariant aspects under certain permutations, composers have not always availed themselves of the total invariant potential of a particular set. For example, the $I_7$ form of the set from Schenberg's Fourth Quartet reproduces the content of each of the three tetrachords of $P_0$ according to the following scheme: tetrachords 1 2 3 of $P_0$ appear in the order 1 3 2 in $I_7$. But Schoenberg did not choose to emphasize that particular invariant property in the quartet. Instead, he chose to exploit the hexachordal combinatorial property—itself an invariant—between a prime form and its inversion at the lower fifth.

---

[17] For an analysis of this work, see George Perle's *Serial Composition and Atonality*, 2nd ed. (Berkeley: University of California Press, 1968), pp. 90–91, 125–131.

**EXAMPLE 6-21.** Stravinsky: Movements for Piano and Orchestra (1958–59), II, mm. 62–67. Copyright 1960 by Hawkes & Son (London) Ltd. Reprinted by permission of Boosey & Hawkes, Inc.

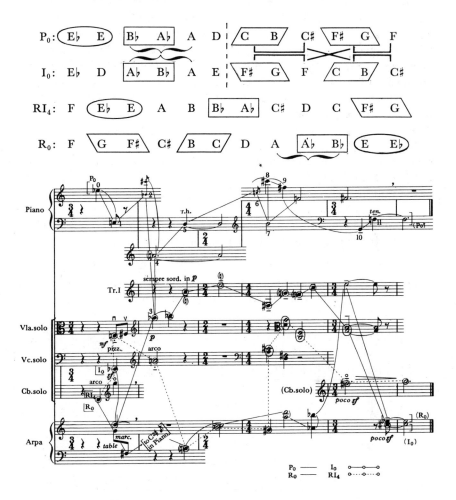

## 5.0 DETAILS OF SET SUCCESSION

The previous discussion has been limited to details of the single set in linear presentation and to the simultaneous combination of parts of one or more set forms. The following discussion is concerned with the structural use of sets, in particular with certain ways in which set forms follow one another and to relationships among compositional statements of successive set forms.

Among the easier methods of guaranteeing continuity by means of a twelve-note set is to present one form continuously, a procedure Schoenberg followed in one of his earliest attempts at twelve-note writing. The fourth piece from his Serenade, Op. 24, for solo voice and instruments, derives its text from a Petrarch sonnet, each line of which has eleven syllables. By setting the text syllabically, Schoenberg is able to overlap text lines and set statements so that thirteen statements of the set (the last of which is incomplete) are necessary to set the fourteen lines of text. In the excerpt shown in Ex. 6-22, the numbers of the set statements are shown above the voice line and the numbers of the sonnet lines below. The instruments also employ set materials but not in a strict ordering.

The linking of set forms by common tones is demonstrated in Ex. 6-23, a passage for alto voice and strings from the second movement of *A Sermon, A Narrative and A Prayer*, by Stravinsky, who adopted the twelve-note method in the middle 1950s. The $R_0$—$I_0$ succession in the alto solo is linked by the common tone E♭, while the set pairs $P_0/I_0$ and $R_0/RI_4$ in the strings utilize common first notes, E♭ and F♮, the same notes which serve, respectively, as terminal and initial notes of the first set of the solo line.

**EXAMPLE 6-22.** Schoenberg: Serenade, Op. 24 (1923), (Petrarch Sonnet, No. 217), mm. 11–14. With permission by Edition Wilhelm Hansen, Copenhagen.

**EXAMPLE 6-22** continued.

**EXAMPLE 6-23.** Stravinsky : *A Sermon, A Narrative and A Prayer* (1960–61), II, mm. 130–137.
Copyright 1961 by Boosey & Hawkes, Ltd. Reprinted by permission.

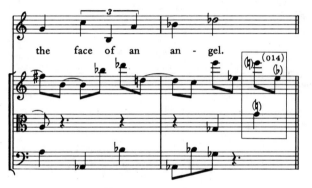

The passage is further unified by reiteration and/or registral stress of invariant elements, particularly the dyads $(E\flat E)$ and $(FA\flat)$, and by the reversed presentation in the strings of the $R_0$-$I_0$ succession of the voice. The choice of $RI_4$ for the fourth set form in the strings is probably explained by its common-tone connection with $R_0$, by the fact that its last two notes $(G\flat G)$ are stressed elsewhere in the passage, and because the last note of $RI_4$ joins with the final two notes of $R_0$ in the last measure to form a $(0\ 1\ 4)$ type trichord, the set type of the first, second, and fourth trichords of the basic set.

The excerpt from the beginning of the third movement of Schoenberg's Fourth Quartet shown in Ex. 6-24 demonstrates several structural details common to classical twelve-note works.

**EXAMPLE 6-24.** Schoenberg: String Quartet No. 4, III, mm. 614–631. Copyright 1939 by G. Schirmer, Inc. Used by permission.

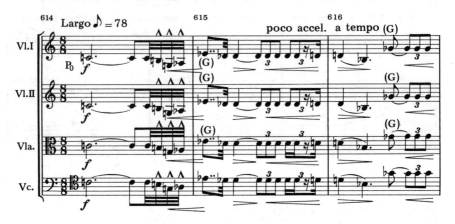

**EXAMPLE 6-24** continued.

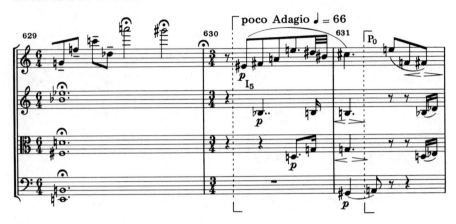

In mm. 617–619, the connection between set forms is made by common set type. The circled segments in the following brief diagram each form a (0 1 5) type trichord common to the first and last trichords of this particular set:[18]

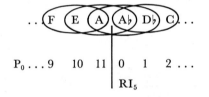

This type of connection between two collections is a carryover from procedures found in pre-serial atonal works, particularly those by Schoenberg and his followers. (Examples from this body of literature are considered in Section 8.0 of this chapter.)

Another aspect of the structure of this passage is the formation of a *secondary set*[19] by the second hexachords of $RI_5$ and of the succeeding form, $R_0$ (mm. 620–623, first violin). A secondary set is created by a succession of pitch classes which are parts of set forms defined by the matrix derived from the basic set of a work. It is an ordered presentation of twelve pitch classes but it is not one of the forms in the matrix. Such sets can be formed in any

---

[18]In that the movement considered here begins with a linear presentation of the basic set beginning on C, this form may be considered $P_0$ for this movement, even though it is actually the $P_{10}$ form relative to the first movement.

[19]The term originates with Milton Babbitt; see "Some Aspects of Twelve-Tone Composition," *op. cit.*, p. 57. Much of the discussion of this passage is taken from Babbitt's analysis in "Set Structure as a Compositional Determinant," *op. cit.*, pp. 83–94.

number of ways, as for example in this set by following $R_0Hb$ by $I_5Ha$, $I_5Hb$ by $R_0Ha$, etc. Notice that the isolation of the first violin pitches from the rest of the texture defines the secondary set clearly.

The combination of set forms in this movement is controlled by combinatorial relations. Furthermore, in the particular section of the movement shown in the example, the succession of set forms is governed by a transpositional scheme given in the diagram below. Combinatorially related collections are bracketed. The first pitch class of each P form is given below each transposition. From the example it is seen that the P form representatives of each combinatorial pair trace a cycle of transpositions outlining a diminished seventh chord. The cycle becomes complete at the beginning of the following section (mm. 630 ff.) with the return of the original combinatorial pair (the hexachordal content of the $I_5/R_0$ combination is the same as that of $P_0$ combined with $RI_5$, though the hexachords are reversed).

| measure(s) | 614–618 | | 621 | 623 | 624 | 625 | | 626 | 627 | 628–29 | 630–31 |
|---|---|---|---|---|---|---|---|---|---|---|---|
| | $P_0$ $RI_5$ | | $R_0$ | $P_9/I_2$ | $I_2R_9$ | $P_9$ $RI_2$ | | $P_6$ | $I_{11}$ | $P_3$ $RI_8$ | $I_5$ $R_0$ |

C - - - - - - - - - - - - - - - A- - - - - - - - - - - - - - - - F♯ - - - - - - - - E♭ - - - - - - - - - C

This kind of cyclical structure involving combinatorial pairs of set forms also appears in other works by Schoenberg, e.g., the Phantasy for Violin, Op. 47.

Before leaving this excerpt, there are several other structural details that deserve mention. First, the length of the statements of the various set forms bears an analogy with harmonic rhythm, as it changes typically at or near a cadence or on the way to a new section. Observe that there are successive reductions of lengths of the statements from $4\frac{1}{2}$ measures ($P_0$ beginning in m. 614) to one measure at the point at which two forms are presented simultaneously (mm. 629). Second, by means of repetition or registral placement, certain invariant dyads are stressed, e.g., the dyad (G♭F) in $P_0$ (m. 617), in $RI_5$ (first violin, m. 621) and as (FG♭) (cello, m. 621); the dyad (CB) in $P_0$ (m. 614), in $RI_5$ (viola, m. 619), and as (BC) in $I_2$ (second violin, m. 623); and the dyad (AG♯) in $P_9$ (cello, m. 623, and first violin, m. 625), in $RI_2$ (second violin, m. 625), in $P_6$ (cello, m. 626), in $RI_8$ (first violin, m. 629), and as (G♯A) as the last note of $I_5$ and the first of $R_0$ in the second section of the movement (cello, m. 631). Each of these dyads plays a referential role. The repeated (G♭F) in $P_0$ is the concluding dyad of $RI_5$, while the dyad (CB) repeated in $RI_5$ begins $P_0$ (in the latter case, the repetition preserves the register of the opening statement); and the notes A and A♭, respectively, conclude $P_0$ and begin $RI_5$. Finally, symmetry plays a role: in the opening statement of $P_0$, the interval span is g—f$^1$♯, with the pitches c$^1$—d$^1$♭ at the exact midpoint of the span being emphasized durationally. At the point of the first simultaneous presentation of two set forms (m. 623), the span is E♭—c$^1$, and the exact mid-pitches are c♯ and d, the only registrally fixed pitches common to the viola and cello lines. That this was a conscious act by Schoenberg is demonstrated by the single change made in the cello line from the opening $P_0$ statement: to preserve the contour of that statement, the E♭ of the $P_9$ form would have to be stated an octave higher. (For other works by Schoenberg employing this kind of symmetry, see the opening sections of the Variations for Orchestra, Op. 31, the String Trio, Op. 45, and the Phantasy for Violin, Op. 47.)

In works by other composers, especially those by Webern, the connection of set forms is very often by one or more common notes. In the second movement of his Variations for Piano (see Ex. 6-19), Webern makes all connections between successive set forms by common note. In the first movement of Cantata No. 1, with a single exception, all set forms are connected by a two-note segment in the manner shown in the excerpt in Ex. 6-18. (The single exception is in m. 13, in which the orchestra completes its assigned forms before the entrance of the chorus.) Beginning with the first choral section, the succession of forms in each of the four voice parts traces a series of minor thirds (or major sixths) similar to the cyclic process found in the Schoenberg quartet movement discussed earlier. In this case, the scheme traces six of these intervals, or a cycle and a half.

Another procedure of set connection employed by Webern and others closely related to the one above is to use an interior segment of one set as a part of another. In Ex. 6-25 from Webern's orchestral Variations, Op. 30, the second tetrachords of $P_0$ and $R_0$ (symbolized here $_2P_0$ and $_2R_0$) are expressed by the common verticalized segment played by the brasses, after which $P_0$ resumes its linear statement begun at the outset of the variation. By employing a vertical presentation for the tetrachords, linear ordering is not a factor in the two retrograde related segments, and therefore the two set forms can make use of a common element.

A more extreme example of the same procedure is found in Webern's Symphony, Op. 21, II, Variation V, in which four-voice chords common to tritone-related set forms provide an ostinato against which a single line, itself derived from notes common to the two forms, is played.[20] As in other examples cited from Webern's works, the effect is one of harmonic stasis in a context of changing dynamics, timbres, and accentual patterns.

To conclude this brief look at the structural uses of sets, a word about form in twelve-note music is in order. The primary formal process in twentieth-century music is variation, and this is particularly true in twelve-note music since every twelve-note work is, in its most elementary sense, a set of varia-

---

[20]See Perle, *op. cit.,* pp. 90–91.

**EXAMPLE 6-25.** Webern : Variations, Op. 30 (1940), Variation I, mm. 21–31 (piano reduction). © 1956, Universal Edition. Used by permission of the publisher. Theodore Presser Company sole representative United States, Canada and Mexico.

tions on a continuously reiterated collection of intervals expressible in any of four forms. It is obvious that the use of a reiterated series guarantees at least a minimal degree of foreground unity of the pitch dimension. As for larger structures, it is generally considered that the invention of the twelve-note method made possible the creation of logical structures of much greater length than seemed plausible in pre-serial atonality. At the very least, the method gave composers a conceptual framework for systematizing pitch and interval relations; it provided limits within which composers could fashion coherent and yet individual musical structures.

But revolutions are rarely complete; something is generally retained from the past, whether because of reason or sentiment. So it was with Schoenberg who, in spite of his revolutionary invention, chose to organize many of his works in traditional forms, as for example in the Fourth Quartet whose first movement is a kind of sonata form, or the first of his Three Songs, Op. 48, which is an ABA structure. Even in his more radical departures from tradition, as in his String Trio and the Phantasy for Violin, one encounters frequent traditional formal processes, such as antecedent-consequent phrase relationships, recurrent melodic contours, traditional textural types, and so forth. And the same is true to an extent with Webern, who generally is regarded as the more influential of the two on later twentieth-century composition. His Symphony retains the traditional double bar structure for the first movement, and his Variations for Piano employs a clear two-part design (with each part repeated) for its second movement. Yet some of his other works, as well as other features of the Symphony and the Variations, are more truly iconoclastic formally. In general, the works of twelve-note composers demonstrate a wide variety of formal processes and designs ranging from traditional to novel. It is doubtful whether any necessary relationship can be drawn between the twelve-note method and procedures of formal structuring.

## 6.0 ELEMENTS OF FREEDOM IN TWELVE-NOTE COMPOSITION

To conclude this presentation of basic details of twelve-note music, the following discussion is concerned with deviation from strict twelve-note compositional practices, in particular with matters of ordering. In some works, after the basic set has been exposed, there is a reordering of notes within segments, generally in order to give prominence to certain pitch elements that might otherwise go unstressed in their original order. In other works, note ordering as such is secondary to the invariance of segmental content. In some instances composers have used the set more as a source of motives than as a strictly ordered and reiterated structural agent. And some works employ two or more sets as pitch bases, while others alternate strictly ordered and freer sections. Examples of some of these approaches to twelve-note composition are included below.

One example in which the reasons for certain departures from classical twelve-note procedures are particularly clear is the Praeludium from Schoenberg's Suite, Op. 25, three excerpts from which are given here. In general, Schoenberg avoided octave duplications of pitch classes in vertical combinations. But within the first three measures of the Suite (Ex. 6-26(a)) the combination of $P_0$ and $P_6$ juxtapose the tritone (GD♭) in two octave positions. The reason for this duplication, which does not occur with other pitches, is that G and D♭, along with E and B♭, serve as a secondary organizing factor in the piece: in mm. 15, 18–19, and 22–24, these notes are used as points around which the other notes are symmetrically placed. The reorderings found in $P_0$ in mm. 5–7 (Ex. 6-26(b)) and in m. 15 (Ex. 26(c)) were no doubt made in order to bring D♭ and G into more prominence in the former case and to structure the materials symmetrically around the two tritones (EB♭) and (GD♭) in the latter. Also, the only forms used in the Suite are

**EXAMPLE 6-26.** Schoenberg: Suite for Piano, Op. 25 (1923), Praeludium. Copyright 1925 by Wien Universal Edition. Renewed 1952 by Gertrude Schoenberg. Used by permission of Belmont Music Publishers, Los Angeles, California 90049.

(With each tetrachord retrograded or Ro with first and third tetrachords interchanged)

$P_0$, $P_6$, $I_0$ and $I_8$ and their R forms, all of which hold the two tritones invariant (to within order reversal) as shown below:

|  | 0 | 1 | 2 | 3 | 4 | 5 | 6 | 7 | 8 | 9 | 10 | 11 |
|---|---|---|---|---|---|---|---|---|---|---|---|---|
| $P_0$: | E | . | G | D♭ | . | . | . | . | . | . | . | B♭ |
| $P_6$: | B♭ | . | D♭ | G | . | . | . | . | . | . | . | E |
| $I_0$: | E | . | D♭ | G | . | . | . | . | . | . | . | B♭ |
| $I_8$: | B♭ | . | G | D♭ | . | . | . | . | . | . | . | E |

A work that demonstrates a borderline case between strict and free twelve-note composition is Alban Berg's *Schliesse mir die Augen beide* ("Close My Eyes"), his first attempt at applying Schoenberg's method with any degree of rigor.[21] The vocal line consists of five complete statements of $P_0$ (a symmetrical all-interval set used also in Berg's *Lyric* Suite) in a presentation similar to that of the fourth piece of Schoenberg's Serenade (see Ex. 6-22). Through the first half of the song, the piano accompaniment employs $P_0$ and $R_0$ forms rather strictly. But in the second half the piano part becomes much freer, and in some places the only demonstrable relationship of its pitch materials to those of the basic set lies in the reiteration of two tetrachords (marked X and Y in the excerpt) and on the formation of certain set types formed by adjacent

**EXAMPLE 6-27.** Berg: *Schliesse mir die Augen beiden.* (1925), mm. 11–20. © 1955, Universal Edition. Used by permission of the publisher. Theodore Presser sole representative United States, Canada and Mexico.

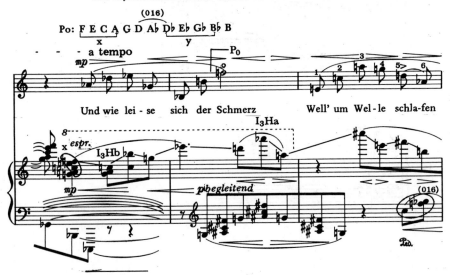

le - get, wie der letz - te Schlag ___ sich re - get, ___

*sempre espress.* - - - - - -

(016)

*poco pesante*

*cresc.* - - - - -

fül - lest du mein gan - zes

basically R₀

*poco cresc. ma*
*sempre tranquillo* - - -

*espress.*

(016)

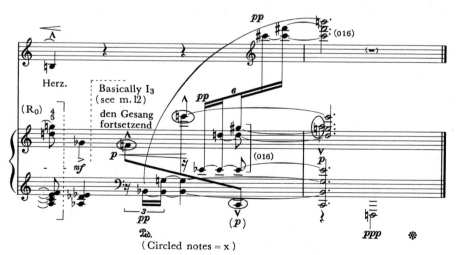

Herz.

Basically I₃
( see m. 12 )

den Gesang
fortsetzend

(R₀)

(016)

( Circled notes = x )

notes in the basic set, especially the (0 1 6) type trichord. Observe also the numerous triads and triads with added notes (e.g., the X and Y tetrachords) that derive from the set, the two hexachords of which suggest tonal centers of F and B (see also Ex. 6-4). The example given above shows a portion of the second half of the song.

Simultaneous strictness and freedom as regards basic set order is also provided by a principle of reordering called *rotation*, which is defined by Ernst Křenek as:

> . . . a procedure in which elements of a given series systematically and progressively change their relative positions according to a plan which in itself is serially conceived in that the changes occur in regular phases.[22]

A particularly interesting and characteristic example of rotation is demonstrated in Ex. 6-28(a). Here each of the hexachords of the basic set from Stravinsky's *Abraham and Isaac* for baritone voice and orchestra is submitted to a rotation scheme in which, for example, the first note of $P_0$Ha (Ha0 in the chart) is rotated to become last. Then the collection is transposed to begin on G, and this hexachord becomes the second in the chart (Ha1). Similarly, Ha2 is derived from Ha1, Ha3 is derived from Ha2, and Ha4 is derived from Ha3. The same procedure applied to Ha5 would restore Ha0. The procedure is applied as well to the Hb hexachords.

In order to grasp the nature of this rotation-transposition scheme, it may help to think of the hexachords as circular arrangements, each beginning with the same note and with the intervals between notes being successively moved one place to the left through five moves. The sixth move would restore the original hexachord structure. The diagram shows Ha hexachords through two successive moves. Intervals measured in semitones are indicated between the notes.

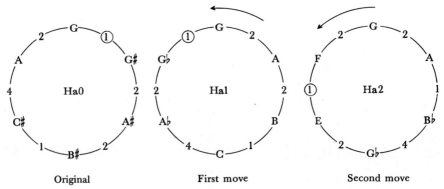

Original        First move        Second move

[22]Ernst Křenek, "Extents and Limits of Serial Techniques," *Problems of Modern Music*, ed. Paul Henry Lang, p. 73. Copyright by G. Schirmer, Inc. Used by permission.

**EXAMPLE 6-28(a).** Rotation of Hexachords in the Basic Set of Stravinsky's *Abraham and Isaac.*

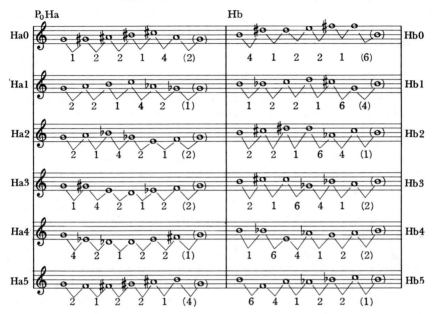

Example 28(b) shows rotation in practice in an excerpt from the work. Three rotations are shown, each in a retrograde ordering of Hb hexachords in transposition: $\overleftarrow{Hb1}_{10}$ symbolizes the retrograde of Hb1 transposed ten semitones; $\overleftarrow{Hb2}_5$ is the retrograde of Hb2 transposed by five semitones, etc. Note that in the excerpt each of these transposed rotations preserves the interval classes of the model while keeping invariant the note F. Elsewhere in the work other rotation schemes are used along with some freer ordering procedures. According to Claudio Spies, from whose review of *Abraham and*

**EXAMPLE 6-28(b).** Stravinsky: *Abraham and Isaac* (1962–63) mm. 211–216 (baritone voice only). Copyright 1954 by Boosey & Hawkes Music Publishers Ltd. Reprinted by permission of Boosey & Hawkes, Inc.

*Isaac* the present examples derive, Stravinsky's interest in rotation lay in the multiplicity of possible successions of hexachord members.[23] His use of rotation in numerous works (e.g., Movements for Piano and Orchestra, *The Flood*, and *A Sermon, A Narrative and A Prayer*) appears to be similar to procedures employed by Křenek, who writes that:

> The purpose of the operation was not so much to make serial design stricter, but to relax it, insofar as the wide variety of available six-tone patterns made it possible to remain within the frame of reference of the twelve-tone serial technique without constantly having to use complete twelve-tone rows.[24]

Schoenberg, primarily in his later works, began to employ the twelve-note set with freedom in terms of linear ordering yet with strictness as regards segmental content. In a sense it might be said that he combined his own method with procedures derived from Joseph Hauer's principles of composition with tropes.[25] An early example of this kind of departure from classical twelve-note procedures is found in the first of Schoenberg's Three Songs, Op. 48 (Ex. 6-29). Linear ordering is maintained only within segments in the vocal line, whereas the piano employs numerous permutations of the other tetrachords. The procedure as employed here insures aggregate control while at the same time allowing freedom in the presentation of set segments. In the String Trio, the Phantasy for Violin, and in his last completed work, *De Profundis*, this procedure is applied to hexachords, in the last case throughout the whole composition.

Karlheinz Stockhausen employs a similar method of organization in his *Klavierstück I*, the opening of which appears in Ex. 6-30. Here the entire pitch material is derived from two complementary (0 1 2 3 4 5) type hexachords (marked Ha and Hb) which alternate throughout the piece (with some overlapping). Thus aggregate control is assured while ordering is, analytically speaking, immaterial.

---

[23]Claudio Spies, "Notes on Stravinsky's *Abraham and Isaac*," *Perspectives of New Music* (Spring-Summer, 1965), pp. 104–126.

[24]Křenek, *op. cit.*, p. 75. For an early example of rotation, see Perle's discussion of Berg's *Lyric* Suite, third movement (*op. cit.*, pp. 69–70).

[25]Hauer devised a method of composing with twelve-note "tropes" in which hexachordal content was preserved but in which ordering within the hexachords was immaterial. Hauer's method, which appeared at about the same time as Schoenberg's, is discussed by Karl Eschmann in his book, *Changing Forms of Modern Music*, (Boston: E. G. Schirmer Music Co.), pp. 81–110.

**EXAMPLE 6-29.** Schoenberg: Three Songs, Op. 48 (1933), "Sommermüd," mm. 1–6. Used by permission of Boelke-Bomart, Inc., Hillsdale, N. Y. 12529.

**EXAMPLE 6-30.** Karlheinz Stockhausen: *Klavierstück* I (1952), mm. 1–12. © 1954, Universal Edition. Used by permission of the publisher. Theodore Presser Company sole representative United States, Canada and Mexico.

The concluding example is taken from the opening section of Gunther Schuller's Fantasy for solo cello (Ex. 6-31). In the first two measures the set upon which the work is based is stated linearly. The set stresses primarily major thirds, along with minor thirds and major and minor seconds. Throughout the work these intervals or their complements receive emphasis by frequent reiteration and thus provide reference to the basic set, although the set itself does not appear in its original ordering after this section. Pitch unity in the work is provided by the generally consistent association of the dyad adjacencies of the set: (GEb), (F#D), (FDb), (EC), (BA) and (AbBb). An added unifying aspect is the tonal role that accrues to the note C. Notice that the first hexachord is a series of chromatically descending thirds leading to the (CE) dyad. Throughout the work C appears frequently by itself, as the lowest note of a chord, or with its upper fifth, G. This tonic is further confirmed by the strong final cadence, a C major triad.

**EXAMPLE 6-31.** Gunther Schuller: Fantasy for Violoncello Solo, Op. 19, mm. 1–12. Copyright 1960 by Rongwen Music, New York.

## 7.0 ORDERING OF OTHER DIMENSIONS: MULTI-SERIALISM

Twelve-note composition took two separate paths during the 1940s, one in the direction of freer applications as discussed above, the other toward what is often called *multi-* (or *total*) *serialism*. In addition to precompositional control of pitch, duration is frequently organized rigorously, either by procedures similar to those applied in serializing pitch or by other numerical schemes that are not serial in the twelve-note sense. Some works strictly order other aspects, such as dynamics, timbre, mode of attack and meter, though in general, pitch and duration are the dimensions most often subjected to rigorously ordered schemes.[26] As a point of departure for our brief examination of some ways in which dimensions other than pitch are strictly organized, we return to the second movement of Webern's Variations for Piano (see Ex. 6-19), which is one of several works by this composer that served as a catalyst for the short-lived but significant history of multi-serialism in music.

In addition to the serial pitch structure discussed earlier in this chapter, Webern has organized very carefully the registral, rhythmic, dynamic, and articulative details of the movement so that it appears to be multi-serialized. Foreground unity is provided primarily by the rhythm, which emphasizes two-note units (defined by rests and/or changing dynamics) throughout the piece. Each unit has one of three dynamics and one of four modes of articulation associated with it (see Ex. 6-32). The consistent succession of two-note units provides coherence, but within a context of constant variation: no two statements of any unit are the same in terms of associated details or manner of continuation. Moreover, the two-note units can be arranged in a pattern of rhythmic cells (i.e., units or combinations of units separated by rests)[27] as shown at the bottom right of the example. The unity of the structure is apparent, but again no two patterns are exactly the same.

Registral details demonstrate similar characteristics. The registral plan displays total symmetry of attacks about the axis pitch, $a^1$. Of the attacked pitches, seven are registrally invariant, three on either side and equidistant from $a^1$. However, the succession of attacks with their associated dynamics and modes of articulation is essentially asymmetrical.

The suggestions of precompositional control of several dimensions evident in this and others of Webern's works (e.g., the Symphony, Op. 21, Concerto, Op. 24, and String Quartet, Op. 28)[28] led other composers to similar experiments. We turn now to some of these works.

---

[26]The reader is referred to Leonard Meyer's recent book *Music, The Arts and Ideas* (Chicago: University of Chicago Press, 1967), especially pp. 236–316, for a penetrating discussion of this music and the problems attending its perception.

[27]The rhythmic groupings are taken from a more extensive discussion of this movement appearing in Wilbur Ogdon's unpublished doctoral dissertation *Series and Structure: An Investigation Into the Purpose of the Twelve-Note Row in Selected Works of Schoenberg, Webern, Křenek, and Leibowitz* (Indiana University, 1955).

[28]See Stockhausen's analysis of the Concerto (in *Melos*, Vol. 20, 1953) and various articles in *die Reihe 2* for discussion of the structure of Webern's music and its influence on serial technique, especially as applied by European composers.

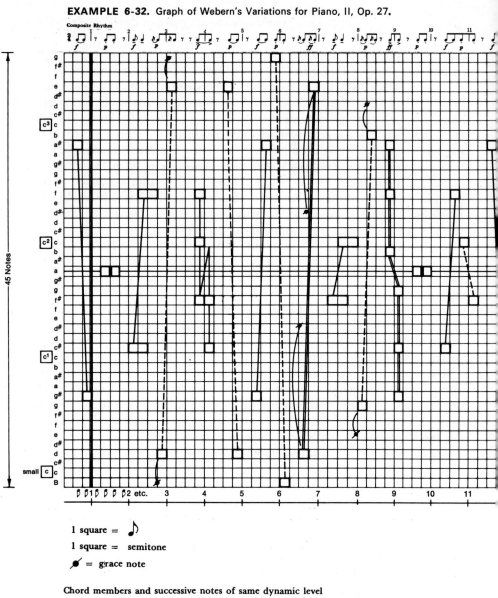

**EXAMPLE 6-32.** Graph of Webern's Variations for Piano, II, Op. 27.

1 square = ♪

1 square = semitone

♪ = grace note

Chord members and successive notes of same dynamic level
connected by lines:

- - - - - - - = *p*

──────── = *f*

════════ = *ff*

Range: 45 notes (B—g³)

Duration: 45 quarter notes (excl. repetitions)

Registrally invariant:    g♯, c1♯, f1♯, a', c2, f2, b2♭,

Modes of Articulation:          ⌢ —m¹

                                · —m²

                                – —m³

                                > —m⁴

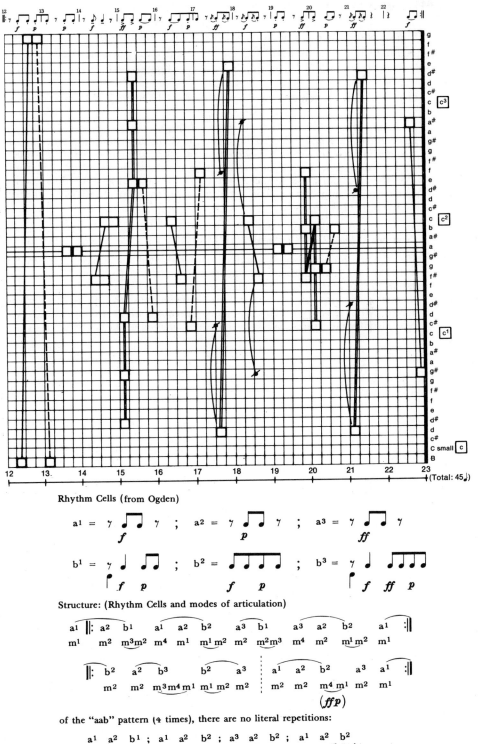

**Rhythm Cells (from Ogden)**

$$a^1 = \text{♪} \quad ; \quad a^2 = \text{♪} \quad ; \quad a^3 = \text{♪}$$
$$\quad f \quad\quad\quad\quad p \quad\quad\quad\quad ff$$

$$b^1 = \text{♪} \quad ; \quad b^2 = \text{♪} \quad ; \quad b^3 = \text{♪}$$
$$\quad f \; p \quad\quad\quad f \quad p \quad\quad\quad f \; ff \; p$$

**Structure: (Rhythm Cells and modes of articulation)**

$$a^1 \; \|: \; a^2 \quad b^1 \quad a^1 \quad a^2 \quad b^2 \quad a^3 \quad b^1 \quad a^3 \quad a^2 \quad b^2 \quad a^1 \; :\|$$
$$m^1 \quad\; m^2 \quad m^3 m^2 \quad m^4 \quad m^1 \quad m^1 m^2 \quad m^2 \quad m^2 m^3 \quad m^4 \quad m^2 \quad m^1 m^2 \quad m^1$$

$$\|: \; b^2 \quad a^2 \quad b^3 \quad b^2 \quad a^3 \quad a^1 \quad a^2 \quad b^2 \quad a^3 \quad a^1 \; :\|$$
$$\quad m^2 \quad m^2 \quad m^3 m^4 m^1 \quad m^1 \; m^2 \quad m^2 \quad m^2 \quad m^2 \quad m^4 m^1 \quad m^2 \quad m^1$$
$$(\textit{ffp})$$

of the "aab" pattern (4 times), there are no literal repetitions:

$$a^1 \quad a^2 \quad b^1 \quad ; \quad a^1 \quad a^2 \quad b^2 \quad ; \quad a^3 \quad a^2 \quad b^2 \quad ; \quad a^1 \quad a^2 \quad b^2$$
$$(\textit{ffp})$$

The second movement of Nono's *Il canto sospeso* employs a duration scheme determined by multiplying numbers selected from a portion of a Fibonacci series[29] by a set of four basic duration units. The procedure is as follows:[30]

The number series contains twelve numbers: 1 2 3 5 8 13 13 8 5 3 2 1. The basic duration units are: (a) ♪ (b) $\overline{\phantom{x}3\phantom{x}}$ ♪ (c) ♪ (d) $\overline{\phantom{x}5\phantom{x}}$ ♪ .
The numbers are multiplied by the basic durations according to a scheme that provides four contrapuntal voices distributed over the eight voices of the unaccompanied chorus. The particular duration unit used as a multiplier depends upon the voice part, that is, voice part 1 will use unit (a) as a multiplier, voice part 2 will use unit (b), etc. The initial presentation of the durations assigned to the pitch set of the work is:

| notes: | A | B♭ | A♭ | B | G | C | F♯ | C♯ | F | D | E | E♭ |
|---|---|---|---|---|---|---|---|---|---|---|---|---|
| durations: | 1(a) | 2(b) | 3(c) | 5(d) | 8(a) | 13(b) | 13(c) | 8(d) | 5(d) | 3(d) | 2(c) | 1(d) |

After the first presentation, the number series is rotated one degree to give 2 3 5 8 13 13 8 5 3 2 1 1. Subsequent statements are similarly rotated. As in the initial statement, the numbers are multiplied by the duration units and assigned to the pitch classes of the set. Pitch class ordering remains constant (that is, there are no transformations of the set). This procedure determines the rhythmic texture of the first thirty-four measures. Ex. 6–33 shows the opening of the movement.

---

[29]The Fibonacci series is a set of numbers in which, starting with 1, each successive number is the sum of the previous two: 1 1 2 3 5 8 13 21 . . .

[30]This résumé is taken from a more complete description of the movement given by Jonathan Kramer in an article, "The Fibonacci Series in Twentieth-Century Music," in *Journal of Music Theory* 17/1 (Spring 1973), pp. 126–130. See also Karlheinz Stockhausen's "Music and Speech," in *die Reihe 6*, pp. 47–57.

**EXAMPLE 6-33.** Nono: *Il Canto sospeso* (1956), II, mm. 1–3. Copyright © 1957 by Ars Viva Verlag GMBH. Used with permission of Belwin-Mills Publishing Corp., agent for U.S.A.

**EXAMPLE 6-33** continued.

The rhythmic texture of the remaining sixteen bars of the movement is determined by applying the number series horizontally as shown in the diagram below. The pitch series, however, is assigned to the voices in the order of entry (see the dotted lines in the diagram). The second half of the section (not shown in the example) is a mirror of the first.

**EXAMPLE 6-34.** Nono: *Il Canto Sospeso,* II, mm. 35ff. Copyright © 1957 by Ars Viva Verlag GMBH. Used with permission of Belwin-Mills Publishing Corp., agent for U.S.A.

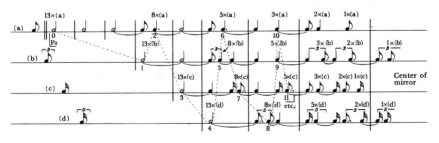

Order nos. of pitch set: - - - - - - - (one statement only marked)

In the first piece of Boulez's *Structures I* for two pianos, pitch, duration, dynamics and mode of attack are precompositionally determined. The chart below shows the sets of the piece.

**EXAMPLE 6-35.** Boulez. *Structures Ia* (1951–52), Sets.

| | 1 | 2 | 3 | 4 | 5 | 6 | 7 | 8 | 9 | 10 | 11 | 12 |
|---|---|---|---|---|---|---|---|---|---|---|---|---|
| Notes (Po) | E♭ | D | A | A♭ | G | F♯ | E | C♯ | C | B♭ | E | B |
| Durations | ♪ | ♪ | ♪. | ♪ | ♪♪ | ♪. | ♪.. | ♩ | ♩♪ | ♩♪ | ♩♪. | ♩. |
| Dynamics | *pppp* | *ppp* | *pp* | *p* | quasi *p* | *mp* | *mf* | quasi *f* | *f* | *ff* | *fff* | *ffff* |
| Mode of Attack | > | >. | • | | normal | ⌢ | ' | *sfz* ∧ | >ᵥ | | ·· | ⌢ |

The duration set in the chart is determined by associating one durational unit (the thiry-second note) with the first note in the basic pitch set, and increasing the subsequent durations in turn by the addition of one unit. Thus the twelfth note has a dotted quarter duration (twelve units). In the matrix of set forms, the durations remain fixed to the notes with which they originally associate.[31] In the composition, however, pitch series and duration series are derived from different transformations within the matrix. For example, in the excerpt that follows (Ex. 6-36), the pitch set $P_6$ appears with the duration set derived from the $RI_5$ form. This is symbolized $P_1, D(RI_5)$. Notice that the duration series may be expressed totally in sounding values or as a combination of notes and rests.

The choice of dynamics (two of which, quasi-*p* and quasi-*f*, had to be invented to complete the set of twelve) and modes of attack are similarly arbitrary. Within the composition each statement of a pitch set form is assigned one dynamic level and one mode of attack. The choice of each is made from a number series derived from a scheme of diagonals in the matrices of order (not pitch-class) numbers of prime and inversion forms of the pitch sets. The reason for having ten rather than twelve modes of attack resides in the particular set of numbers arising from the diagonals determining the attack series; the numbers four and ten do not appear. A typical passage is shown in Ex. 6-36.

In contrast to the arbitrary procedures employed by Boulez, a somewhat more plausible method of multi-serial organization is found in the first of Babbitt's Three Compositions for Piano, which is generally considered to be

---

[31]For a discussion of this piece and its serial details, see György Ligeti's article "Pierre Boulez," in *die Reihe* 4, pp. 36–72. The pitch set for the work is the same as that used by Boulez's teacher, Olivier Messiaen, in his early total serial work *Modes de valeurs et d'intensité* (1948).

**EXAMPLE 6-36.** Boulez: *Structures Ia*, mm. 8–15. © 1955, Universal Edition. Used by permission of the publisher. Theodore Presser Company sole representative United States, Canada and Mexico.

the first multi-serial work. In this piece Babbitt used four forms of a number series to determine the number of attacks of different pitches. Each of the forms of the attack set is assigned consistently to a similarly designated form of the twelve-note set of the piece, and each of these pairs of forms is assigned a particular dynamic level. Mode of attack does not appear to be serialized.

**EXAMPLE 6-37.** Babbitt: Three Compositions for Piano (1948), I.

```
Attack set:  P  5  1  4  2  R
             I  1  5  2  4  RI
```

Associated forms:

| | | | | |
|---|---|---|---|---|
| Pitch set: | P | R | I | RI |
| Attack set: | P | R | I | RI |
| Dynamics set: | mp | mf | f | p |

The I form of the attack set is found by subtracting the numbers of the P form from six. Several examples of the attack set as used within the work appear below. The basic unit of the attack set is the sixteenth note.

**EXAMPLE 6-38.** Attack Sets in Babbitt's Three Compositions for Piano, I.

(a) mm1−2  Attack set: P

(b) m10  Attack set: RI

(c) m11  (chords)  Attack set: I

(d) m41  (chords)  Attack set: R

In Ex. 6-38(a), the last note of each attack group is extended, by sustention or rest, to separate the groups of the form. In Ex. 6-38(b), slurring defines the form. In the final two examples chords are stated and sustained or are accompanied by rests to articulate the particular groupings desired, though perception of the last version as a particular form is tenuous; appropriately, this version appears at a later point in the piece after the basic forms have been well established.[32]

Soon after his initial attempt at multi-serialism, Babbitt wrote two other works, Composition for Four Instruments and Composition for Twelve Instruments, both of which are remarkable in terms of their serial details. In Composition for Four Instruments, in addition to complex pitch serialism, a duration series based on the set (1 4 3 2) is used. At the outset of the piece

---

[32]See Perle's analysis (*op. cit.,* pp. 134–141) for a fuller description of the structure of this work.

the series is based on a sixteenth-note unit, but the continuation involves restatement of the series using, in turn, basic units of a quarter note, a dotted eighth and an eighth note. The opening rhythm is shown in the following example. Notice that the succession of changing units ( ♪ ♩ ♪. ♪ ) is

                                                  1    4    3    2

itself a manifestation of the basic number series (based on a sixteenth note.)[33]

**EXAMPLE 6-39.** Babbitt: Composition for Four Instruments (1949), mm. 1–7. Copyright 1949, Merion Music, Inc. Used by permission.

Duration set: 1 4 3 2

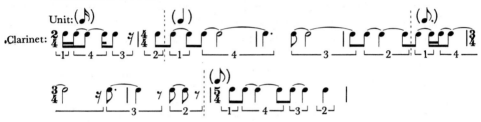

Also appearing in this work is a rigorous scheme of timbres. In the example below notice that each instrument appears in a solo passage and that every possible combination of instruments, including all four instruments, appears once and only once. Further, within the bracketed pairs, each instrument appears once and only once.

**EXAMPLE 6-40.** Timbre Set of Babbitt's Composition for Four Instruments.

| mm. | | | | |
|---|---|---|---|---|
| | 1– 35 | cl | 206–228 | fl, cl, cello |
| | 36– 59 | fl, vln, cello | 228–250 | vln |
| | 60– 88 | cl, cello | 251–289 | vln, cello |
| | 89–118 | fl, vln | 289–327 | fl, cl |
| | 119–138 | fl, cl, vln | 328–350 | fl |
| | 139–163 | cello | 350–368 | cl, vln, cello |
| | 164–185 | fl, cello | 368–405 | fl, cl, vln, |
| | 186–206 | cl, vln | | cello |

In Composition for Twelve Instruments, durations are determined by pitch class numbers. For example, the $P_0$ form of the pitch set is (0 1 4 9 5 8 3 10 2 11 6 7). The associated duration set, predicated on a sixteenth-

---

[33]Peter Westergaard, "Some Problems Raised by the Rhythmic Procedures in Milton Babbitt's Composition for Twelve Instruments," in *Perspectives of New Music* (Fall-Winter, 1965), p. 112, fn. 4.

note unit, is the same set, except that the durational equivalent of pitch class 0 is 12. Similarly, inversion of the duration set involves complementation of the duration numbers, e.g., $I_0$ is (12 11 8 3 7 4 9 2 10 1 6 5). It follows then that combinatoriality, secondary set structure, aggregate formation, etc., can be extended to include sets of durations as well as pitches. For example, the set is a third order all-combinatorial type. In this work $P_0$ combined with $I_3$, $I_7$, or $I_{11}$, or with $P_2$, $P_6$, or $P_{10}$ will create hexachordal aggregates of durations as well as pitch classes. However, in this work as in Boulez's *Structures Ia*, perception of duration relationships is difficult, if not in reality impossible, for while in the pitch domain we can distinguish pitch (frequency) and interval, it is much more difficult to apprehend the analogues of these features in the duration scheme employed in this work: absolute duration and duration interval as defined by pitch class numbers. As an example, consider the durational equivalents of the following pitch-class adjacencies extracted from the set of this piece:

Pitch classes: - - - - - - - 8    3    10 - - - - - - - - -11    6

Duration:

$(8 \, \flat)$    $(3 \, \flat)$    $(10 \, \flat)$      $(11 \, \flat)$    $(6 \, \flat)$

In each case, subtracting the left pitch class from the right of each bracketed pair (adding twelve where necessary) gives a constant interval of seven semitones. But it is doubtful that even the most skillful listener can apprehend this constant in terms of durational relationships. Our experience (at least at this point in the twentieth century) simply has not provided us a basis for this kind of perception.[34]

As a final example of the extension of the twelve-note principle to the control of other dimensions, we consider some recent suggestions of Babbitt regarding the control of duration that serve, at least in part, to correct some of the deficiencies mentioned in the preceding paragraph. In a discussion of rhythmic structure within the electronic medium,[35] he suggests equating duration intervals and pitch intervals, thereby creating sets of durations, called *time-point sets*, that are isomorphic to pitch sets. The examples below give a brief (and admittedly incomplete) view of time-point sets as they appear in Babbitt's proposed system. In each case the measure is the modulus (as the octave is the modulus in the pitch class system) and the unit

---

[34]For a more detailed look at the rhythmic structure of this work, including a criticism of the procedures from the point of view of perception, see Westergaard, *Ibid.*, pp. 109–118.

[35]See Milton Babbitt's "Twelve-Tone Rhythmic Structure and the Electronic Medium," in *Perspectives of New Music 1* (Fall-Winter, 1962), pp. 49–72.

of duration is 1/12 measure. The duration intervals are found by subtracting in turn each pitch-class number from the one on its right (adding twelve where necessary).

**EXAMPLE 6-41.** Time-Point Sets.

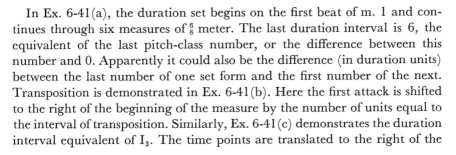

In Ex. 6-41(a), the duration set begins on the first beat of m. 1 and continues through six measures of $\frac{6}{8}$ meter. The last duration interval is 6, the equivalent of the last pitch-class number, or the difference between this number and 0. Apparently it could also be the difference (in duration units) between the last number of one set form and the first number of the next. Transposition is demonstrated in Ex. 6-41(b). Here the first attack is shifted to the right of the beginning of the measure by the number of units equal to the interval of transposition. Similarly, Ex. 6-41(c) demonstrates the duration interval equivalent of $I_3$. The time points are translated to the right of the downbeat by the number of units represented by the index of transposition, and the duration intervals, like pitch intervals under inversion, are the complements of corresponding intervals of the $P_0$ ($= D_0$) form. Finally, Ex. 6-41(d) demonstrates the time-point equivalent of a transposed retrograde form. As retrograding complements order numbers (i.e., the first order number of P is the last order number of R, the second of P is the penultimate of R, etc.), so it is with time points. Here, however, the first point of the duration set is translated to the right by eight units, that is, by the durational equivalent of the first pitch-class number of $R_2$ (recall that the index of R refers to its last element, not its first as in P or I forms). As in most duration schemes applied in serial music, a duration interval can be filled out in part by a rest as shown in Ex. 6-41(d). And as somewhat of an analogue of octave equivalence of pitches, any duration can be increased by an integral number of modular units. In $D_0$, for example, the first duration could be fifteen units $(12 + 3)$. Further, derivation, combinatoriality, secondary set formation, etc., can be applied to duration sets as well as to pitch sets.

It has been our purpose in the preceding portion of this chapter to set forth the basic elements of the twelve-note compositional method, including extension of the twelve-note concept to the systematic organization of dimensions other than (and usually in addition to) pitch. Because this is merely an introduction to serial technique, we have not considered how serial procedures are applied in electronic and computer music (e.g., Stockhausen's *Studie II* and Babbitt's Ensembles for Synthesizer). And we have purposely avoided the significant and very refractory questions that might be (and frequently have been) raised about the perception of this generally complex music.[36] Suffice it to say here that the serial concept has had a very great impact on twentieth-century composition. Indeed, it would be easier to count those composers who have *not* employed serial procedures, however freely, than it would be to count those who have. That serial composition is no longer in vogue should in no way be construed as minimizing its importance in the development of atonal music in this century. In this regard we conclude our examination of serial music with the remarks of Ernst Křenek written more than thirty years ago:

> It is the belief of this author that, in a later stage of development, atonal music may not need the strict regulations of the twelve-tone technique. He anticipates that the essentials of this technique will grow into a sort of second nature. This consummation, however, will materialize only if the twelve-tone technique is constantly used as a training for composing in the atonal idiom, just as the theory of classical harmony is taught as an introduction to "free" tonal composition.[37]

---

[36]In this regard see Meyer, *op. cit.*
[37]Křenek, *op. cit.*, ix.

### 8.0 PRE-SERIAL ATONALITY

Having looked in some detail at serial procedures of organization, we turn now to a body of music that preceded and led to Schoenberg's twelve-note method. This music, generally called *free atonality* but in reality far from free in its structure, spans the period of about 1908–1923, or from the time of Schoenberg's Three Pieces for Piano, Op. 11, to his Suite for Piano, Op. 25. Also included in this corpus are compositions by Schoenberg's students, Webern and Berg, and by others such as Bartók and Scriabin.

The essence of these compositions is as difficult to define as the works themselves are to analyze. Each work is different, yet each has in common the avoidance of tonality and, generally, the reliance on unordered pitch sets of from two to seven notes and motivic rather than thematic organization. We will investigate movements from three pre-serial atonal works in the following pages using some of the notions developed in the earlier portions of this chapter.

We begin our investigation with the fourth of Webern's Five Movements for String Quartet, Op. 5 (1909).

**EXAMPLE 6-42.** Webern: Five Movements for String Quartet (1909), IV (complete). Copyright 1922, Universal Edition. Used by permission of the publisher. Theodore Presser Company sole representative United States, Canada and Mexico.

**EXAMPLE 6-42** continued.

The contrast provided by comparison of this piece with earlier music organized according to triadic tonal principles is striking. On first hearing there appears to be no consistent principle governing pitch details. There is no melody to speak of, there are no traditional chord structures, there are no cadences in the traditional sense of the term, and because of the piece's brevity and relative lack of reiterated materials, there is little apparent unity. Further, rhythm and meter play very little if any obvious formative role in the piece. In short, compared with traditionally organized music, the effect here is one of mere juxtaposition rather than interrelation of events. Yet, careful study of the score reveals a high degree of pitch and interval organization that begins to come through to the listener once he becomes familiar with the organizational principles.

The piece may be divided into four sections as delineated by tempo changes, a typical sectionalizing agent in much twentieth-century music. In the first section three of the sets of the piece are exposed. These are marked A, B, and C on the score and are shown below in the normal form versions of their initial appearances. Set types are included beneath the sets.

**EXAMPLE 6-43.** Sets of Webern's Five Movements for String Quartet, Op. 5, IV.

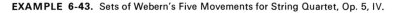
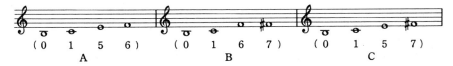

The A and B sets are typical of Webern's music and of atonal music in general. Both sets consist of semitone neighbors to larger intervals, which in Webern's music are commonly major thirds or perfect fourths.[38] The opening sets, $A_0$ and $B_0$, the latter of which may be viewed as a semitone expansion of the former, have three notes in common. The unique notes from each set form the dyad (EF♯), the sole pitch content of the viola through the first four measures. The pitch and interval materials for most of the remaining measures of the piece can be derived from these two sets and from a third, $C_0$, which is formed by the highest notes of the first two measures.

In triadic tonal music the vertical alignment of pitches is crucial to the definition of chord and non-chord tones. Similarly, in most atonal music this alignment is no less important for the creation and definition of significant interval relationships, even though consonance and dissonance as traditionally defined are not features of this music (except insofar as certain intervals

---

[38]A fuller description of Webern's choice of pitch sets is given in Walter Kolneder's *Anton Webern*, tr. Humphrey Searle (Berkeley: University of California Press, 1968), pp. 39–40.

and interval combinations are inherently more or less dissonant, or tension-creating, than others). In the example below, abstracted from the opening section, observe how the various intervals are formed by vertical alignment or by oblique association of parts. (For clarity and because of their importance to this and to other atonal music, only major sevenths and minor ninths are marked.)

**EXAMPLE 6-44.** Interval Structure in Webern, Ibid., mm. 1–3.

Often in atonal music the general impression of intervallic similarity created by the use of intervals from a particular interval class seems to be the intention of the composer. In particular, the intervals of class 1 are prominent in many compositions, especially in this one. In fact, it seems likely that the choice of E♭ for the lone cello pitch in the first three measures was made in order to form a minor ninth (compounded two octaves) with the E of the first violin. Other intervals present in the example are the major second and third, the perfect fourth and fifth, and the tritone. Excluded are the minor second, minor third and major sixth. Excluded intervals become important in the following sections. Throughout the piece Webern carefully aligns his parts to create intervals and interval combinations presented in this section.

In section II of this piece, the B set, which appeared chordally in the previous section, now appears linearly in a brief canon between the two violins and the cello. The first statement is $B_0$, which provides pitch unity with the previous section. The first note of the following canonic voice, whose pitch classes comprise $B_5$, creates again the dyad (BC) (found in m. 1) with the last note of $B_0$. The last note of $B_5$ forms the dyad (FF♯) (from m. 2) with the first note of the cello line, the contents of which restores $B_0$. Notice also that $B_1$ appears on the first beat of m. 4, and that three new notes, B♭, C♯, and G are introduced by the $B_1$ and $B_5$ sets.

The combination of parts in the fifth measure demonstrates another way in which sets are formed in much atonal music. Here the viola plays a dual role in that its pitches combine with those of the first violin and cello to form transposed versions of A and B. The transpositions employed here suggest an analogy with the notion of modulation in tonal music: $A_1$ has two notes in common with $A_0$, while $A_2$ has none. If $A_0$ is regarded as a point of departure tonally, then the motion to $A_2$ is not unlike motion to an "unrelated" key. Other elements providing contrast in the section are the new note D (in addition to the B♭, C♯, and G already mentioned) and the minor second intervals of mm. 5 and 6. The minor second was not present in section I.

The second section concludes with a seven-note set, $D_0$, which is comprised of the members of $C_0$ and three of the four new notes of the second section. As in the previous section, the first note of $D_0$ relates to the last note of the other sounding voice, the cello, by an interval class 1 member.

The third section provides contrast with the previous two by its texture and by emphasis on minor thirds in the first violin (minor thirds have not appeared previously, except for the last interval of the $D_0$ set in m. 6). The other pitch materials of the section, however, refer back to the first section (with the exception of two new notes, G♯ in mm. 8–9 and A in m. 10): the accompaniment sustains the notes B and E (the pitch extrema of $A_0$ in the first section), emphasizes major thirds, and includes an inverted version of $C_0$, (E G♭ B♭ B). The ascending version of $D_5$ in m. 10 brings back all the notes of the first section (plus the new note A) and thus provides a capsule version of section I by way of introduction to the final section.

The final section inverts the texture and varies somewhat the materials of section II. The pizzicato chord in m. 12 provides a timbral and textural referent to the chord at the end of section I and a transpositional parallel to the $A_2$ set: $A_2$ and $A_0$ include no common tones, and this is true also for $B_2$ and $B_0$ (the contents of $B_2$ are three of the four notes of section II not in section I and the G♯ of section III). The statement of $D_8$ in the final measure concludes with the dyad (E♭F♯), the two notes representing the pitch extrema of section I. The figure opens with the dyad that concludes the first violin line in m. 9, (G♯C). A connection between the two separate statements of this pitch class pair is pointed out by George Perle:[39] in m. 8, G♯ is associated with B by a slur, while in m. 9, G♯ is slurred to the following C, which thus anticipates subtly the beginning of the $D_8$ set statement.

To conclude our rather detailed look at the structure of this brief piece, we direct the reader's attention to other subtleties of construction which are common to Webern's style in particular and to much atonal music in general. A concern for balance and symmetry is very much in evidence, as is shown by the arch-like registral structure of the piece (from high to middle to high), by the opposition of registers for certain pitch classes and sets (e.g., E♭ is lowest note of section I and the highest of section III, and the two pizzicato chords balance each other registrally and in terms of distance from beginning and end of the piece), and by the choice of pitch sets (the sets A and B and the sets made up of the viola notes in the accompaniment and the violin notes of the upper part of section III are symmetrical).

Equally important to this style (and to the body of music with which we

---

[39]Perle, *op. cit.*, p. 18.

are concerned in this chapter) is Webern's use of variation. Note, for example, that there is absolutely no literal restatement of any of the materials in this piece. A good indication of Webern's concern for subtle contrast is the rhythmic variation that the seven-note ascending figure undergoes on each of its reappearances; its contour is always the same, but each time it is transposed, it is rhythmically varied, it appears in a different part of the measure, and it is either changed dynamically or in its manner of presentation (recall the subtle variation of repeated elements in Webern's Variations for Piano discussed earlier).

Having seen how sets may appear in one atonal composition, we turn now to another and slightly earlier work, the first of Schoenberg's Three Pieces for Piano, Op. 11, composed in 1908. This piece, which is generally considered to be the first truly atonal composition, contrasts markedly with Webern's string quartet movement in its textural and iterative details, yet both pieces rely on pitch and interval sets to organize their structure and both point to the later twelve-note method. Ex. 6-45 shows the complete piece and indicates some of its set details.

On the basis of set deployment, changes of procedure and reiteration of materials, the piece may be divided into the five sections shown on the score. Sections I and II serve roles rather analogous to those of first and second theme areas of a sonata movement exposition. The third and the major part of the fourth sections are developmental, and the concluding portion of the fourth along with the fifth section is much like an inverted and varied recapitulation.[40]

**EXAMPLE 6-45.** Schoenberg: Three Pieces for Piano, Op. 11 (1908), 1 (complete). Copyright 1910 by Universal Edition. Renewed 1938 by Arnold Schoenberg. Used by permission of Belmont Music Publishers, Los Angeles, California 90049.

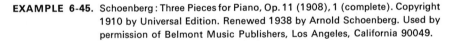
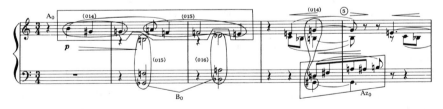

---

[40]Perle, *op. cit.*, pp. 10–16, discusses this piece also. However, his formal delineation differs from the one given here, and his attention to set structure is limited to the role of one of the trichordal sets of the piece.

**EXAMPLE 6-45** continued.

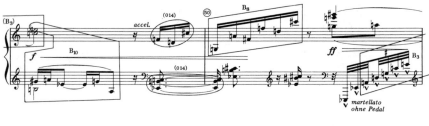

Schoenberg presents the basic materials of the piece in the first three measures. To demonstrate the complex web of set relations exposed in these measures, the following numerical diagrams of the passage are given. The note C is arbitrarily chosen as 0. For convenience in subsequent references, letters are assigned to the tetrachords and hexachords of the example.

**EXAMPLE 6-46.** Schoenberg: Op. 11, I, mm. 1–3.

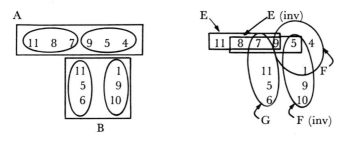

Table 2 below shows each of the sets of the example in normal form followed by its set type.

**TABLE 2**

| Set | Normal Form | Set Type |
|-----|-------------|----------|
| | (7 8 11) | (0 1 4) |
| | (9 10 1) | (0 1 4) |
| | (4 5 9) | (0 1 5) |
| | (5 6 11) | (0 1 6) |
| E | (7 8 9 11) | (0 1 2 4) |
| E (inv) | (5 7 8 9) | (0 1 2 4) |
| F | (1 4 5 9) | (0 1 4 8) |
| F (inv) | (5 9 10 1) | (0 1 4 8) |
| G | (5 6 7 11) | (0 1 2 6) |
| A | (4 5 7 8 9 11) | (0 1 3 4 5 7) |
| B | (5 6 9 10 11 1) | (0 1 4 5 6 8) |

Observation of the sets reveals that all contain at least one (0 1) dyad which represents the most prominent interval class of the piece. All but the (0 1 6) type contain the intervals (and thus the interval classes) 1 and 4, the latter of which is also prominent in the piece. And all of the larger sets, except G, contain the (0 1 4) set type, which is the most prominent of several trichordal set types to appear. Trichords, especially the (0 1 4) type, organize much of the foreground vertical and linear activity. The background appears to be organized by the pitch and interval relations inherent in the hexachordal structures of section I. Also prominent are tetrachords, especially those of mm. 1–3. In general, unity is provided by unordered pitch class sets, along with recurring melodic contours and rhythmic patterns.[41]

After the opening three measures discussed above, a contrasting passage appears. In mm. 4–8, the right hand states two more important trichordal types, (0 2 6) and (0 1 2). These culminate in a (GB) dyad which combines with the sustained lowest note of the left hand, G♯, to give the pitch content of the opening (0 1 4) trichord. The left hand articulates the two new trichords in the formation of a hexachord, $A_z$, so symbolized because it is identical to A in terms of interval-class content but is not a transposition or

---

[41]A most important characteristic of Schoenberg's music is the basic shape or structure, the *Grundgestalt,* of his primary materials. This shape is reflected throughout a composition by recurrent melodic and rhythmic motives and by pitch and interval sets. For a discussion of this, see Joseph Rufer's *Composition With Twelve Notes . . . ,* trans. Humphrey Searle. (London: Barrie and Rockcliff, 1954), esp. Chapter 3.

transposed inversion of it.[42] The numerical diagram below shows the structure and set types of the passage.

**EXAMPLE 6-47.** Schoenberg: Op. 11, I, mm. 4–8.

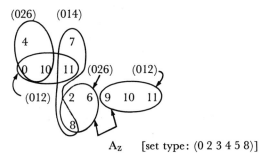

$A_Z$    [set type: (0 2 3 4 5 8)]

The texture of the first three measures returns in the concluding portion of the first section, but with changed pitch content and with two new hexachords, C and D, which are intervallically dissimilar to the corresponding A and B sets (see Table 3). By presenting dissimilar pitch and interval details in this otherwise repeated passage Schoenberg avoids the effect of closure that would be provided by a literal return of the opening materials.

Section II is noteworthy for its linear presentation of sets that were vertically deployed in the previous section. Another configuration of the prominent (0 1 4) set type is given by the opening three notes, B, C, and E♭, the last of which is the only member of the total chromatic missing from the first section. To point up this new element, Schoenberg separates it spatially from the following materials and prolongs it over an octave through the second quarter note of m. 14 (see the circled single notes in Ex. 6-45). Following this trichord is a new rhythmic figure which juxtaposes linear versions of B and D sets, both of which played accompanimental roles in section I. The major seventh and minor ninth intervals of the D set statement appear frequently in other parts of the piece, especially in section IV. Beginning with m. 12, the tetrachords E, F, and G appear as foreground materials. An important inclusion of the materials comprising the succession of E sets in the thirteenth measure is $B_8$, which reappears at the end of section IV prior to the return of the opening materials (see m. 50).

The details of the pitch structure of mm. 12–17 are indicative of the control exercised by Schoenberg over his materials. In m. 12, eleven different pitch classes appear. Aside from the immediate repetition of the note B,

---

[42]See fn. 12, p. 406.

three notes, A, G♯, and C, appear twice, with each duplication displaced one or two octaves from its initial position. In m. 13, the missing note from the previous measure, F, is the only one to appear twice in the right hand, with duplication again at the octave, and ten pitch classes are present. One of the missing notes, G♯, is then prolonged through the following mm. 15–18, and it appears in three octave positions. Though this scheme does not appear to be continued, it points to a concern for detail and control that eventually culminated in the more systematic procedures of the twelve-note method.

The concluding measures of section II are like those of the previous section, though with two significant changes: the accompanimental set is now the Z-related $D_Z$ collection, and the last note of $C_0$, B♭, is supplanted momentarily by a repeated element from within the set. The B♭ appears in the first measure of the third section and thus provides a subtle connection between sections (see mm. 17–19). Such overlapping of set elements is a common procedure in atonal music. The hexachords of the opening two sections of the piece are given below along with their interval-class contents.

**TABLE 3**

| Set | Type | Interval Class Contents* |
|-----|------|--------------------------|
| A   | (0 1 3 4 5 7) | 3 3 3 3 2 1 |
| $A_Z$ | (0 2 3 4 5 8) | 3 3 3 3 2 1 |
| B   | (0 1 4 5 6 8) | 3 2 2 4 3 1 |
| C   | (0 2 3 4 6 8) | 2 4 2 4 1 2 |
| D   | (0 1 2 3 4 7) | 4 3 3 2 2 1 |
| $D_Z$ | (0 1 2 3 5 6) | 4 3 3 2 2 1 |

*The numbers represent the multiplicity of interval classes in order beginning with interval class 1.

The set structure of the third and fourth sections is evident from Ex. 6-45, and as such it will not be discussed in detail. Observe particularly in section IV the freedom of structure characteristic of traditional development sections.

Recalling the discussion of Webern's modulatory scheme in the fourth piece of his Op. 5, a similar plan is operative in section III of this piece. Among its other materials, the following sets appear in the order listed: a five-note subset of $A_{Z_1}$; $C_9$, $C_6$, and $C_1$; and $B_6$, $B_3$, $B_{10}$, $B_3$, and $B_1$. The minimum number of common notes possible between any one of these sets and its parent set of section I is two.[43] Of the sets given, all but $B_1$ and $C_6$

_____

[43]Transposition of any set by any member of the interval classes 1 to 5 will produce the number of common tones indicated by the multiplicity of that

manifest this property. Since these two exceptions appear as the second parts of sequences ($C_6$ in m. 26, $B_1$ in m. 30), they might be regarded as less significant than the other transpositions, particularly since there is only one instance of each. Further, the opening portion of the fourth section appears to continue this scheme of "remoteness." Section IV begins with successive (0 1 4) trichords which combine to present three simultaneous transpositions of A. The top line, which because of tradition tends to stand out above the lower two coupled voices, is $A_6$, the most distant transposition of the A set (only two common notes with $A_0$). Appropriately, this transposition stands at the approximate midpoint of the piece (m. 34), the most distant point from the beginning or end.

Preceding the return of the opening theme at the beginning of the final section are $B_8$ and $B_3$[44] sets of section II (mm. 50–51), the latter of which recalls the opening of the earlier section by its contour and pitch class content. Notice also that the trichord of the left hand of m. 49 is the same one that opens section II. Also present are new versions of A (in inversion) accompanied by B sets (mm. 51–52). Here again, pitch relationship to the $A_0$ and $B_0$ sets seems significant, though not particularly systematic: $I_1A$ (the semitone transposition of the inversion of $A_0$) has four notes in common with $A_0$, while $I_{11}A$ and $I_{10}A$ have two each; $B_1$ and $B_5$ have three notes in common with $B_0$. It appears that there is a tonal motion back towards the original pitch class content of the parent A and B sets.

The final section is reminiscent of the first, but with a significant change which finds $A_{Z_0}$ rather than $B_0$ accompanying the $A_0$ collection in the opening measures (m. 54). This brings into close association the two sets with common interval-class content of section I. Also prominent in this section is the (0 4 8) trichord, originally part of F, but also prominent in its own right (see mm. 20, 22, and 24 in particular). In keeping with other details of pitch-class control mentioned above, the four successive semitone transpositions of (0 4 8) found in mm. 55–56 produce the twelve pitch classes.[45] The concluding measures again present $A_0$, though with some reordering and with an interpolated A♯. The interpolation creates an (0 1 6) trichord with the following E and E♭, which along with the two other (0 1 6) trichords formed in the last two measures (see Ex. 6-45) provides emphasis on the trichord associated with the first appearance of B, the set whose role is supplanted in this section by $A_Z$. Note that the last sounding notes are the octave statement of

interval class in the set. For the tritone (interval class 6), the number is double. For example, the set A (see Table 3) transposed one semitone is (*1* 2 *4 5* 6 8). Transposed by tritone the set A is (6 *7* 9 10 11 *1*). The italicized numbers show common elements with set type A. (This property does not hold for transposed inversion.)

[44]The G in m. 50 (left hand) should probably be G♯, which would then restore the pitch class materials that open section II (m. 12).

[45]The C♯ in measure 55 is a misprint for B♯ according to Perle (*op. cit.*, p. 15, fn. 4).

E♭ which provides a final reference to the note introduced in section II (recall also the previous comments about octave duplications of "unique" notes in that section).

In conclusion, the following diagram is given to demonstrate one aspect of the control and balance achieved by the two hexachords A and B and their transpositions. It is interesting and, in view of the frequency of such details in this and other atonal examples, seemingly significant that the B sets shown in the diagram are located nearly equidistantly from the $A_0$ set that opens the first and closes the final sections of the piece.

| Hexachord | $A_0$ | $B_3$, $B_8$ | $A_6$ | $B_8$, $B_3$ | $A_0$ |
|-----------|-------|--------------|-------|--------------|-------|
| Measures | 1–3 | 12–13 | 34–35 | 50–51 | 62–63 |

The two pieces we have discussed played an important role in launching the period of atonal music composition, but they do not break totally with tradition. Both works rely on the traditional practice of preserving contours (of primary thematic and/or motivic materials) and pitch levels (for returns of materials in concluding portions). Further, transpositional details appear in part to be motivated by traditional practices of tonal change from near to more remote regions and back. However, subsequent compositions by both composers produced works that carried their initial experiments further. Schoenberg, for example, in his Six Little Pieces for Piano, Op. 19 (1911), approached the brevity characteristic of Webern in the second and third pieces, each of which is only nine measures long. Moreover, none of the pieces in this collection contains themes in the sense evident in the first of the Op. 11 pieces. To conclude this discussion, we consider the piece given below, the third of Webern's Three Little Pieces for Cello and Piano, Op. 11 (1914), one of the most concentrated compositions of this period.

**EXAMPLE 6-48.** Webern : Three Little Pieces for Cello and Piano Op. 11 (1914), III (complete). Copyright 1924, Universal Edition. Used by permission of the publisher. Theodore Presser Company, sole representative United States, Canada and Mexico.

This piece appears to be the ultimate in non-repetition. To the listener, at least at first, there is little to provide cohesiveness. Nevertheless, as the diagram below shows, there is a consistency in the types of interval sets presented. (The pitch class numbers are arranged to approximate the shapes of the parts. The note C is 0.)

**EXAMPLE 6-49.** Numerical diagram of Webern's Op. 11, III.

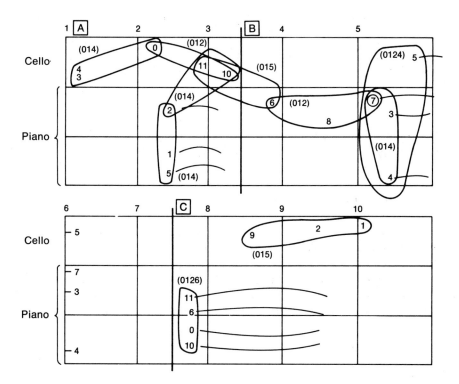

In view of its brevity, the piece might be considered as consisting of three 'sound events' (marked A, B, and C) rather than sections. Within each event there are no notes in common between the instruments, and there are no notes in common between successive events within each part. The piece consists of an eleven-note collection followed by a collection of all twelve notes, the two joined by the common pitch class, 7, at the middle of the piece.[46]

Unity is provided essentially by intervals, to a lesser extent by pitch. Dyads of interval class 1 are formed by the opening and closing notes in the cello, (4 3) and (2 1), and by the highest and lowest elements of the fifth measure, (5 4). Trichords, especially (0 1 2), (0 1 4), and (0 1 5) types, are structurally important (note that these same types also appear prominently in the other two pieces discussed) and are primary subsets of larger collections (see especially mm. 5 and 8). Certain invariant combinations of pitch classes are likewise important, e.g., the dyads (4 3), (2 1), and (11 10), and the trichord (10 11 0). Notice also that E is the lowest note of both the cello and the piano (mm. 1 and 5) and that the F of the piano (mm. 2–3) registrally opposes the F of the cello (mm. 5–6). The subtlety of the iterative details of this and other non-thematic atonal pieces is summarized by George Perle:

> Any aspect of a musical idea—melodic contour, harmonic formation, texture, dynamics, rhythm, even the octave position of an individual note—may serve as the momentary referential basis of a nonliteral restatement. The extreme brevity of these works is not an idiosyncratic feature but a necessary and logical consequent of the multiplicity of function of every single element.[47]

## CONCLUSION

As was mentioned at the outset of this chapter, much of the compositional activity of this century has been devoted to finding ways to organize musical materials without the trappings of traditional triadic tonality and its system of functional relationships. For this purpose the serial principle was conceived for the organization of pitch materials and was later extended to include other dimensions. The tremendous influence of the serial concept on compositional thought in this century cannot be denied. Even composers such as Stravinsky, Copland, and Bartók, whose mature styles seemed sufficiently substantive without employing serial procedures, turned to serialism in one way or another and in varying degrees. Yet at the same time, serialism as a principle has been vigorously attacked, especially as a result of certain practices in which several dimensions are serialized according to rather

[46]Because of this feature, Kolneder (*op. cit.,* p. 80), suggests that this might be considered the first twelve-note piece.

[47]Perle, *op. cit.,* p. 21.

arbitrary procedures (recall the comments about multi-serialism in Boulez's *Structures* Ia in section 7.0). It became clear to most composers that to assign a note, a durational value, an articulative detail, or a timbral combination a particular location in a composition only because it is ordained by the pre-compositional scheme upon which the work is based leads to an uncontrollable compositional result. Thus it is that many composers have produced works during the past twenty-five years that exhibit a free use of serialism or the application of procedures of pitch organization not at all unlike those found in the pre-serial atonal pieces examined in the last section of this chapter. Still other composers have turned completely away from serialism and its rigors to aleatory practices or to procedures of composition not readily classifiable under any one methodological category. However, regardless of the future of serialism, whether it will find application only in the training of composers, as Křenek suggests, or whether it will be absorbed ultimately as a part of some more all-embracing compositional procedure, its role in shaping musical thought in the twentieth century cannot be underestimated. It seems no exaggeration to say that, in one way or another, every Western composer alive today has been influenced by serial thought and that subsequent generations will likely also be influenced by Schoenberg's invention.


## SUGGESTIONS FOR FURTHER STUDY


In addition to the works cited in this chapter, the reader is referred to the following list which includes a variety of serial and non-serial compositions.


Babbitt, Milton: *All Set;* Three Compositions for Piano.

Berg, Alban: *Lyric* Suite.

Berio, Luciano: *Nones.*

Boulez, Pierre: *Le Soleil des Eaux; Le Marteau sans maitre.*

Křenek, Ernst: *Eleven Transparencies; Sestina.*

Nono, Luigi: *Incontri.*

Schoenberg, Arnold: Five Orchestral Pieces, Op. 16; Six Little Piano Pieces, Op. 19; *Ode to Napoleon Buonaparte,* Op. 41; Piano Concerto, Op. 42; String Trio, Op. 45.

Schuller, Gunther: Music for Brass Quintet.

Spies, Claudio: *Times Two.*

Stockhausen, Karlheinz: *Studie Nr. II.*

Stravinsky, Igor: Octet for Winds; Cantata; *Canticum Sacrum; In memoriam Dylan Thomas.*

Webern, Anton: Six Pieces for Orchestra, Op. 6; Bagatelles for String Quartet, Op. 9; Quartet, Op. 22.

Wuorinen, Charles: *The Politics of Harmony.*

## SUGGESTIONS FOR FURTHER READING

The following books are to be regarded as a source of sources for further reading on serialism and pre-serial atonality to supplement the writings cited in the body of the chapter. A brief annotation appears with each source by way of summarizing its contents.

*Books*

Basart, Ann P., *Serial Music: A Classified Bibliography of Writings on Twelve-Tone and Electronic Music*. Berkeley: University of California Press, 1963.

This book contains a comprehensive bibliography organized into sections on philosophy and criticism, history, analysis and theory, and specific writings on the works of 23 major composers, including special emphasis on Schoenberg, Berg, and Webern. While it covers writings only up to the first years of the 1960s, it is nevertheless a very helpful source, especially for the beginning student of serial compositional practice.

Brindle, Reginald Smith, *Serial Music*. London: Oxford University Press, 1966.

This is essentially a book on composition using serial procedures, but even the general reader can glean a great deal from it about serial music in general. Included are the details of twelve-note writing, more recent practices of multi-serialism, and a concluding chapter on free atonality.

Carlson, Effie B., *A Bio-Bibliographical Dictionary of Twelve-Tone and Serial Composers*. Metuchen, N.J.: The Scarecrow Press, 1970.

The avowed purpose of this book is to extract an understanding of serial composition through piano literature of the twentieth century. There are four sections: (1) a discussion of the emergence of the serial concept and the piano music of the Viennese composers, (2) composers of serial piano music since Schoenberg (eighty composers are included), (3) a geographical survey of serial composers; and (4) a bibliography. Like the Basart book, the main value of Carlson's work is in the list of sources about the music and the serial method.

Forte, Allen, *The Structure of Atonal Music*. New Haven: Yale University Press, 1973.

Forte's book is divided into two parts. The first part deals with basic concepts of pitch class set structure and relationships. The second deals with more complex relationships among the sets of a composition. Arising out of his earlier work on the topic, Forte's main concern is set structure in non-serial atonal music, especially in music by Schoenberg, Webern, Berg, and Stravinsky.

Křenek, Ernst, *Studies in Counterpoint*. New York: G. Schirmer, Inc., 1940.

Křenek's book is a brief source on counterpoint using the twelve-note technique. One-, two- and three-part writing are considered and numerous examples are included.

Perle, George, *Serial Composition and Atonality*, 2d ed. Berkeley: University of California Press, 1967.

Perle's was one of the first books to investigate in detail both serial and pre-serial atonal composition. It is a thoughtful, comprehensive work that should be required reading for serious music students. The numerous examples emphasize the works of the Viennese composers but include pertinent citations from the works of other composers. Of particular value is the fact that the book is periodically updated by the author.

Rufer, Josef, *Composition with 12 Notes*, trans. Humphrey Searle. London: Barrie and Rockcliff, 1954.

Rufer was Schoenberg's pupil and assistant at the Prussian Academy of the Arts in the 1920s. The book represents the efforts of the author over a period of years to summarize Schoenberg's thoughts not only about twelve-note writing but about composition in general. In this regard the first three chapters are valuable reading, particularly the third which deals with antecedents of the twelve-note compositional technique. The remaining six chapters deal with the method as reflected in Schoenberg's music.

*Periodicals*

Below are a few of the almost countless English-language periodicals in which may be found significant writings about serial and pre-serial atonal music.

*die Reihe* (in translation from Theodore Presser, Bryn Mawr, Pa; 1955–62)
*Journal of Music Theory* (Yale School of Music, 1957–   )
*Music Review* (W. Heffer and Sons, Cambridge, England, 1940–   )
*Perspectives of New Music* (Princeton University, 1962–   )
*The Score and I.M.A. Magazine* (The Score Publishing Co., London, 1954–
   61)
*Tempo* (Boosey and Hawkes, London, 1940–   )

Of those above, *die Reihe* and *The Score* have ceased publication but are available in many libraries. *Die Reihe* is important because of its currency to the European musical scene (especially Germany) during its period of publication. Most of the significant composers and theorists writing today are represented in one or another of the journals listed.

## SETS AND ORDERING PROCEDURES . . .
## DEFINITIONS OF TERMS

**Aggregate:** a collection of the twelve pitch classes formed by two or more voice parts in a relatively short space of time, e.g., the simultaneous presentation of the two hexachords of a set.

**All-combinatoriality:** a special case of combinatoriality resulting when a set is complement-producing under transposition and transposed inversion and is also symmetrical. The concept is generally applied to hexachords, though smaller equal-part partitions of twelve-note sets may also have all-combinatorial properties, e.g., the trichord (0 1 2).

**All-interval set:** a twelve-note set that will permit an arrangement such that all eleven intervals (from 1-11) can be represented.

**Combinatoriality:** commonly applied to hexachords, an instance of combinatoriality exists when transposition and/or transposed inversion of a hexachord produces its complement. Combinatoriality may also be extended to other equal-part partitions of a twelve-note set, i.e., to dyads, trichords, tetrachords, and to single notes.

**Complement:** (a) the complement of any interval from 1–11 is its inversion; (b) a pair of pitch class sets are complementary when they contain no common members and when combined they produce all twelve pitch classes.

**Derived set:** a twelve-note set derived from systematic operations on one of its subsets, e.g., the set (B B♭ D E♭ G F♯ G♯ E F C C♯ A) from Webern's Concerto, Op. 24, in which the second,

third, and fourth trichords are derived from the first.

**Dyad:** any set of two different notes.

**Fibonacci series:** a number series in which, beginning with 1, all subsequent terms are sums of the preceding pair: 1 1 2 3 5 8 13 21 . . .

**Hexachord:** any set of six different pitch classes.

**Index number:** index numbers (subscripts) associated with P and I set forms denote the pitch class number on which the form begins. For retrograde forms, the index number denotes the pitch class number on which the form ends.

**Interval class:** an interval class (IC) consists of an interval (only simple intervals are considered) and its complement. There are six interval classes: 1 (m2/M7), 2 (M2/m7), 3 (m3/M6), 4 (M3/m6), 5 (P4/P5), 6 (+4, °5).

**Invariance:** the preservation of one or more segments of a set under transposition or transposed inversion, e.g. $I_4$ of (0 1 3 4 5 7) is (4 3 1 0 11 9), which preserves the content of the initial tetrachord.

**Inversion:** symbolized I, the inversion of a pitch class (except for 0) is found by subtracting its pitch class number from 12. The inversion of 0 is 0. Inversion complements intervals with respect to 0, e.g., 7 inverts to 5: the set (0 1 4) inverts to (0 11 8); the set (3 5 7) inverts to (9 7 5). The inversion of a set preserves interval class succession while complementing intervals.

**Matrix:** also called a 'magic square,' a matrix of set forms is a convenient method of representing the forms deriving from transposition and transposed inversion of a set. Read from top to bottom, each row in the matrix is a prime form beginning on the various members of the original inversion form, and the columns read left to right are inversions beginning on the various members of the original prime form. Retrograde forms are found by reading in opposite directions.

**Multi-serialism:** multi-serialism exists when two or more dimensions of a work are organized according to a serial procedure. An equivalent term is *total serialism*

**Normal form:** a particular arrangement of a set of pitch classes such that the order is ascending and the span (the interval between the first and last pitch classes) is the smallest possible, e.g., the normal form of (1 8 9) is (8 9 1).

**Order numbers:** the set of numbers 0–11 may be assigned to the ordinal positions of pitch classes in a set. This set, rather than the set 1–12, is used in order to correspond with the set used for numbering pitch classes.

**Permutation:** a reordering of the contents of a set.

**Pitch class:** refers to a note and any and all of its octave duplications (including enharmonic equivalents).

**Pitch class numbers:** the numbers 0–11 assigned to a set of pitch classes as a means of specifying semitone distances *above* the (arbitrarily chosen) zero element. The set (D C♯ A B♭ F E♭ E C A♭ G F♯ B) in pitch-class numbers is (0 11 7 8 3 1 2 10 6 5 4 9).

**Prime:** symbolized P, a prime form of a set is the original form or any of its simple transpositions. The original prime form is generally symbolized $P_0$.

**Retrograde:** symbolized R, a retrograde form is any prime form read in reverse order. Retrograde inversion, symbolized RI, is the inversion in reverse order.

**Rotation:** a reordering procedure in which the relative positions of notes of a set are systematically changed according to a scheme. Rotation most commonly is applied to hexachords by rotating first elements to last for five rotations. Often the resultant hexachords are then transposed to begin on the same note.

**Secondary set:** a set formed by the juxtaposition of parts of set forms generated by the basic set of a work. Secondary sets, however, are not found in the matrix of set forms. One example is the succession $R_0$Ha—$P_0$Ha, where Ha signifies the first hexachord of a set.

**Serial:** a term applied to music in which one or more of its dimensions (e.g., pitch, duration, timbre) derives its organization from an ordered set.

**Set:** a collection of discrete entities. In music we may speak of pitch sets, duration sets, timbre sets, etc.

**Set form:** refers to any of the four standard arrangements of an ordered set: prime, inversion, retrograde, and retrograde inversion.

**Set type:** a convenient abstraction for symbolizing generic collections of intervals. To determine a set type, the pitch class members are arranged in *normal form* and numbered in terms of semitone distances above the first element, 0, e.g., (E F A) becomes (0 1 5). If the smaller intervals are not to the left in the resultant set, 0 is associated with the rightmost element and the set is read backwards intervallically, rearranging the numbers in ascending order. For example, given (E G♯ A) the numerical set is (0 4 5). Here the smallest interval is to the right (between 4 and 5). Associating 0 with the rightmost pitch class and numbering from right to left gives (0 1 5).

**Symmetrical set:** any set whose contents can be reproduced under some transposition or some inversion. All set types of symmetrical sets have the property that the interval class succession of its members is the same read in either direction, e.g., (0 1 5 6).

**Tetrachord:** any set of four different pitch classes.

**Time-point set:** duration sets which are isomorphic to pitch sets in that the distance in time units between attack points (time-points) is equal to the semitone distance between pitch classes (i.e., duration interval = pitch interval).

**Transposition:** often symbolized T, transposition can be defined as the addition of a constant number repre-senting an interval from 0–11 to each member of a pitch-class set. If any of the resulting numbers is greater than 11, 12 is subtracted from it, e.g., (3 5 8) transposed a perfect fifth higher is (7 12 15). If 12 is subtracted from the second and third members, the set is (7 0 3).

**Trichord:** any set of three different pitch classes.

# Index